TERROR OVER AFRICA

THE SHOCKING TRUE STORY OF THE ATTEMPTED HI-JACKING OF BRITISH AIRWAYS' FLIGHT BA2069

TERROR OVER AFRICA

THE SHOCKING TRUE STORY OF THE ATTEMPTED HI-JACKING OF BRITISH AIRWAYS' FLIGHT BA2069

STANLEY STEWART

First published in Great Britain in 2025 by
Pen & Sword Airworld
An imprint of
Pen & Sword Books Ltd
Yorkshire - Philadelphia

ISBN 978 1 03614 026 7

A CIP catalogue record for this book is available from the British Library.

Typeset in INDIA by IMPEC eSolutions
Printed and bound in England by CPI Group (UK) Ltd, Croydon, CRO 4YY

The Publisher's authorised representative in the EU for product safety is Authorised Rep Compliance Ltd., Ground Floor, 71 Lower Baggot Street, Dublin D02 P593, Ireland.
www.arccompliance.com

For a complete list of Pen & Sword titles please contact

PEN & SWORD BOOKS LIMITED
47 Church Street, Barnsley, South Yorkshire, S70 2AS, England
E-mail: enquiries@pen-and-sword.co.uk
Website: www.pen-and-sword.co.uk

or

PEN AND SWORD BOOKS
1950 Lawrence Rd, Havertown, PA 19083, USA
E-mail: uspen-and-sword@casematepublishers.com
Website: www.penandswordbooks.com

Contents

PART 2: THE COVER-UP

Acknowledgements

I would like to express a monumental thank you to Captain Bill Hagan for all the time, effort and knowledge he provided for the writing of this book over many years. Without his massive contribution it can truly be said that this book could not have been written. I would also like to say a huge thank you to Stewardess Kim Parker for all the information she so helpfully provided of her injury and of her experiences. Her contribution was significant and greatly helped turn the facts uncovered into a story. I would also like to say a big thank you to all those, too many to mention, who, over the years, provided information, some just snippets and some more important, but all with contributions that helped enrich the telling of this story.

Foreword

BA was contacted by letter with the relevant details before publication and given the opportunity to review the manuscript, which they declined; while BA said that some of the details set out were 'factually incorrect', they did not identify any specific allegations that had been referred to them. What they did mention was that 'As is self-evident from the existence of information in the public domain about this matter, British Airways denies any allegations of such a cover up.'

Abbreviations

AAIB	Air Accident Investigation Branch, UK
AAICD	Air Accident Investigation Central Directorate, Sudan
ADI	Aviation Defence International
ALPA	Air Line Pilots Association, USA
AOC	Air Operating Certificate, CAA
ARP O50	Association of Retired and Persons over 50
ATC	Air Traffic Control
BA	British Airways
BALPA	British Airline Pilots Association, UK
BASI-4	BA Standing instruction No4
CAA	Civil Aviation Authority, UK
CEO	Chief Executive Officer
CGI	Computer-Generated Images, BA
CPS	Crown Prosecution Service, UK
CSD	Cabin Services Director
CVR	Cockpit Voice Recorder, BA
DCA	Directorate of Civil Aviation, Kenya
DERA	Defence Evaluation and Research Agency
DETR	Department of the Environment, Transport and the Regions, UK
DFDR	Digital Flight Data Recorder, BA
D for T	Department for Transport
DME	Distance Measuring Equipment

DTLR	Department for Transport, Local government and the Regions, UK
ETA	Estimated Time of Arrival
ETD	Estimated Time of Departure
FDR	Flight Data Recorder, BA
FDS	Flight Data Simulation, BA
FL	Flight level
FMS	Flight Management System
FOD	Flight Operations Department, CAA
FODCOM	Flight Operations Department communication, CAA
FOI	Freedom of information, UK
FTSG	Flight Technical Safety Group, BA
GAPAN	Guild of Air Pilots and Air Navigators
GMT	Greenwich Mean Time
HF	High Frequency radio
IAS	Indicated Air Speed
ICAO	International Civil Aviation Organisation, Montreal
IFALPA	International Federation of Air Line Pilots Associations
LOC	Loss of Control
MLD	Multilateral Division, DETR/DTLR, DETR/DTLR
MLD A/G	Multilateral Division Aviation Group, DETR/DTLR
MOR	Mandatory Occurrence Report, CAA
NASC	National Aviation Security Committee, UK
NASP	National Aviation Security Programme, UK
OCIC	Operational Crisis Incident Centre, BA
OSG	Operating Standards Group, BA
PA	Public Address, captain
PAG	Passenger Action Group
PTSD	Post Traumatic Stress Disorder

QUB	Queen's University Belfast
RADAR	Royal Association for the Disabled and Rehabilitation
SESMA	Special Event Search and Master Analysis, BA
SFO	Senior First Officer
SOP	Standard Operating Procedures, BA
SRG	Safety Regulation Group, CAA
TCAS	Traffic Collision Avoidance System
TRANSEC	Transport Security Directorate, DETR/DTLR
UTC	Universal time co-ordinated
VHF	Very high frequency radio

PART 1

THE ATTACK

Preamble

Captain Hagan's day on 28 December 2000 had been long and tiring, but flight BA2069 from Gatwick to Nairobi, although a little late, was proceeding well. Now it was the middle of the night over Sudan and he was completely exhausted. He had elected to take the third rest period and finally it was his turn for a break. Quickly he got ready, crawled into the lower bunk and, in the darkness, was soon deeply asleep.

Before long, his sleep was disturbed by movement and he could sense that he was sliding about in the bunk. One moment he was slipping head down with feet up and the next he was slipping the other way. He could hear the loud, whining sound of engines, in spite of the noise being muffled by the ear plugs he used to help with sleeping, and, as he tried to open his eyes in response to these alarming sensations, all he could see was blackness. It was all very confusing and he struggled to comprehend.

As the aircraft violently banked, climbed and dived he felt as if he was being tossed around in a small boat in a force 10 gale and then, for a brief moment, he was horrified to feel the airframe buffeting severely and shaking violently, for he knew instantly that the aircraft was in the process of stalling and was in great danger.

Now rudely awakened, he was completely baffled by the severe jerking of the controls that was creating such extreme and violent jolting. He had left the flight in charge of two very competent co-pilots but what kind of emergency had demanded such turbulent inputs? The level of violence had shaken Captain Hagan very badly, but now he was fully alert.

The story, however, began a few days earlier in Lyon, France.

Chapter 1

Lyon to London Gatwick

There was now no doubt in Paul's mind. He had suspected for some time that people were following him but now he was certain. Paul also believed that those stalking him were intent on harm and he was fearful of their attention. What made matters worse was that exam time was approaching and the pressure was becoming intolerable.

Paul's exams were scheduled for 9 January 2001, but the young 27-year-old was only one of about 120,000 students attending the three main universities and thirteen institutions that comprised the campus of Lyon University who were also anxious about their forthcoming exams. The university is one of the most important centres for higher education and research outside the Paris region and a year back in September 1999, Paul had enrolled as a postgraduate student at Lumière University Lyon 2, which focused on the social sciences.

Paul Kefa Mukonyi had been identified from an early age as a bright pupil and in the 1990s had attended the prestigious Moi University, founded by the Kenyan president, Daniel Arap Moi, where he graduated with a 1st class honours BSc degree in Science and Tourism. He also had a flair for languages and, as well as speaking English and Swahili naturally, he had learned German and French. His fluent French had resulted in him being granted a French Government scholarship in 1999 for postgraduate study in France and it was that award that had brought him to Lyon.

Mukonyi successfully completed the first year of his postgraduate studies but he was having difficulties integrating into French society and he was becoming increasingly sensitive to what he perceived as racial inequalities in Lyon. Studying in one's own country with family and friends within reach and in a familiar environment is one thing but studying abroad, far from those close to you and in an alien culture, is another, and Paul was not coping well. In the period of just over a year that he had been there he had become increasingly unsettled by the colour prejudice he had encountered on occasions from both outside and within the university. In particular, what affected him most was the attitude of those of Arab origin from North Africa, mostly Algerians, who seemed to treat him as a black African with contempt. This was the group that was spying on him and their behaviour disturbed him. He was also frightened by their derogatory remarks and threats.

Not only was Paul nervous about the forthcoming exams, therefore, but the actions of this Algerian group also made him nervous, and the dreams of this bright young man were beginning to turn sour. He began to feel unwell, he became more agitated, his stomach ached with fear and his life became very uncomfortable. More than anything he needed to talk to someone about his concerns but he felt isolated in this hostile arena. Previously he had seen his doctor for an unrelated medical matter but had not mentioned his present predicament so he arranged for a second appointment. He resolved then to discuss his concerns at this next visit and to ask the doctor for help.

He wasn't sure if involving the doctor was the right thing to do, especially since people seemed to be threatening his life, but, when he finally got the chance to explain, the doctor, to his relief, proved sympathetic. A course of action was decided upon and the doctor arranged a visit by the University social department. Paul was immediately found new accommodation and the change of his room now prevented the people he feared from being in daily contact with him. They could no longer follow or threaten him and the improved circumstances would enable him to study for his exams once more.

By Christmas 2000, however, Paul's condition was deteriorating again and his behaviour was becoming more extreme and irrational. To his consternation he also felt unwell. The disturbing feeling of being spied upon returned and he was at a loss as to how this could have happened. How had this group of Algerians managed to find him? They were real enough and he did not like them but he didn't know why they treated him this way. The last time he encountered them he had seen one of their guns a little too closely as one of the Algerians had held the weapon to his head while the others had watched and laughed. He had no idea what they wanted of him and once again he was afraid. Hopefully this time they would just go away but they always seemed to be there, never far away, and he dreaded that they would keep appearing.

But what would happen if he challenged them, or if they made demands and he refused? Would they kill him, and how would they do it? The answer, he resolved, was to do as they bid and he would be OK. He knew deep down, however, that they would keep following him. They had even followed him to the medical centre for his doctor's last appointment and all he could do was let them. The only real solution to the problem was to get them to stop following him but how this was to be achieved was beyond him.

He kept a diary of his fears and wrote to those he knew about his anxiety but he felt very alone trying to cope with the stress on his own. On at least three occasions in the past, he had reported his concerns to the police but, as he had no evidence of verbal or physical abuse, they were unable to do anything. As his fears increased, he became more disturbed so he decided his best course of action was to make a break for it by returning immediately to his parents' home in Kenya, and he planned his escape.

On 27 December he withdrew sufficient cash to purchase a ticket the next day but, with night falling, he felt it too dangerous to go back to his own room. He desperately needed somewhere to stay so he begged a fellow African friend to let him spend the night with him. He told his friend the whole story, about when and how he was first threatened and that he knew they would be waiting for him if he went back to his accommodation in Rue Pasteur. He would have to sleep on his friend's floor and it was going to be another cold night but he was wearing his warm, black hooded jacket and he would be OK – provided they didn't find him!

In the early morning of 28 December he checked that the €1,300 he had withdrawn the previous day was still in his pocket but by then he couldn't remember how he had acquired the money. He had been told it would buy him a return ticket to Kenya and he knew he had to go there straight away. He wasn't going to risk returning to his room and it would be easier for him to travel light with no suitcase. Outside it was cold and there were more flurries of snow, a precipitation he had only experienced after arriving in Lyon a year or so ago, having spent all of his previous life in Kenya. While waiting at the bus stop to take him to Part-Dieu railway station for the express train to the airport he was aware he was being watched and that once again they were shadowing him. As he boarded the bus, he sensed they were following and they would know where he was going.

From Part-Dieu station it was a rapid journey to Lyon Saint Exupéry Airport where he went straight to the Air France ticket counter and, with a look over his shoulder, asked to buy in cash a return flight to Nairobi, outbound with the first available flight and inbound with the flight from Nairobi on 9 January. A ticket with British Airways was prepared via London Gatwick and, conveniently, flight BA2357, operated by a Boeing 737 with registration G-BSNV, was departing Lyon at 1115 local and, with the UK being one hour behind, arriving in Gatwick at 1125 local. Not so conveniently, however, flight BA2069 from London Gatwick to Nairobi, operated by a Boeing 747-400, was not scheduled to depart until late that evening at 2225, a transit of eleven hours. Even with time spent disembarking and boarding there would be at least a long, nine to ten hours layover to endure, and that would be followed by an overnight flight to Nairobi of eight and a half hours with a scheduled arrival, allowing for the three hours' time change, of 1000 local. Mukonyi was pleased to be soon on his way but, as he handed over his €1,300, he was oblivious to the Gatwick transit time this journey entailed for his attention was drawn again to his stalkers, who he was sure were in the terminal and still keeping an eye on him. Paul went across to the British Airways check-in desk where he spoke in French to the clerk. Quickly he was processed and the check-in clerk politely wished him, 'Bon voyage Monsieur Mukonyi.' Paul didn't reply, in fact he didn't even hear his name, for he could now see his pursuers, but this time he had a plan and they would not beat him.

He went to the office of the commissariat de police and informed them he was being followed. He described the group stalking him and took care to warn the police that they were armed. One of the policemen was very helpful and joined Paul to say he was imagining things but that he would remain with him for a while. The terminal building was now very crowded and Paul recognised two of the people there. They both were members of that group and one of them had held a gun to his right temple a few days before, but he felt safe with the police escort. The policeman, however, only waited for a short time then returned to his office.

Paul was now very nervous and, when he heard, but mostly missed, the content of an announcement about his flight, BA2357 to London Gatwick, he immediately returned to the BA desk to enquire. While Mukonyi had been anxiously waiting in the terminal to board, however, unfortunately for him the BA flight outbound from Gatwick to Lyon was still on its way owing to its very late departure from Gatwick, and it was the same aircraft and crew that would operate the return flight on which Mukonyi would travel. As this would have a knock-on effect of also delaying the Lyon departure, the crew had radioed ahead on the BA company frequency of 131.8 MHz to inform the Lyon operations staff that heavy snow in Gatwick had caused their delay.

On receipt of this information, it was announced to the waiting passengers that the departure to London of BA2357 would be delayed because of weather and, on only partly hearing the message, Mukonyi had become alarmed. The BA clerk at the desk explained to him that the departure had been delayed and when he anxiously asked for the reason he was told, 'It's because of the weather, Sir.' The reference had obviously been to the weather in London but, as far as Paul could observe, there was nothing unusual about the weather outside and he quickly became suspicious. Somehow the pursuing group had managed to orchestrate this delay and it was clear they were still after him! He knew that, if he returned to the police, he would be safe for they were aware of his predicament and they had said they were there to help. Very carefully he made his way back, making sure he wasn't seen en route. This time the police wanted to check his documents, which reassured him, and another policeman was appointed to look after him until he boarded. He also asked if a police escort could be waiting for him on the aircraft to accompany him to his seat.

The problem for Paul now was that not only did the Boeing 737 aircraft operating BA2357 back to Gatwick arrive very late in Lyon owing to the disruption of heavy snow in the UK, but the snowing persisted and was causing a further long delay to flight BA2357's departure from Lyon. The delay was proving to be very extensive indeed but Mukonyi felt reassured with the protection provided by the police officer. It also gave the BA airport duty manager the chance to mingle with passengers in the terminal to help explain the delay and on his walk round he noticed Paul being escorted by a policeman. Paul's behaviour was clearly attracting attention even before he had boarded the aircraft.

Eventually, after a delay of about nine hours, flight BA2357 began to board and, with the policeman by his side, Paul was able to jump to the front of the queue and be chaperoned to the door of the aircraft. The airport duty manager was there when he arrived but, as Paul was still being accompanied by the police, the manager once again assumed he was a deportee. The policeman told him that was not the case but he mentioned nothing of Mukonyi's previous conduct and the manager, who didn't ask why he had been escorted, considered there was no reason to deny him boarding. This was an opportunity lost, for had he enquired he may have reached a different conclusion. Neither of the police officers involved with the young Kenyan had considered that his behaviour merited noting in their daily log so vital information that might have warned of Paul's condition had not been shared.

As Mukonyi boarded he showed his pass to one of the cabin crew, who handed him over to the Senior Cabin Crew Member. She had been alerted by him arriving accompanied by a policeman so had decided she would seat the passenger herself and Paul, assuming that he had been expected, was pleased he was being taken personally to his seat. The accompanying policeman had left him by the door but then, on board, he became distressed when he realised that, in spite of his request, there was no police escort on the aircraft. While the Senior Cabin Crew Member was taking him to his seat, he had asked why no there was no one from the police on board to be with him but was told she didn't know. He also asked bizarre questions such as 'Where is the flight deck?' and 'Is it possible to hijack the aircraft?' Although he appeared passive, he was very nervous and he also told her that he was being pursued by a group of people and that he wished to remain out of sight. He also requested that she ask for a police escort for him at Gatwick. As they had a light load, she decided that the best thing to do was to sit him out of the way at the back of the cabin. As they proceeded to the rear of the aircraft, he looked around at his fellow passengers boarding and was alarmed to see the same pair following him he had spotted in the terminal. They had got on board too! It was obvious they were trying to disguise themselves but he knew it was them in spite of their attempts to change their appearance. He ducked his head down as he made his way to his seat hoping they wouldn't see him but, in spite of this setback, he already had another plan in his head and this time he was sure he could stop them.

Before take-off the Senior Cabin Crew Member visited the flight deck to inform the captain about Mukonyi's conduct and his strange questions and the captain instructed her to keep him at the back of the cabin and to monitor his behaviour throughout the flight. BA2357 finally departed Lyon at 2107 local, almost ten hours late, and after take-off Paul got up to look round to check if any police were on board and soon a stewardess approached him to ask if he needed assistance. He was surprised she was so nice to him and it encouraged him to ask her the questions again that were still going around in his head. As a crew member she would know the answers. 'Where is the cockpit?' he enquired, 'and how difficult is it to hijack an aircraft?' Rather than answer his unusual questions she gently showed him back to his seat and left him there. As she walked away Paul watched her go all the way up the cabin and he thought she had entered the flight deck at the front of the aircraft, but he wondered where the cockpit would be on the Nairobi flight. Would it be in the same place as on this aircraft or on a bigger aircraft would it be upstairs? He would be able to make certain by asking the question on that flight as well.

Soon the flight was well on its way to London and Paul decided to call the police to make sure he was being met at Gatwick. He had already told the Senior Cabin Crew Member but he wanted to make sure. He went to the rear galley and picked up the handset of the interphone in an attempt to call the police but he didn't know how to operate it or that it only connected with other stations on the aircraft, so he got no response. Once more the flight attendant approached him and this time asked him to leave the phone alone and not to touch the handset again. Paul settled back into his seat but he was not idle. He decided to use his time productively and, as a precaution, he removed the lifejacket from the stowage beneath his seat to read the instructions on how to don it in an emergency. Fortunately, the stewardess was still keeping a close eye on him and she told him firmly to put it back.

The unusual conduct of Paul Mukonyi was no less so on the flight than it had been in the terminal and from the outset he had attracted the cabin crew's attention. They became concerned by his manner and the Senior Cabin Crew Member visited the flight deck once more to update the captain on his behaviour. He again instructed her to keep an eye on Mukonyi, to report periodically back to him and to ensure he did not approach the flight deck. The captain also asked if she knew what had happened in Lyon but all she could report was that he had been escorted to the flight by a policeman and that he had requested a police escort in Gatwick. He tried to radio back to BA Operations in Lyon on the company frequency for more information but in spite of repeated attempts he received no reply. The cabin crew liaised well with the captain and kept him fully informed and, when within radio range of Gatwick, he transmitted the details to BA Operations.

'We have a strange one,' reported the captain. 'A gentleman was escorted by security to the aircraft. Apparently, he was set upon in Lyon and is catching a flight to Nairobi. He's very, very nervous and he believes there is a chance that he will be set upon again. He is requesting some kind of escort.'

BA Operations, instead of relaying the details to BA Security where the situation may have been easier to manage internally, had called Aviation Defence International, an agency that BA could use as a back-up as the company's staff were trained to deal with security events of this nature. Operations had called them to request an agent to escort Mukonyi in the terminal from arrival to departure and they had provided the details received from the BA2357 captain. It was now up to Aviation Defence International to inform the appointed agent of the circumstances.

BA2357 arrived at Gate 49 at Gatwick at 2112 on the late evening of 28 December, only 1 hour and 13 minutes before the scheduled departure of BA2069 at 2225. Although the incoming flight's delay had drastically reduced Paul's transit time at Gatwick, it didn't leave much time to transfer to an international service. Fortunately, the Nairobi flight was departing from Gate 54, only a short distance from Gate 49 and, with no hold luggage, he had no problem transferring in time. It was also unlikely, with so many delays in the present difficulties, that BA2069 would depart on time.

When BA2357's forward door was opened for disembarkation Mukonyi noticed the same stewardess coming towards him and stopping beside him at his seat row. A few minutes later the passengers in front of Paul vacated their seats to follow those leaving and he also stood up but was asked politely by the stewardess to wait for a short time. This was just what he wanted to hear, for now he was reassured that someone must have been in contact with the Gatwick police and that shortly he would be under their protection.

Aviation Defence International's agent had turned up at Gate 49 only a few minutes after the Lyon flight's arrival so was waiting to meet Mukonyi at the door. As the Kenyan had been delayed from disembarking, before handover a cabin crew member was able to brief the agent about the young man's conduct on the flight and, in particular, his request for a police escort at Gatwick. Whatever had happened to the information provided by BA Operations was not known, but it had certainly not reached the Aviation Defence International agent who was going 'to work at the coalface' as Mukonyi's escort. She was under the impression that her task was to perform a customer service role with a nervous passenger, but it was not clear who had issued this instruction. The agent had known nothing of Mukonyi's bizarre behaviour on the flight from Lyon until being informed by the stewardess at the aircraft door. At least she had now been alerted by the crew that there was a bit more to her task than just holding a nervous passenger's hand. The cabin crew member who had remained with Mukonyi then accompanied him to the forward door and, when he finally exited, the uniformed Aviation Defence International agent approached him and enquired, 'Mr Paul Mukonyi?' Paul nodded, and together with his escort they proceeded along the airbridge towards the terminal. This time his plan was working and he was going to defeat his pursuers.

Once in the terminal area Mukonyi began identifying people that he believed were following him and, at the transfer desk, started claiming that people from the Lyon flight, whom he feared, were also checking in for the Nairobi flight. The presence of the Aviation Defence International agent made the BA ground staff at the desk think he was a deportee but, as he was clearly spoken and coherent, a staff member quickly compared the passenger manifests and was able to reassure him that he was the only passenger transferring from Lyon. Paul was not convinced and, still concerned, he continued to point out passengers he thought were going to harm him. Mukonyi and the agent then proceeded through security screening while the young Kenyan persisted in spotting passengers, including VIPs and those being screened for other flights, who he thought were following him with the intention of causing injury. During their entire period together Paul's only dialogue had been in reference to those who intended him harm and at no time did he engage in normal conversation. After due process they finally arrived at Gate 54 where they were met by the flight dispatcher, and the Aviation Defence International agent let him know that her charge was not a deportee but that his behaviour had been unusual. She mentioned Mukonyi's strange comments about people he claimed were following him with intent to do harm, but he had not committed any offence. What additional information she did impart to the dispatcher is not known for she had been at pains to point out she was only doing 'a babysitting job'.

After listening to the agent, the dispatcher decided to talk to Paul himself, but the young Kenyan then began mumbling about 'arms' and 'drugs' which sufficiently alarmed the dispatcher to call for police assistance but, in spite of such serious remarks, he did not call the BA station manager, who may have been able to assist with mediation. Over the phone he relayed to an officer at Gatwick Police Station what the agent had told him and what mumbling he had heard from the Kenyan. Two constables were then dispatched to have a word with Mukonyi, to assess his demeanour and to check whether or not he was safe to fly.

When the two uniformed policemen arrived at Gate 54 in the terminal, they were met by the flight dispatcher, the Aviation Defence International agent and Mukonyi and, as they had already been briefed at the station, they only had a few words with the dispatcher before approaching Mukonyi to interview him. As the details they had received from the dispatcher had originally been provided by the agent, it appeared that they did not question her. However, the agent was the one most aware of Paul's actions and was the one person who, more than anyone else, may have been able to provide insight into Paul's bizarre manner. The Aviation Defence International agent had been well briefed by the BA2357 crew and, during the one and a half hours she had been in close company with Mukonyi, she had witnessed primary evidence of his behaviour and had observed his distress when commenting on imaginary assailants. She, of all those in the chain, was best placed to report on the young Kenyan's conduct. If the two constables had spoken to her and had encouraged the agent to offer an opinion, she may have told them about Mukonyi's very strange conduct. The agent, of course, could have volunteered the information to the police, but, since they had taken charge, she may have considered it was not her place as a 'babysitter' to intervene. With the police only having limited information from the dispatcher via the recipient of his call to the police station, more than likely no detailed evidence from the agent and, perhaps, little or no appropriate training or experience, they did not appear best qualified to assess the young Kenyan's suitability for carriage, and it couldn't be said it was fair to leave any decision to them.

The policemen then interviewed the Kenyan for about 10 minutes and afterwards informed the dispatcher that they 'considered him OK to fly and we will escort him to the aircraft and speak to the crew'. The flight dispatcher was aware that, whatever the police concluded about permitting Mukonyi to travel, it was the captain who would make the final decision and that he could refuse to accept the Kenyan on board if he considered him a risk. While the Aviation Defence International agent, the two policemen and Mukonyi proceeded to Door 2 Left, therefore, the dispatcher returned to his duties of closing the flight. Paul was pleased to have another police escort, this time to the aircraft side, but as they walked down the airbridge, he now expressed concerns that someone might have smuggled a bomb on board the flight.

'The accompanying officers convinced him of the security arrangements at Gatwick,' Chief Inspector Alan Wingrove, the commander of police at the airport, later stated. 'Although he was confused, he was not disruptive and showed no signs of mental health problems. They deemed he was nervous of flying.'

In charge of the cabin crew on BA2069 was Cabin Services Director Laura Boyd and she was at Door 2 Left when the four men arrived. While the Aviation Defence International agent waited with Mukonyi on the airbridge by the door, the two police officers approached Laura and one of them explained the situation. The policeman told her that it was their opinion that the Kenyan was a nervous and confused passenger who, although apparently distressed at seeing people he thought were following him, had not broken any rules or had been in breach of the law. The police officer said that they had interviewed Mukonyi, he did not appear to be under any influence of alcohol or drugs and that they considered he was 'OK to fly'. They acknowledged that the final decision would rest with the captain but they suggested that, if the young Kenyan was accepted for travel, he should be monitored by the crew. By then the flight dispatcher had re-joined the group by the door and Cabin Services Director Boyd left for the cockpit to inform the captain of what she had been told.

Chapter 2

Glasgow to London Gatwick

Captain Bill Hagan was in command of the BA2069 flight to Nairobi that late evening and he had arrived on board earlier with his crew. Bill was from Northern Ireland but lived in Glasgow and, like Mukonyi's delayed journey with the heavy snow that morning, he had faced the same ordeal trying to fly to Gatwick. He had planned to take his family with him on this trip and they were also trying to fly down in the late afternoon to join him on the Nairobi flight, but they were having the same problem.

In British Airways in 2000 there was a system for distributing work called Bidline whereby pilots submitted bids for published lines of work for the following month. These bids were then processed on a seniority basis and Captain Hagan was somewhere in the middle. In 2000 he was pleased to have been awarded Christmas at home and then, on 28 December, a nine-day trip to Nairobi on which he planned to take his family and they could celebrate New Year there together. He would then fly three one-day shuttles from Nairobi and back while his wife and children could remain in the hotel and enjoy their time in Nairobi.

On the morning of the 28th, Bill had heard an early warning bulletin of the snow on the radio so he quickly grabbed his already packed suitcase and headed for Glasgow Airport, where he found Gatwick flights cancelled and the few flights for Heathrow already full. On these flights, extra cockpit seats, known as jump seats, were being offered to crew members but other pilots, whose own flights were departing earlier than his from Heathrow, were being taken first, so he had to wait. He then had good fortune, as the captain operating the Los Angeles flight from Heathrow was told that his flight had been cancelled so Bill was given his place and soon he was on his way.

After his arrival at Heathrow, he boarded the transfer coach to Gatwick but the journey was slow as the driver was proceeding with care on the snow-covered M25 motorway. At the airport he hurried to BA Operations in Concorde House and checked in at 2110 with only 5 minutes to spare before the deadline. Luck had most certainly been on his side.

Captain Hagan was now concerned about his family's journey so he checked flight arrivals. To his surprise he noticed that a flight in-bound from Glasgow had an estimated arrival time of 2215, ten minutes before the Nairobi scheduled departure of 2225, and he hoped his wife and children would be on it. He mentioned this to the BA duty manager who said that, as BA2069 was likely to be delayed they might just make it, and he would do what he could to expedite their transfer if his family was on board the flight from Glasgow. Their two suitcases, however, would need to wait until the next day. Captain Hagan was also informed that his cabin crew on BA2069 had checked in earlier and, as Gate 54 was nearby, they had walked ahead to the aircraft. In the meantime, he met his two co-pilots, Senior First Officers Richard Webb and Phil Watson, and they had already started printing the flight briefing paperwork.

The crew list for BA2069:

Captain	William Hagan
Senior First Officer	Philip Watson
Senior First Officer	Richard Webb

Cabin crew:

Cabin Services Director (CSD)	Laura Boyd
	Christine Wetton
	Ian Saunders
	Philip Andrews
	Rowena Teager
	David Lonergan
	Eva Osle
	Kimberley Parker
	Caroline Rankin
	Kate Donello
	Alison Sheridan
	Wilson Roveri
	Collette Manning
	Ben Marshall
	Penny Lester
	Victoria Underwood

SFO Richard Webb was a 35-year-old ex-Royal Air Force pilot and he and the captain were scheduled to fly together for the whole round trip operating out from and back to Nairobi, twice to Dar-es-Salaam and once to the Seychelles. As these duty days were shorter, they could be operated by only two pilots.

The overnight flight down to Nairobi could, in fact, also be operated by two pilots but, on this occasion, SFO Phil Watson was the third pilot on the crew. Although he was not essential on this sector, he was positioning down to Nairobi as his presence was needed as relief pilot for crew rest requirements on the longer overnight flight back to Gatwick the following evening when he would join the crew operating the return. Phil, now 38, had also served for years in the Royal Air Force, latterly flying Phantoms, and had spent a lot of time in the world of aerobatics. Later that night he was to tell the captain that he had spent 'half his life upside down'.

As Phil's trip had been planned for only two flights he would operate as co-pilot on the way down and relief co-pilot on the way back. Richard, the second co-pilot on this overnight trip, would, although not strictly required, act as relief pilot. He would have his chance to do more flying on the 'Dar' and 'Seychelles' return trips. Richard, in the role of third pilot, would occupy the third seat for take-off and climb and descent and landing, and would usually take the first rest period. He would then fill in for the others taking the middle and last periods and, as the captain was the handling pilot on this sector, he had elected to take his rest last.

The three pilots assembled at the briefing desk and checked the departure airfield details, the planned route for any problems, and the weather forecasts for airports locally, en route, at destination and at the designated alternate, Mombasa. All seemed satisfactory, as were the conditions now at Gatwick, and, as there was no turbulence anticipated on the sector, a smooth flight could be anticipated. On viewing the defects, it was noted that one flap track fairing for streamlining was missing from the left wing which would cause slightly more drag but, on checking the fuel, this had been taken into account so the calculated fuel figure of 92,000kgs, or 92 tonnes, or metric tons, was agreed. To the layperson, however, the missing fairing could look like a part of the wing was missing and, although it would not be seen overnight, it could be spotted at first light. Richard, as the relief pilot, would undertake the 'walk-around' checks before boarding and he offered to brief the cabin crew afterwards on his way to the flight deck. They could then reassure any passengers in the cabin section adjacent to the missing component that this was a known defect and that it did not affect the flight. Also, on inspecting the operational notices, it was observed that a new entry stated that, if the aircraft had been de-iced at departure, this detail had to be recorded in the Technical Log after landing at destination.

Captain Hagan and Senior First Officer Watson then boarded the aircraft and the captain stopped briefly to speak to the flight dispatcher who was managing their departure. They discussed the passenger total, the fuel load, the de-icing of the aircraft and concurred that the departure delay was down to the weather. The captain also mentioned that his family of three was trying to join the flight from Glasgow and might arrive at the last minute so could he please keep Door 2 Left open for as long as possible? He then walked round the aircraft to greet the cabin crew and to brief Cabin Services Director Laura Boyd, saying that there would be a short delay loading the baggage, that they should have a smooth journey and that his family might be able to catch the flight.

On the upper deck he said hello to the rest of the cabin crew before joining Phil on the flight deck and then, a short time later, Richard arrived having completed the external walk-around checks. He had visually confirmed that the de-icing had been completed and was able to tell them that the baggage loading would be finished in about half an hour. This was good news for the captain's family for now they had a chance of getting on board. As Bill had been lucky earlier on his trip to Gatwick, so had his family, for suddenly he could see from the flight deck that his wife and two children had arrived at the desk in the terminal. As they entered the airbridge he assumed they were the last to board, but there was still one passenger waiting, a Mr Mukonyi, and as the three entered the aircraft they barely noticed the young Kenyan by the door with his escort, two constables and the flight dispatcher.

Phil called Air Traffic Control (ATC) for departure clearance with the call sign Speedbird 2069 and, as he finished copying it down, a Midhurst Departure from runway 26L, the captain made a short introductory PA to the passengers. He told them of the short delay to load the baggage and that, when ready, they would be departing towards the west then turning over Brighton. He continued by saying that the conditions were clear so a smooth flight could be anticipated but that they should keep their seat belts fastened at all times during the flight, even if the seat belt sign was off, in case of unexpected turbulence. Little could anyone at the time have realised the dire importance of the captain's warning!

As the pilots on the flight deck were busy preparing the aircraft and completing the departure checks, Laura, the Cabin Services Director, was on her way from Door 2 Left to speak to the captain. He, however, knew nothing of the long chain of Mukonyi's bizarre behaviour that had stretched from the Lyon terminal to BA2069's Door 2 Left, or of the many links in the chain that had been broken.

Captain Hagan, about to be asked to decide, was not helped by the fact that the detail he was about to receive had not in any way been communicated in a direct line, for what he was about to hear from Laura was now sixth hand. Not only that, but the greatest impediment to the captain making any informed decision was that he had checked in about the same time as BA2357's arrival from Lyon and he was oblivious to the drama that had been unfolding with Mukonyi. Through no fault of his own he was also not best placed to make a decision of such importance and had he been better apprised of the circumstances he would have handled the situation differently. When the BA2357 captain from Lyon was later asked if, with his knowledge of events, he would have accepted Paul on BA 2069, he replied that he would most certainly have not. Captain Hagan had no such privilege.

The Cabin Services Director, Laura, then entered the flight deck to confirm the passenger count of 379 passengers plus 6 infants, and to mention that the captain's wife was in First Class and his children were in Club World. She then informed the captain that they were almost ready to close the doors but there was an unusual situation at Door 2 Left as the dispatcher was waiting with the police who were holding a transfer passenger from another flight. The police had escorted him to the aircraft as he thought he was being followed.

'The police say he is OK to travel,' she continued, 'with no sign of drugs or alcohol. The dispatcher would like to know if you are happy to take him?'

Captain Bill Hagan was reluctant to overrule the police so, having ascertained that the Cabin Services Director was prepared to accept him, so was he, and between them they agreed to take the man. Laura then conveyed that decision to the dispatcher and the police, who were still waiting with the Aviation Defence International agent and Mukonyi by the door, and shortly afterwards Door 2 Left was closed. The Cabin Services Director then spoke to the purser in charge of the World Traveller section and asked, 'Please ensure that Mr Mukonyi is escorted to his seat, keep an eye on him so you can monitor his state and report back, but only if there are any concerns.'

A cabin crew member was then instructed to escort Paul to his seat and, as they walked to the rear of the aircraft, the steward thought him to be an inexperienced traveler of a nervous disposition. He showed the young Kenyan his seat and paused to assist him stow his hand baggage, then he left to pass on his opinion of this passenger to his colleagues. Paul's seat number was 32H and he was pleased that he had been allocated an aisle seat as it would make it easier for him to move around without disturbing fellow passengers in the same row. Quickly he settled into his seat and fastened his seat belt. Mukonyi was on board!

Chapter 3

Airborne

A few minutes later the last cargo door was finally closed and, after clearance from Ground Control was received, BA2069 pushed back from Gate 54 at 2302, only 37 minutes late on the scheduled departure time of 2225. A good result considering the earlier extreme conditions. The arrival in Nairobi the next day, however, would also be late on the scheduled time of 0700, 1000 local, on the morning of Friday, 29 December, but there was a chance of making up some lost time along the way.

On the push back the captain started the engines and, with all engines running, the checks were completed. The push back truck was then detached and, when the all-clear signal had been given, clearance to taxi was requested and received. The aircraft, registration G-BNLM, or Lima Mike for short, was now ready to proceed under its own power and the captain began taxying the aircraft by easing the four thrust levers forward a little. The BA2069 take-off weight was 327,000kgs, 327 tonnes, well short of the maximum take-off weight of about 400 tonnes, depending on conditions, but the 747-400 still needed a nudge to start rolling. The captain then followed the taxi route to runway 26L for take-off and remarked on the way that 'he would do his best to catch up for lost time on the way'.

BA's standard operating procedure, referred to as a monitored approach, was a mandatory practice to be adhered to on every flight. On this sector to Nairobi, Captain Hagan had elected to be the handling pilot so he would fly the take-off out of London and the initial climb. At an appropriate moment, he would hand over to the co-pilot, Senior First Officer Watson, referred to as the non-handling pilot, which was something of an oxymoron, and he would then fly the aircraft for the remainder of the climb, the cruise, the descent and the initial approach when, once again, at a suitable point, the captain would regain control and fly the final approach and landing. Such a procedure provided effective monitoring by both pilots of the take-off and departure and the approach and landing phases of the flight.

Approaching the holding point for 26L the Tower Controller cleared BA2069 to line up and, as they turned on to the centreline, further cleared them for an immediate take-off. Without stopping, when lined up on the runway the captain advanced the thrust levers to take-off power and, when set, the airspeed began to increase rapidly. At 150 knots the captain eased back on the control column, rotated the nose gently towards 12 degrees and, passing about 10 degrees nose-up, Lima Mike lifted off the runway with an airborne time of 2319. Following the Midhurst Departure, the captain climbed straight ahead for 6 miles, banked left for Brighton on the south coast and then, with the autopilot now engaged, turned towards central France. Already BA2069 was making up time.

Passing 10,000 feet, about ten minutes after take-off, the captain switched off the landing lights which, as was normal practice, had been left on as a 'see and be seen' precaution, switched off the seat belt signs as the sky was clear and the ride was smooth and then handed control of the aircraft to Phil. It had been decided that about two hours rest period for each pilot would be suitable for the flight time remaining as that would allow for all three pilots to be back on the fight deck about an hour before landing, so Richard announced his departure and went off for the first break. The captain and co-pilot, except for rest periods, would now remain in their designated seats for the remainder of the flight, captain on the left and senior first officer on the right, and Richard, as relief pilot, would play musical chairs when the others had their rests.

The visibility was excellent and, thirty minutes on their way, they had an outstanding view of Paris. Captain Hagan took the opportunity to speak again to the passengers, telling those on the left that the Eiffel Tower could be clearly seen, then informing all that the route from Paris was towards Nice, down the west coast of Italy past Rome to overhead Sicily, across the Mediterranean passing over Malta and, at the far coast, crossing into Libya. From there the route would proceed south east across Libya, then across southern Sudan and finally into Kenyan airspace. They were making good progress and were now hoping for only a 15 minutes delay with an estimated arrival time of 0715 UTC (Universal Time Coordinated – same as GMT), 1015 local.

Top of climb was reached on the way to Nice and Lima Mike settled at the initial planned cruise height of Flight Level 330 (FL330), which was equivalent to an altitude of 33,000 feet with standard pressure setting selected on the altimeters. FL330 would then be maintained until fuel consumption reduced the weight sufficiently to reach the next available higher level of FL370, 37,000 feet, which was expected to be achieved just before entering Libyan airspace. At such high levels speed is measured as a Mach number where Mach 1.00 is the speed of sound in the ambient atmosphere. Mach 0.85, a fairly standard cruising speed at which BA2069 was flying, represents a speed of 85% of the speed of sound in the prevailing environment, and the actual Mach number being flown is shown as a digital readout at the bottom of the speed tape. Captain Hagan thought that his passengers had been through a lot so to try and arrive as near schedule as possible he increased the speed to Mach 0.87.

Dinner was being served in the cabin and all was proceeding as normal except for one large gentleman sitting at the back and on the right of the World Traveller section in aisle seat 32H. Mr Mukonyi was once again attracting attention and his constant restlessness was upsetting his two fellow passengers sitting in seats 32J and 32K in the same row. They were two Americans, both worked for Boeing and both had travelled extensively. Both had noticed him when boarding as he had been accompanied to his seat by a cabin crew member and he seemed to be acting strangely. They noticed he had requested the same meal as them and that he had not ordered alcohol but he was very nervous and agitated.

In the cockpit the flight was progressing well as traffic was light and Air Traffic Control (ATC) had been able to offer BA2069 a direct routing to the Italian island of Elba, from where they could see the lights of Rome and Naples in the distance. The passengers now began to settle down for the night so the main cabin lights were dimmed and the blinds were shut to prevent the early morning sun from waking those asleep. Soon afterwards the Cabin Services Director, Laura, called the flight deck to confirm the ETA of 0715 UTC for Nairobi as she wished to plan the cabin crew rest periods.

The flight continued to cruise at FL 330 but, to take advantage of the more efficient level of FL370, it was a requirement for the aircraft to be at that level before entering Libyan airspace. To reach the level, a lower weight, preferably below 300 tonnes, would also be needed, so a close eye would have to be kept on when the climb could start. Italian radar control was contacted with a request to maintain FL330 for the time being and that was approved with the proviso that the higher level of FL370 was reached just before Malta.

Prior to climbing to a higher level, it is necessary to check the aircraft's performance data to confirm that the aircraft can operate safely within the required parameters. If an aircraft flies too fast and close to the speed of sound, high speed buffeting occurs, caused by shock waves forming on the wings. If it flies too slowly and close to the aerodynamic stall, low speed buffeting occurs caused by turbulent airflow on the wing and some lift is lost. If the speed is allowed to drop further, a point is reached at which all lift is lost and, as the wings are unable to sustain flight, a full aerodynamic stall occurs. The nose dips below the horizon and the aircraft plummets vertically downwards very rapidly. Recovery to a safe flying speed is achieved by converting height to speed by pushing the nose down a bit further to a shallow angle and by applying full power until the required flying speed is regained. The aircraft can then be gradually pulled out of the descent and flown straight and level. Early recognition of and swift recovery from an impending aerodynamic stall is an essential part of basic pilot training and is periodically practiced on the simulator throughout a pilot's career.

In the cruise, indicated airspeed is shown on a vertical speed tape on the left of the primary flight display and the required indicated airspeed is displayed on the tape in a little window in slightly larger digits than other speeds marked on the tape. Airspeed indicated on the instrument is much lower than the true airspeed owing to the thin atmosphere but it can be used to certify that the aircraft is flying at the safest and most economical speed for the prevailing conditions. A bit above and below the required indicated airspeed are little red squares shown vertically in line on the tape and they mark the segments of danger if approaching the maximum and minimum speeds. As long as the speed is maintained in the vertical space between the little red chequers, the aircraft is flying at a safe speed. BA2069's weight by Malta was calculated to be 298 tonnes and a check of the data for FL370 confirmed that a climb could be initiated and that Mach 0.85 would be the best and safest speed to maintain at the higher level. Passing over Sicily Captain Hagan had already made up 20 minutes so cruising at 37,000 feet at a slightly lower Mach 0.85 with an arrival of about 15 minutes late was better than expected under the circumstances.

Approaching Malta, a climb to FL370 was initiated and at 0150 UTC Lima Mike passed overhead the island at the new cruise level. The second rest period now began and Phil vacated his position to start his rest while Richard took his place in the co-pilot seat. From Malta the flight continued over the Mediterranean and on towards the Libya border.

In the cabin, the crew had earlier commenced their rest rotation, which had been arranged to finish at 0515 UTC, about two hours before arrival, as CSD Laura had planned that by then the full cabin crew complement would be back on duty to prepare the breakfast service. Another person, however, had also taken an interest in the rest schedule, and other procedural details, and that was the nervous Kenyan gentleman by the name of Paul Mukonyi who was sitting in seat 32H. He had taken advantage of his aisle seat to walk around without disturbing his fellow travellers and through the night he had been away from his seat a lot. He constantly pestered the cabin crew working in the mid to rear sections of the aircraft, and crew members complained to one another about Mukonyi's behaviour. He would go to one galley for a while and ask questions and then go to another galley and ask the same questions again. He enquired about the location of the flight deck, the number of cabins in the aircraft, the number of passengers on board and tried to glean information about crewing levels such as how many men were on the crew.

The young Kenyan had also asked about breakfast and had been told that he would be wakened about two hours before arrival to be served, so he was aware that a full cabin crew would not be on duty till then. The time of arrival now seemed to have become a fixation for him as he frequently checked his watch and persistently asked others for the landing time. Mukonyi was a big man, six feet tall, muscular and weighing about 200lbs/91kgs. He wore a black, hooded, weatherproof jacket with a shiny, nylon appearance and was conspicuous by his size but, as he wandered in World Traveller, it was his behaviour that was now drawing attention. One passenger who noticed his unusual conduct was Mary Kevari. She was on her way from the United States for a three-week photography safari in East Africa and this was her dream trip. She was trying to settle down to sleep when she reported seeing 'a hooded man walking up and down the plane, mumbling things, being rude'.

'They told me I could have a nicer seat,' she heard the man grumble. 'I come on the plane and you want to treat me like this?'

'A flight attendant asked him to keep his voice down,' Mary added, 'and "Don't touch me" was his reply'.

'I'm not touching you, sir,' she remembered the attendant replying, 'just please keep your voice down.'

'Everyone around had noticed his behaviour,' she reported, 'but I was exhausted and it wasn't important to me at the time.'

It was also thought that earlier he had reconnoitred his route by wandering up towards the rear of First Class, had climbed the stairs that led to the upper deck and had waited there for a short time within sight of the cockpit door. But now he once again made his way to the rear galley where he approached one of the stewards he had spoken to earlier and asked him what he was doing. Mukonyi was politely requested to return to his seat and having done so he still appeared fidgety and uneasy to the two Americans sitting beside him.

Libya now lay ahead and, as BA2069 proceeded at FL370 along airway UB512, at 0307 UTC it then crossed into Libyan airspace. In the darkness could be seen the first yellow glows of burning gas marking the numerous oil wells scattered into the distance over the vast expanse of the desert. In such remote regions encountered in Africa it is normal practice to fly a track offset 1nm to the right of the airway centreline. With the advent of very precise navigation systems this prevents conflict between opposite direction traffic that is proceeding precisely on the centreline where, owing to error or malfunction, aircraft may be flying in different directions at the same level and in great danger of collision. With each tracking 1nm to the right the two aircraft can pass safely 2nm apart. The offset was now keyed into the Flight Management System and, as the aircraft flew deeper into the desert, it made a slight adjustment to pick up the new track 1nm to the right. At this stage of the journey the flight was going well, and the estimated landing time of about 0700 UTC with on chocks at 0715 UTC/1015 local still looked good.

Mukonyi had once again been attracting attention, however, but nothing untoward had been reported by the cabin crew, which was unusual for such a busy flight. Compared to the actions of the crew on the Lyon–Gatwick flight, the lack of crew communication on BA2069 was more than a little inadequate. It was, of course, a bigger aircraft, more crew, longer flight, busy cabins, flying overnight, changing shifts, tiredness, etc and these probably contributed to the breakdown of communications. Some of the junior crew members, however, who had earlier been irritated by the young Kenyan's annoying conduct, had expressed concern within their group about his mental well-being but, unacceptably, had not shared this information. This scenario, however, only related to information not being relayed from the bottom to the top and it is surprising that no one at the top, even out of simple curiosity, had felt compelled to reach out to junior members of the crew. Had the Cabin Services Director enquired, that may have triggered some action. The response may also have been sufficiently alarming for her to report immediately to the captain what she had been told, and precautions could have been taken. What is clear, however, is that, for whatever reason, the Cabin Services Director knew nothing of Mukonyi's strange conduct or of his restless wandering and, by consequence, neither did the captain.

At about this time, Laura had decided to take her break and she called the flight deck to let the captain know that all was quiet in the cabin, that she was starting her rest break and the name of the crew member who would be in charge in her absence. She also checked if the arrival estimate had changed, which it had not, and then she, along with some other crew members, retired to the crew rest seats at the very rear of the aircraft. In the upper rest area, in a section above the last ten rows of passenger seats, some more crew were already resting in bunks.

Mukonyi's restless behaviour had continued and his conduct had prevented the Americans sitting in the same row from catching any sleep. He had also been asking them repeatedly about the landing time but now, as he settled into his seat for what turned out to be a short spell, he enquired what the local time was at that moment in Nairobi. The Americans told him it was just after seven o'clock local time, three hours ahead of British time.

About three hours remained now till landing and it was time for the captain's rest so the musical chairs began again. Richard, as the relief pilot, vacated his position and Phil then sat in his designated seat as co-pilot once again. As he settled in, the captain gave him a quick briefing to bring him up to date. He told him that Laura had called to say she was going on her break and that she had not reported anything untoward in the cabin. Bill also asked to be wakened about an hour before landing, to call him at any time if needs be and he then vacated his seat for Richard to occupy.

BA2069 was now in a remote south east region of Libya and contact with their Air Traffic Control (ATC) centre had to be maintained using High Frequency (HF) radio. HF had been in use since the Second World War but, at the start of the Millennium, it was still the only means of long-distance communication in most of the isolated areas of Africa. HF transmissions bounce off the ionosphere and then return to earth where the signal is received, but the level of the ionosphere changes between day and night, with greater range at night, so several frequencies had to be available.

Depending on the circumstances, the pilot had to find the best frequency, of which Libyan ATC had five, but these frequencies were also used by numerous other long-distance ATC centres, so it could be difficult to communicate by HF and its reliability could be uncertain.

Lima Mike was soon to cross into the northwest corner of Sudan where the flight would proceed southeast over northern Sudan and ahead on its track lay the remote town of El Obeid with its reasonably large airport. When within 200 nautical miles range of the town, communications by the much clearer Very High Frequency (VHF) radio would once again be available for a short period for reporting to El Obeid Control Tower but, when outside of the range on the far side of the airport, it would be back to HF radio.

The pilots' bunk area was inside the cockpit, on the left side aft of the captain's seat, and could be accessed directly. The entrance was only two or three paces from the pilots' seats so a sleeping colleague could be shaken awake in a few seconds if quickly required back on duty. A short central corridor ran down the side of the bunk area and that led to the flight deck door at the back. The captain's day had been very tiring so he quickly stripped down to his underwear, inserted his earplugs and fell into the lower bunk. He pulled a blanket over himself, loosely fastened the restraining belt across his waist and, with the time at about 0400 UTC, he instantly fell deeply asleep.

Unknown to Bill Hagan, at almost exactly the same moment in the passenger cabin, Paul Mukonyi, the Kenyan man who had been escorted to the departure gate by the police, was about to wander once more.

Chapter 4

The Attack

As the captain slumbered in the bunk, Mukonyi stirred from his seat. He stood up, calmly folded his blanket, carefully wound the cable wire around his headset to lay it on top, and placed his pillow beside it. He then tidied away all his personal belongings except for a small green notebook or folder that he kept in one hand. Before leaving, he spoke briefly again to the two American passengers sitting with him, reputedly muttering, 'My time has come, I must go now,' then slowly he walked forwards from the row of seats. His fellow passengers were pleased to see him go for his restless and nervous behaviour had made it almost impossible for them to sleep. They would not see him again.

Over the next forty minutes his whereabouts are still something of a mystery for only a few people observed his movements and he went largely unnoticed by the cabin crew as he had stopped asking them questions. He paused briefly in Galley 2 by the bottom of the stairs so it is surmised that he then climbed the stairs to the upper deck and remained there for about 10 minutes. If he did so he did not attract attention to himself and it is possible he spent some of the time unnoticed in the passenger toilet located on the right just outside the flight deck door.

As Mukonyi wandered in the cabin and lingered on the upper deck, the aircraft left Libyan airspace at the country's southeast corner and crossed the border into Sudan. The flight then headed southeast across the Western Desert of northern Sudan towards the Nuba Mountains in the south of the country. The region is arid and desolate with no habitation until interrupted by the small city of El Obeid with its 747 usable airport with a 10,000 feet runway situated about 200 miles southwest of Khartoum.

In the passenger cabin it was still dark with the blinds closed and few would have been aware of the impending sunrise. If someone on the left by an east-facing window had lifted the blind to peer towards the horizon, they would have noticed the approach of day, but otherwise darkness prevailed throughout the cabin.

The flight now approached position Delam and, on the flight deck, the Distance Measuring Equipment (DME) of the navigation beacon situated at El Obeid, Morse identification OBD, indicated 115 miles to run to the airport, about 13 minutes flying time away. The first red hint of sunrise, like a growing semi-circular glow, suddenly became visible from the cockpit under the low cloud layer far beyond the left wing. At altitude, especially flying towards the equator, it can be an awesome sight. As the sun began to appear over the distant horizon about 100 miles to the east, the distant horizon to the west was still shrouded in complete darkness and the blue-black shadow cast by the earth continued to blacken most of the sky above. The sun rises faster at lower latitudes and within ten minutes it would soon bathe the landscape below in sunshine and light the sky above to a bright blue. For the moment it was still mostly dark but shortly the breath-taking spectacle would unfold and would be a rewarding compensation for the pilots awake at such an early hour. Richard, the relief pilot, still occupied the captain's seat, and he would soon have the piercing sun fill the large window immediately to his left. This would be a good time to leave the flight deck and stretch his legs for a few minutes so he unfastened his seat belt and prepared to go. He decided to take the chance to go briefly to the cabin to remind crew members near the wing about the missing flap fairing and what to say if a passenger commented. He would be back in no time.

Before leaving the flight deck Richard waited until Phil had transmitted their position report to El Obeid Tower on the VHF frequency of 124.1 MHz for relay to Khartoum. 'El Obeid Tower, Speedbird 2069 good morning. Delam at 0447, level 370, El Obeid at 0500.'

Breaks for brief periods on an aircraft designed to be operated by only two flight crew members was normal practice and Richard intended to return in time for the next report at El Obeid at 0500. Before departing, however, Richard checked with Phil that he was happy to be left on his own for a few minutes and he waited for the other co-pilot to put on his shoulder straps as required by company regulations. He then pushed the captain's seat fully back and to the left side to make space to get out and, on leaving, gently closed the flight deck door behind him. As only one pilot was now being left in charge for a short period a cabin crew member should have been informed to monitor the flight deck but, as Richard did not intend to be absent for long, he left without saying anything. He then slowly descended the stairs to the main cabin deck, walked back to the rear galley at Door 4 Left and spoke to the crew member on duty there. On Richard's sojourn through the mostly sleeping passengers, it is highly possible that he and Mukonyi's paths crossed but, if so, it must have been like ships in the night for the Kenyan's movements went unnoticed by the co-pilot.

As Mukonyi lingered on the upper deck, Isaac Ferry, one of the sons of Brian Ferry, singer of the 70s band Roxy Music, noticed the Kenyan's strange behaviour. The Ferry family of Brian, his wife Lucy and three sons Isaac, Tara and Merlin were sitting next to the flight deck and 15-year-old Isaac was able to observe the man's movements.

'He was holding a prayer book', thought Isaac. 'He seemed to be delirious, talking away to himself. He walked up the aisle towards the cockpit', Isaac continued, 'and was hanging around the toilets.'

Now Mukonyi's 'hanging around' was over and he nervously approached the flight deck door, still muttering, possibly praying, and then hesitated outside. Why he chose this moment is not clear but it may have been as a consequence of his constant enquiries. He may have unexpectedly witnessed Richard leaving and, with three silver stripes on his jacket arm, Mukonyi may have mistaken him for the captain who had four stripes, as did some other passengers. If so, he may have thought this was his best opportunity. It may, of course, just have been by chance but, for whatever reason, after a few moments he was ready. Slowly the large Kenyan turned the handle, gently swung the door open and, still clutching his notebook, stepped forward to pass through the narrow doorway. The cockpit door opened into an equally narrow corridor which was confined on the right by the door of the crew toilet, now obscured by the fully open flight deck door, and further forwards on the right by the aircraft library manuals stowage. On the left the corridor was formed by the partition wall of the bunk area behind which the captain was fast asleep, a fact of which Mukonyi, without prior knowledge, would have been oblivious. The entrance to the bunk area was on a section at the forward end of the partition that angled gently towards the rear left window but, from the intruder's position, it would also have been obscured from view. About six feet/1.8 metres ahead from the entrance, the corridor opened onto the rear of the flight deck.

Looking forwards down the corridor into the cockpit from the open entry door Mukonyi would have seen ahead, on the left, part of the back of the captain's vacant seat, in the centre the pedestal with the thrust levers on top and the instrument displays behind and, on the right, the back of the third pilot's seat with, beyond, part of the back of the co-pilot's seat and one side of Phil sitting in it. The Kenyan would only have had a rear-view glimpse of part of the co-pilot's head and left shoulder but would have noticed that he was on his own and that only one pilot was at the controls. Now was his chance! At 0453 he continued through the entrance into the corridor, carefully shut the door behind him and moved silently forwards on his purposeful intrusion.

Phil had heard the noise of the flight deck door clicking shut and now looked round expecting to see Richard returning. To his surprise he saw instead a large African man with a very menacing appearance. Immediately he sensed danger. Phil was aware of the incident with the passenger being escorted by the police just before departure but, like his captain and fellow co-pilot, he had not seen the man and, like his colleagues, had no way of knowing that the passenger now standing in the flight deck, Mukonyi, was the same person. It was evident to Phil that this stranger had a determined, sinister and deadly look about him and, as the intruder stood his ground, they made eye contact. There was now little doubt left in the co-pilot's mind that the man was about to attack and he shouted at him to leave.

'Get out! You can't come in here, get out!' he yelled.

Mukonyi now stepped forwards into the open space by the captain's parked seat on the left side of the cockpit and, without any warning or uttering a word he suddenly threw himself at the co-pilot with his note book tumbling from his hand. He dived on his side to the right, flew over the central pedestal and squeezed his large bulk in a crash between Phil and the control column. The attacker landed heavily on the co-pilot with his right upper torso on Phil's lap, his back partly on the pilot's chest and his head and shoulders by Phil's right shoulder. The large Kenyan's upper body completely blocked the co-pilot's view of the instrument panel, as well as the glimmer of a horizon to the east in the still less than half light, and, in an instant, Phil lost all visual and instrument sight. In the same movement, like a goalkeeper diving to the side to snatch a ball, the attacker locked both his hands and arms on the control column and aggressively pulled it into his chest, tugging the control wheel to the left as he did so. The effect of the heavy pull rearwards on the column was immediate and the aircraft suddenly jerked forcefully upwards. Phil's initial sense of imminent danger had alerted him to the threat and he was braced for the attack. His reactions were fast and, in an instant, he managed quickly to stretch around Mukonyi's bulk and firmly grasp the controls in an attempt to counter the intruder's inputs. The strong backwards pull of the attacker that had jolted the aircraft sharply upwards caused the autopilot to disconnect as the pressure on the column exceeded the design limit break out force of 25lbs/11.4kgs. The disconnect warning system activated and instantly a red light flashed accompanied by a loud, undulating siren that filled the air. With the increase in nose-up angle the aircraft climbed rapidly and instantly the 'beep', 'beep', 'beep' of the altitude deviation caution also sounded as the aircraft ascended more than 300 feet above the selected cruise level of FL370 (37,000 feet). The piercing noise of the autopilot disconnect drowned the flight deck and was so all embracing and uncomfortable to the ears it demanded to be silenced. The intensity of the sound was such that it could even be heard in the First Class cabin below.

Amongst the passengers travelling in First Class was Jemima Khan and she had made it known to the crew she was a nervous flyer. On this trip she was travelling on holiday with her mother, Lady Annabel Goldsmith, her two young sons, Sulaiman and Kasim, and her brother Benjamin. Her husband, Imran Khan, was not on board but he had planned to join them later. They had felt the jar as the aircraft had first lurched upwards but, as they were all sitting directly beneath the flight deck, to add to their discomfort they could clearly hear the penetrating wail of the autopilot warning. 'This is it,' was her first thought.

On the flight deck the co-pilot was still without any visual reference but Mukonyi, from his position, was able to see a glimmer of light outside and he knew exactly what he was doing and what mayhem he was causing. Phil continued his struggling with the attacker but the co-pilot was also a strong and well-built man and a match for Mukonyi. Somehow, he managed to depress the autopilot disconnect button on the control wheel to extinguish the loud warning and the overwhelming wailing tone ceased. By brute force he also tried to keep the control wheel level and prevent the intruder from fully banking the aircraft to the left but, with the man's heavy bulk on his lap and the Kenyan clutching the control to his chest, it was more difficult to counter the enforced nose-up demand. Like an arm wrestle to the death with the lives of over 400 people at stake, the two opponents grappled for control. This was not a battle that Phil could afford to lose and with all his strength he fought to overcome his assailant. As the nose continued to pitch up sharply and the climb rate to increase rapidly the indicated air speed dropped significantly. The thrust levers on a quadrant at the forward end of the central pedestal had not been disturbed by Mukonyi's dive and the auto-throttle remained engaged. They immediately advanced to full power and, as the engines responded, there was a strong 'push' from the increased thrust and a distinct sound of a high-pitched whine.

Amid this cacophony of noise and still flying blind, Phil overcompensated in his effort to level the wings and the aircraft turned sharply to the right. The speed at which an aircraft stalls is indicated on the speed tape and is computed for the normal force of 1'g' loading when in stable flight but, when an aircraft manoeuvres, such as banking in a turn, there is an increased loading that effectively raises the 'g' force and the stall speed indicator moves higher up the speed tape. As the aircraft banked swiftly in the turn the increased 'g' force raised the minimum manoeuvring speed and the indicated airspeed became enclosed in the danger zone. The low-speed aural warning activated and, as it added its own 'beep,

beep' to the orchestra of noise, the aircraft encountered the pre-stall buffet. The aerodynamic stall warning system activated and vibrated the control column intensely with a loud rattling noise. Suddenly, turning steeply and without warning, the aircraft was severely buffeted by the turbulent airflow from the wings and the entire fuselage vibrated roughly. The result was dramatic. From the smooth conditions of only a few seconds earlier the attacker had propelled the flight into great danger and in an instant all on board had been shaken awake and stunned by the outburst.

In the moments before the attack all had been quiet and calm throughout the darkened cabins. The meal service had been completed some four hours before and the almost perfect flying conditions had induced an unusually tranquil and relaxing environment on the flight. Most passengers were resting, with some sleeping soundly and others dosing, but the serenity was not to last. Abruptly all aboard were rudely awakened from their slumbers by a violent jolt and were greatly shocked. The nose jerked upwards to a high angle, much higher than that experienced on take-off, and continued to rise. With more power being applied the engine noise grew rapidly louder and a distinct 'kick' was felt. As the aircraft continued to climb a steep bank was sensed and then, for some unknown reason, the fuselage had unexpectedly started to judder severely. In a matter of moments their peace was totally shattered.

The outburst had happened so quickly and had alarmed and confused everyone but only the co-pilot on his own on the flight deck was aware of the unfolding drama as he struggled with the attacker. Phil was still without visual reference but he instantly recognised the approach to the stall and sensed the steepness of the right turn. To level the wings, he now eased his grip on the controls and allowed Mukonyi's pull to reduce the bank angle and this had the desired effect. With the steep bank reducing the shaking abruptly stopped, even before the wings had levelled, and the buffeting ended as suddenly as it had started. It had only been a brief moment of intense juddering but it was of sufficient severity to strike fear into everyone.

The relief felt by everyone in the cabin when the shuddering had stopped was genuine but was tempered by the strange sensation of the whole aircraft being lifted up, and up, and up further. The initial shock of being shaken awake appeared to have abated and there was a little less panic in the air. It was also apparent, however, that the alarm generated by the outburst was being replaced by fear of the unknown and a sense of quiet foreboding prevailed. The nose of the aircraft remained very high, now up to 25 degrees, and the passengers were still being pressed into the backs of their seats as the aircraft continued to climb rapidly upwards. But there was no announcement from the captain and, as the 'seat belt' signs stubbornly remained blank, there was no reassuring gesture of them being switched on.

In the bunk area on the left side of the flight deck the captain had been in the deepest slumber, oblivious to the noise owing to his ear plugs, and totally unaware of where he was when he felt the effect of something unusual happening. It is normal when in the bunk to have sleep disturbed by one thing or another but this was different. His body had slipped downwards with his head being forced into the pillow at the rear bulkhead and his forward-facing feet had been tilted upwards as if someone was trying to turn him upside down. The full thrust from the engines only made the feeling worse. With the whining noise piercing his ears even through his earplugs, he had been rudely aroused from his sleep and was now aware he was on an aircraft. As he came round, he felt the aircraft bank steeply to the left and then suddenly he felt the airframe shaking briefly but violently with buffeting at a level he had never before experienced. Instantly he recognised that the aircraft had been on the point of stalling and the danger that represented, but he was at a loss as to what was going on. He could see nothing in the bunk area as it was in complete darkness but he could sense that not only was the nose-up attitude high but that it was increasing. Now he was completely awake.

Passengers on the left side by the windows were aware that the aircraft was in a steep left bank but, when looking out of the windows, were horrified at what they saw in the first hint of dawn. Instead of some rays from a distant horizon they were staring at what appeared to be a vast expanse of black desert. The aircraft was almost completely on its side! Liz Stuart, sitting near a window, had earlier assumed they were experiencing very bad turbulence and now thought 'that they were going through a storm because I looked out the window and saw black. Then I realised I was looking at the ground.'

In the cabin all were extremely concerned and they looked around expectantly as if waiting for reassurance that this had been no more than severe turbulence. In the rear galley Richard, the relief pilot, unaware of the cockpit intrusion during his brief visit to the cabin, was talking to a stewardess in the galley by Door 4 Left when the sudden burst of violent buffeting brought their conversation to an abrupt end. Richard knew immediately this was not weather-related turbulence and instantly recognised the pre-stall buffet but under what circumstances would an aircraft in commercial operation ever experience buffeting of this nature? Alarm bells sounded loudly and clearly in Richard's head but, before he could fully gather his senses, no sooner had the shaking stopped than another bout of even more violent buffeting erupted.

'We are in a ******* stall', he cried as he ran out of the galley.

Chapter 5

Roller Coaster

On the flight deck, in the moments leading to Richard's outburst in the galley, the Kenyan continued to press his attack. Phil's sight of the instruments remained blocked and in the weak, dark grey light of early dawn he still had no visual reference. Once more he had to sense when the wings were level and then to strongly oppose Mukonyi's persistent attempt to aggressively roll the aircraft to the left. The heavy attacker's upper body weight still lay across Phil's lap, pinning him down and trapping him in his seat. To make matters worse, the full safety harness with shoulder straps that Phil was still wearing further restricted his movements and he was unable to pull the attacker away from the controls. It may have been possible for the pilot to push his seat back and sideways to attempt an escape but this would have relinquished full control of the aircraft to Mukonyi so he remained in position to counteract the man's actions.

Mukonyi continued to clutch the control column close to his chest and to force the aircraft into an excessive rate of climb. To remove his grip Phil tried biting him, but to no effect, and he also attempted in vain to peel the Kenyan's fingers away one by one from the control. The assailant remained silent as he pressed his attack and was determined not to relinquish his grasp. For a brief moment Mukonyi was even able to tug the control wheel unopposed and Phil had to muster all his strength to force it to the right again. By now the airspeed had dropped substantially and the 'beep, beep, beep' of the low-speed aural warning sounded continuously. Without sight of a horizon the co-pilot once more overcompensated and for a second time the aircraft banked sharply to the right. Exacerbated again by the additional 'g' force in the steep bank, the big jet entered a full aerodynamic stall and the control column vibrated and rattled in warning. Only moments earlier, at the approach to the stall on the first sharp right turn, the jar and pre-stall buffeting had shocked the passengers. Now, on this second steep right turn, the aerodynamic buffeting that returned was very violent. The vibration and juddering were extremely severe, substantially more so than the initial short outburst had been, and for a longer period. The 747 shook and shuddered wildly from nose to tail. To add to the confusion the shaking had triggered random activation of the passenger call buttons and associated chimes from the galleys could be heard throughout the aircraft. The cabin lights also flashed on and off, like a scene from a horror movie, and by now all on board were completely terrified.

Once more the co-pilot eased on the pressure to allow Mukonyi's pull to reduce the bank angle and again, gradually, the buffeting abated. Phil finally managed to level the wings but with the nose-up attitude remaining excessive the aircraft continued to soar higher, the indicated airspeed plummeted and the buffeting was only pausing for breath. The terror in the cabin that had eased off after the first short burst of shuddering had reignited with a vengeance when the aircraft had banked once more to the right. As the bank angle had steepened with the vibration increasing significantly, many must have thought that the aircraft was about to break up under the strain.

The two outbursts of stalling had occurred rapidly, one after the other, and, as the captain was still lying in the bunk, he found it even more alarming when the aircraft banked right for a second time. Strangely the rhythm was very regular, as if a big hand was grabbing the aircraft and shaking it more and more vigorously. Lima Mike had once again entered the stall regime but this time it felt more like the aircraft had experienced a full aerodynamic stall. On the approach to the stall, buffeting is a warning and all pilot training focuses on the need to immediately initiate stall recovery, but the nose-up attitude had remained high with no attempt to push the nose down to regain speed and the aircraft had progressed deeper in to the stall. 'Why were the pilots not trying to recover?' reverberated in Bill's head. Thoughts of what damage may have thwarted their attempts, and how it may have occurred in the first place, flashed through the captain's mind but no plausible answers were forthcoming.

As the wings moved towards the level once more the buffeting reduced and, once again, the hopes of all in the cabin were raised that the worst was over. The respite, however, was to be short lived. The nose-up attitude was still excessively high and the aircraft climbed swiftly above 40,000 feet. The indicated airspeed fell below 210 knots, substantially less than the critical stalling speed of 230 knots that was marked on the speed tape, and continued to drop rapidly. The stall warning system shook and rattled the control column continuously. The engines were still on full power but the aircraft never exited the stall regime and the big jet was now fully stalled. The speed dropped further to 190 knots and the buffeting and shuddering were unbelievably violent. With all lift lost the aircraft could no longer sustain flight, the nose pitched down and the 747-400 fell flat from the sky like a stone.

In a desperate attempt to initiate the stall recovery procedure Phil shoved the assailant's upper body forwards as hard as he could to force the control column to the fore and push the nose down. The action had the desired effect in arresting the rate of ascent and the altitude peaked at around 41,000 feet. The flight path curved downwards but, as the nose dropped below the horizontal the intruder's upper body rolled onto the control column and his heavy weight drove it fully forwards. As the stalled aircraft went 'over the top' and plummeted earthwards, all on board floated upwards as the 'g' force turned negative and they could feel a heaving sensation in the pits of their stomachs. An American passenger from California sitting by a window at the rear of the aircraft stated that 'the wings looked like a bird's wings flapping up and down'.

Hilary Attenborough and her mum were sitting on the right side of World Traveller and when Mukonyi had walked forward earlier they thought he looked 'rather shifty'. Little did they realize he was now the cause of their plight. They recalled that with the first indication of a stall a male passenger had been seen leaving his seat and a stewardess had called, 'Sir, please sit down', which they thought was very 'English'. Hilary was by a window and now lifted the blind up briefly but quickly pulled it down again so as not to see out. She had a glass of water in her hand and as the aircraft rose and fell the liquid 'jumped out of her glass', paused in mid-air as if in space and then plopped back in again. As the 747 dropped they could hear a 'whooping' noise from the air and the engines that had been 'screaming and whining' now fell silent, as did the passengers. A few moments later the silence was broken by the call of 'brace, brace' uttered by a stewardess and some passengers started screaming again.

The enforced descent had initiated the stall recovery and the speed was increasing but controlling the pitch would now be more difficult with the attacker's full weight lying on the control column. In this dire predicament what Phil needed most was support. If someone could come quickly to his aid and remove the assailant, he would have a chance. With his throat dry he yelled as loudly as he could for assistance.

'Help...help...help...help', he cried out repeatedly.

In the bunk the captain was oblivious to Phil's calls owing to the background noise and his ear plugs. He could, however, sense that the body angle was much too high and it was no surprise to him that the buffeting and shaking continued to intensify. In fact, as the aircraft had rapidly progressed to the full stall condition the buffeting had become so violent that even he began to fear for the integrity of the structure. As far as the captain was aware, there were two ex-Air Force pilots on the flight deck who were very competent and well trained and he could trust them to handle any situation. If he left his position of being strapped to the bunk, he could get tossed around like a loose cannon and make matters worse. And, even if he did manage to reach the co-pilots, they would be strapped into their seats and there wouldn't be much he could do to help with the flying anyway. Bill Hagan had experienced nothing like this before, and his head was in turmoil as all sorts of damaging scenarios raced through his mind, from a structural stress failure, to an engine departing the wing, to a catastrophic control loss or to the aircraft being struck by something, but none of these seemed plausible. Whatever the incident, it was clearly serious so, initially, it would be difficult to manage the emergency and contain the situation, but they would soon complete procedures and have the aircraft under control. Tough as his decision was, he felt the safest option was to remain in place and he further tightened the bunk safety belt.

For those in the cabin the excessive nose-up angle and the rapidly dropping airspeed, in spite of full power thrust, were extremely alarming. As the aircraft went deeper into the stall, they could feel the lurch when the high rate of climb evolved into a descent. The violent shaking worsened by the second and, as it did so, so did the terror in the cabin. One passenger in the rear section of the cabin described the noise as 'like large rocks being thrown at the aircraft'. When the nose had been pushed down it felt like they were going over the crest of a giant roller coaster and they floated upwards out of their seats in the weightlessness. On an actual roller coaster ride the same sensation of weightlessness lasts only a few seconds but, on the aircraft, the negative 'g' was experienced for almost 20 seconds and the drop was twenty times greater than the world's biggest ride. And just like in a roller coaster some screamed, but the difference was that they were screaming for their lives. Most passengers had their seat belts fastened whilst asleep and they hovered in the air above their seats restrained by their belts, but one small group on the right side had not strapped themselves in and they began to float towards the ceiling. Many passengers had found the violent upset and the rapidly changing 'g' forces overwhelming and, with it all being too much, had lost consciousness and passed out.

As Phil's attention on the flight deck was preoccupied with the recovery from the stall, Mukonyi, still clutching the control wheel, was able to turn it rapidly and fully to the left. The aircraft immediately banked sharply to the left and Phil was certain he was trying to turn the 747-400 on its back. The rate of the roll to the left quickly reached a fast ten degrees per second, much higher than before and, as the bank continued to increase sharply, the speed fell back to 180 knots, 50 knots below the indicated stall speed. The entire fuselage continued to shake violently from nose to tail. As the bank increased beyond 45 degrees an aural warning sounded in a loud American voice repeating the words 'Bank angle! Bank angle!' every few seconds. The wings continued to roll through almost 90 degrees and hovered close to the vertical. The indicated airspeed dropped back even more and hesitated around 170 knots. The aircraft was slipping sideways towards the ground faster than it was moving forwards and it seemed to settle into that attitude!

In the first-class galley, Stewardess Kimberley Parker had been shocked by the aircraft being tossed around violently. The sudden shuddering, lurching and pitching was something she had never experienced before and it had been extremely frightening. When the turbulence had erupted, Kim and Rowena Teager, the first-class purser, had managed to hold on by wedging themselves in the first glass galley but then, suddenly, the aircraft seemed to plunge towards the ground, diving steeply. The dive then appeared to slow for a moment and Kim crawled towards Door 1 Right to reach a crew rest seat where she hoped to catch sight from the small door window of how far they were from the ground. Rowena had also moved to a crew seat and had managed to strap in just before the aircraft, once again, hurtled rapidly earthwards. The descent then seemed to ease again and the 747 appeared to be levelling off when, suddenly, there was a violent roll to the left and the bank angle increased rapidly as the aircraft continued to roll. Kim, caught unawares, had been thrown through the air, right across the galley, and had crashed down by Door 2 Left. She landed heavily on the hard floor with her back, leg and ankle striking the surface with force, and she winced with severe pain as her right ankle cracked and, unknown to her at the time, her right leg fractured. Overcome by the impact and the pain, she then passed out. Rowena was nearby and she also heard what had sounded like a bone cracking as Kim struck the solid floor. When Kim came to, the pain was excruciating, even worse than at the moment of injury. Somehow Kim was able to pick herself up and get to safety but now, in terrible pain, she had to weather the 'storm' as the upset continued.

Kim's husband, Chris Parker, was accompanying her on the trip and he was sitting in seat 29C in the middle section of World Traveller. He had been shocked at the sudden violent nature of the disturbance but he could only assume it was severe turbulence and he kept looking for the unlit seat belt sign to illuminate to confirm he was right. In his stress, the seat belt sign became a focus of his attention but it remained stubbornly dark and, when the aircraft plunged in a steep dive, he felt his heart in his mouth, his head spinning and then he, too, like many others, succumbed to the 'g' forces and passed out.

At the same time Richard, the relief co-pilot, was desperately trying to make his way through the cabin on what was now a long journey from the rear galley back to the flight deck. With the aircraft churning like a tumble dryer, it turned out to be more of a battle than a sprint. He had to clamber over the seats and, when the bank angle became excessive, he had to walk along on the edges of the seats, but he knew he had to make it back to the cockpit.

The breaking light of dawn only worsened the passengers' ordeal for not only could they sense the aggressive banking, high roll rate, wings tilting to the vertical and sideways free-fall but many cabin blinds had been raised and they could now witness their dire predicament through the windows. And all accompanied by the entire structure of the 747 buffeting, jolting and shaking uncontrollably. To the passengers it seemed that the whole aircraft was breaking apart and many were praying. In the cabin absolute terror reigned and a number on board were screaming loudly.

At the top of the climb the aircraft's trajectory had curved downwards with negative 'g' being experienced and the prolonged feeling of weightlessness had caught everyone by surprise. The sensation was scary and it had a profound effect. As if on cue the screaming stopped, everyone became still and the cabin turned very quiet. Those sitting on the left could see some cloud but their windows were mostly filled with the grey-brown of the desert beneath while those on the right could see only a brightening sky but couldn't resist glancing across at the alarming view of the ground through the opposite windows. One American lady, Zanne Augur, had a seat on the left by a window and in the row in front noticed a man travelling with his two small children. Concerned for the toddlers, especially the boy who was the elder of the two, the father raised his arm to shut the blind to shield him from the view.

'He pulled the shade down and looked at me as if to say "Please do the same thing so my son can't see what is happening." It was a very touching moment and naturally, I complied. I wasn't a mom at the time, but I am now, and I can totally understand what he must have been feeling.'

Jemima Khan described the eerie silence whilst the aircraft dropped sideways in free-fall as more frightening than the shuddering and screaming. As the aircraft plummeted the auto-throttle fully retarded the thrust levers and there was no engine noise and no screams, just a whistling sound from outside and the moans of some of the passengers inside. The aircraft was below the clouds now and she could see the ground clearly but felt as if she was 'falling forever'.

The violent manoeuvring had caused chaos in the cabin with items flying around and overhead storage bins falling open. Oxygen masks dropped and dangled uselessly from the ceiling. Zoe McNaughton, a 19-year-old student from England was going on holiday to Africa.

'Everyone's stuff was flying around. Our stuff went up in the air,' she said. 'People hit their heads on the ceiling. I was scared. I thought we were going to crash.'

James Kalugira, a Tanzanian man who was one a group of 16 truck drivers who had been working in the States, was returning home.

'People were yelling. Some luggage dropped from overhead cabins,' he reported. 'The cabin crew were lying on the floor. I started to pray when I realised the situation was out of control.'

The small group in World Traveller that had failed to fasten their seat belts floated up and struck the ceiling then slipped across the roof of the cabin. Those strapped in their seats tried to catch their arms and legs but found it impossible to help them. The floating passengers then drifted to the opposite side of the aircraft and when the negative 'g' abated they dropped like sacks into the laps of other passengers.

Big jets are flown at all times using flight instruments as, unlike light aircraft, they cannot be flown accurately by just looking out of the window. For airline pilots, being able to see the instrument panel at all stages of flight is very important. For the dire and dark circumstances that Phil found himself in on the flight deck it was critical. Phil's sight of the co-pilot's instrument panel, however, was still blocked by Mukonyi's large body. Although dawn was breaking the earth below was a dull grey-brown colour, the lower sky ahead was still black with a creeping hint of greyness but the upper sky was clearly beginning to lighten. As the aircraft banked very steeply to the left the aircraft turned eastwards towards the rising sun and gave Phil just what he needed to properly assess the seriousness of the aircraft's situation – a real, visible horizon. There was no need now for guidance from the instrument panels for the sight was sufficient to make him entirely aware of the excessive bank angle and the danger it posed. It was obvious that the aircraft remained fully stalled and to avert disaster he knew exactly what was needed to initiate a recovery. This was the third time the passengers had been subjected to severe buffeting but, with the aircraft now fully stalled and the airspeed at 170 knots, 60 knots below the stall speed, it was much worse than before and the very violent shaking continued to terrify all on board.

Phil had so far been able to combat Mukonyi's attacks and had also managed to push him fully forwards when desperately needed. But the assailant, still not having uttered a word, had not released the controls for a second and the aircraft continued to respond to the full left turn demand by banking the wings to a perilous angle. If the rolling motion continued the aircraft would flip on its back and recovery from the inverted stall would be impossible. With no lift being produced by the wings, the airspeed dangerously low and the aircraft fully in the stall, the 747 nose-dived relentlessly on its side in free-fall. In the rare atmosphere at altitude, it rapidly plummeted towards the ground, quickly accelerated sideways to terminal velocity and plunged earthwards at 30,000 feet per minute, a descent rate equivalent to half the muzzle velocity of a pistol bullet. But the indicated airspeed representing the aircraft's forwards motion was still steady at 170 knots and the wings remained close to vertical.

The aircraft was in immediate and extreme danger so it was imperative to reduce the bank angle to allow the nose to drop and the speed to increase by converting altitude to airspeed. Although Phil's recovery actions would be instinctive, it was still possible in the circumstances to mishandle the procedure and the aircraft could spin. The 747 could not be allowed to roll further left and perhaps invert but levelling the wings by rolling right to reduce the excessive bank angle also had its dangers. Too rapid a corrective roll rate could exacerbate the stall and delay recovery.

The recovery from the stall was now in the hands of one pilot whose rescue efforts were being hampered by a very determined and strong attacker and his actions over the next few seconds would be critical to the survival of the aircraft and all on board. As an ex-RAF fast jet pilot, Phil was no stranger to unusual attitudes and inverted flight but a deeply stalled 747 did not form part of his experience. Phil certainly had the skill to fly the aircraft out of danger, even if the wings continued to roll substantially over the vertical, but would the structure of the 747 cope with the stresses? If the 'g' forces became more excessive the aircraft could break up. The fighter jets and aerobatic aircraft the co-pilot had flown were designed to withstand excessive aerodynamic loads but a 280 tonne passenger aircraft with 40 tonnes of fuel in its wings was not built to cope with such stressful manoeuvres.

Phil continued battling to oppose Mukonyi's control demands but now had sight of the earth's horizon to help. The fight to the death continued, however, and in the contest of strength it was touch and go. For a moment the attacker gained the upper hand and the wing tipped over the vertical to 94 degrees. If the rotation continued now, it would be impossible to stop the big jet from rolling inverted but somehow Phil was able to muster all his strength and pull the aircraft back from the abyss. He succeeded in opposing the attacker's efforts by tugging the control wheel to the right and he managed to start gently reducing the bank angle. Phil could have placed his feet on the rudder pedals and could have applied rudder without hindrance from Mukonyi, but the rudder is not used in this manner on a big jet. The powerful control can over-stress the structure and in the stall would not be used to lift a dropped wing. A judicious application of rudder in a bank with the wings in a vertical position could have assisted recovery but the crossed controls of left aileron and right rudder could also have risked inducing a spin.

In the bunk the captain's mind was spiralling and he continued to review what had occurred in an attempt to diagnose the problem. The aircraft had been lurching from side to side, rolling twice sharply to the right and then rolling very fast to the left and to a much steeper angle. Each time the 747 had banked it had approached the stall but now it was much worse for the aircraft had fully stalled and was plummeting earthwards. Seconds seemed to pass like minutes and he had no idea what was going on. On the flight deck, Phil, the co-pilot, started shouting as loudly as he could and then suddenly, in spite of the turbulent shuddering, Bill just manged to pick up through his earplugs the faint sound of someone crying for help. Blind in the blackness of the bunk area and confused and bewildered by being violently tossed around, the cry sent a chill down his spine. He was then shocked to realise that his earplugs were still in place so, now in fear, he quickly dislodged them, unfastened the bunk safety belt, swung round and stood up as quickly in the darkness as he could. Stopping to dress was not an option so, in his underwear, he felt his way in the dark towards the door as best he could, pushed it open and, with great trepidation, peered from the blackness into the grey half-light of the flight deck.

Instantly he was met by a cacophony of sound with the alert of 'Bank angle! Bank angle!' warning of excessive bank, the piercing noise of the stall warning stick shaker incessantly rattling the control column and the loud buffeting of the airframe. But it was not the terrible racket assaulting his ears that terrified him the most but the shock of what he saw, for the scene numbed his brain. Bill had expected to see two co-pilots strapped in their seats but, instead, he had been confronted with the bizarre sight of only Phil in his place and the head and shoulders of another man on his lap. This large individual's midriff was over the centre pedestal and his legs and feet were by the captain's empty seat. Phil seemed to be trapped by the upper part of this other person and momentarily the captain's attention focussed on the dark body shape against the backdrop of the grey half-light. All this, of course, had flashed through the captain's mind in less than an instant but such was his confusion that to his horror it appeared to him for a split second that Richard, the relief pilot, was attacking Phil.

Phil continued his effort to level the wings and when the bank reduced below 45 degrees the bank angle warning fell silent but the stall warning continued to vibrate and rattle the control column. With the wings almost level the nose lowered and immediately the speed began to increase quickly. Soon the aircraft flew out of the stall and to everyone's relief the buffeting ceased. To Phil's dismay, however, the 747 now approached a second critical phase. The aircraft speed continued to increase rapidly, as did the steepness of the dive, and the nose pitched down 35 degrees. No sooner had the 747 escaped from great peril than it was back in extreme danger again for the aircraft was now at serious risk of over speeding.

'Help, help, help', Phil continued to bellow.

Chapter 6

The Captain Joins the Fight

Captain Hagan had only been awake from his deep sleep for about a minute and his mind was still struggling to make sense of the very strong aural and visual signals with which he had been bombarded. On second sight he could now see that the assailant was wearing what appeared be a black balaclava but what he had seen, in fact, was Mukonyi's black jacket with its hood partially raised and the back of his dark-haired head. The imaginary balaclava, however, moved his mind in the right direction for, he surmised, terrorists wear balaclavas so, with Phil still calling for help, he switched straight into anti-terrorist mode.

Phil tried with all his strength to arrest the rate of descent but was unable to pull Mukonyi sufficiently far backwards to have any effect. The steep dive meant that greater force was needed to move the heavy man lying on Phil's lap and the co-pilot could not find sufficient leverage to shift such a big, strong opponent. As the thought of who this 'terrorist' might be flashed through Bill's mind, he knew he had to get this man off the controls and to act quickly. His first thought was to grab a weapon and close by was the jemmy that BA stowed in the flight deck wardrobe in case of emergency. When the captain looked forward through the pilots' windows, however, he was horrified to see what appeared to be the aircraft in a near vertical dive. Although later it was revealed to be 35 degrees nose-down, much less than vertical, it was still a very frightening sight. The flight path was rapidly becoming extremely critical and it was obvious that the 15 or 20 seconds to remove the jemmy from its stowage was going to be too long. It was imperative to pull the 747 from the dive but to do that he first had to remove the terrorist. Bill could now see he was a very big man but he somehow had to prise this large assailant from the controls and he had to do it immediately.

With the speed building up the aircraft's movements became less excessive but the ever- increasing airspeed now hurtled the 747 towards a point of no return. On reaching the intruder Phil became aware of his captain's presence and he hollered at his rescuer to 'get him off'. Bill immediately struck Mukonyi on the head with his right fist as hard as he could but was unable to get a really good swing owing to the restricted area behind the co-pilot. He hit him at least two or three times in a vain attempt to render the attacker unconscious, or at least to force him to release the controls, but it had no effect whatsoever. It was like trying to smash a stone bollard with his fist and it only succeeded in bloodying his knuckles. As Lima Mike continued to plunge earthwards, the rapid increase in air noise emphasised the urgency of the situation as did the increasing loudness and intensity of Phil's demands.

'Get him off ...get him off ...GET HIM OFF'!

As Bill manoeuvred to better press his attack he still struggled with his rude awakening and, initially, he was so bewildered he couldn't even remember what route they were on. Thoughts flashed through his mind as to where they were, what lay beneath and how much time they had before hitting any high terrain below. His vacant seat could be moved on rails and had been pushed back and to the side to allow access and, as he quickly moved into the space provided, he suddenly remembered with relief that they must be some way north of Nairobi in an area where there were no high mountains. He then reached across the central pedestal, grabbed Mukonyi's black 'hoodie' jacket by the shoulders and heaved as hard as he could. The fabric had a shiny, nylon appearance that felt smooth and slippery and, as Bill pulled strongly backwards, the garment simply peeled off his back. What he needed was a better grip so he slipped his hands inside the back of his jacket and under his arm pits, then heaved again. This time the captain managed to lift the assailant and to pull him upwards about two feet, or just over half a metre, but the Kenyan continued to grasp the control column firmly. To counter Bill's backwards pull Mukonyi clutched the control column tightly to his chest and, as he did so, his snatch tugged the controls harshly backwards a bit and the nose pitched upwards sharply. The captain's first reaction was one of alarm as such a violent manoeuvre at high speed could over-stress the aircraft, but his feelings changed instantly from shock to enormous relief when it appeared that the aircraft had not been damaged. Bill now released his grip on the attacker's shoulders with the effect that Mukonyi eased his clutch of the control column and the aircraft resumed the dive, although not as steeply. Captain Hagan suddenly realised that by good fortune he had found a way of controlling pitch so, immediately, he lifted the big Kenyan once more and, as Mukonyi again tugged the control column backwards, the steepness of the dive further reduced. Inadvertently Bill had succeeded in moving the control column back from the fully forward position and had reduced the steep dive by about 15 or 20 degrees.

The captain now turned his efforts to trying to remove the attacker and, as he frantically pulled and pulled on Mukonyi's shoulders, the 747's changes of pitch from bursts of slightly nose up to steeply nose down were terrifying for the passengers and gave them the impression they were in a giant, out of control roller coaster that had just performed a series of dives. As the speed reduced with each nose-up attitude the aircraft once again approached the stall and the buffeting and turbulence resumed. The autothrottle had remained engaged throughout the attack and they could hear the sound of the engine power reducing and increasing as the thrust levers moved backwards and forwards in response to the roller coaster ride. Shoes, handbags, books, pillows, blankets, newspapers and all sorts of loose objects flew about the cabins and a few passengers, struck with emotion, were calling out that they were going to die. In the rear cabin most passengers were quiet and some were holding hands across the aisles.

During the first dive the speed had risen quickly yet had still remained dangerously low but in the second dive the speed improved more rapidly and the indicated airspeed now exceeded the critical stall speed of 230 knots. With the steep dive continuing and the airspeed still increasing the 747 emerged from the stall, the buffeting abated and then it finally stopped. For a moment the aircraft was flying safely but, with the airspeed again increasing swiftly in the steep dive, the situation was once more becoming very threatening. The problem with the oscillating flight path was that the raising of the aircraft's nose when pulling Mukonyi backwards was less than the steep lowering of the nose when he leaned forward on the control column and Lima Mike was hurtling earthwards at an extreme nose-down attitude with speed being rapidly gained and altitude being rapidly lost.

If an aircraft in a steep dive nears the speed of sound, what is known as a 'tuck' can develop whereby the nose tucks down, the steepness of the dive further increases and supersonic speed can be reached in a very short time. Any attempt at recovery by pulling out of such a dive has to be conducted with the greatest of care as too strong a pull could massively increase the stresses and the airframe could break up. The phenomenon is well known to professional pilots and recovery from a steep dive should be attempted immediately. More thoughts now flashed through the captain's mind of the 747 diving all the way down to the ground to impact, with time for all on board stopping, and he could not bring himself to look out of the window. Other reflections raced in his head of being forced to break the golden rule of flying to 'always fly the aircraft first'. In an emergency, a pilot should, as the saying goes, 'Aviate, Navigate, Communicate' – first, check the aircraft is flying safely, second, check that the aircraft is navigating safely, third, communicate the circumstances effectively, then deal with the problem. Captain Hagan's dilemma was Mukonyi and there was no doubt in his mind that he had to deal with him first so he continued to press his attack. With the big Kenyan disabled Phil could 'aviate' the aircraft to safety, together they could navigate a safe flight path and then they could communicate effectively about the incident.

At that moment Phil was still shouting at Bill to 'get him off, get him off' which upset the captain slightly for he really was doing his best to remove the powerful attacker! Once more he heaved with all his strength with exactly the same jerking up of the nose as previously but now in the knowledge that it would not over-stress the fuselage. What should have been obvious earlier also dawned on him: that although the aircraft was diving steeply with sharply increasing speed, the indicated airspeed was still well below the normal safe operating airspeed of 290 knots for the 747's cruising level. It was the low indicated airspeed of the flight that was sparing the structure from excessive strain and saving the day! The captain could now confidently pull him by the shoulders to pull out of the dive and he did so a number of times then, unexpectedly, to his enormous relief, his efforts were rewarded. The aircraft began to respond as intended and each time he dragged Mukonyi backwards he was able to ease the aircraft from plunging further and eventually, with a groaning of the fuselage, the 747 bottomed out of the dive. In the cabin the feeling of weightlessness gave way and was replaced by the rapidly increasing force of positive 'g'. Passengers' possessions and items that had only shortly before been flying and floating around the cabin now fell rapidly to the floor. The passengers soon sensed the weight of their bodies double and they even felt their eyelids droop heavily. The flight data recorder later revealed that the maximum and minimum forces registered during the upset were +2.1 'g', more than twice normal weight, and -1 'g', weightlessness.

Once again, to add further to the passengers' distress, more oxygen masks dropped from the overhead stowage positions and dangled uselessly from the ceiling. The violent upset also triggered spurious calls on the internal telephone system and for no reason phones began sounding in some galleys. Those crew members sitting by the rear galley heard the ringing and noted it was a priority call from the flight deck but when they tried to answer it the aircraft was bottoming out of its dive and they found themselves pinned to their seats and unable to stand up. They stretched to reach upwards and pick up the phone but their efforts were in vain and the phantom calls rang unanswered. Cabin crew in the rear rest area also tried to answer the calls but found that when strapped into the bunks they couldn't reach the phones, even without the 'g' effects.

As Bill continued to coax the aircraft back from diving downwards to flying safely the excessive 'g' forces reduced to normal, and eventually a point was reached at which secure flight was resumed. The aircraft was not stalling, buffeting, or banking and he managed to raise the nose sufficiently to achieve the normal cruise attitude of a few degrees above the horizontal. By now the airspeed had increased to 260 knots, well above the stall speed, and even the engine thrust had returned to the normal cruise power setting.

The long-suffering passengers breathed a huge sigh of relief. At last, the aircraft seemed to be flying normally, just as it had been in the cruise only a short time before. The travellers once more looked around at each other in bewilderment, wondering if whatever had happened would do so again, or if it really was now all over. The evidence for their relief was tangible as the flight was smooth again, and a reassurance from the captain would have helped calm their fears, but he was busy elsewhere. No announcement was forthcoming and the silence only served to increase their trepidation. A short 10 seconds later the drama erupted again.

Mukonyi still attached himself firmly to the control column, the flight was still in mortal danger from another assault and the captain, at all costs, still had to remove him quickly. With the aircraft in a stable state the moment seemed appropriate for a final attempt to try with all his strength to extricate him from the controls. Once again, Bill pulled him up twice with as much force and vigour as he could muster but his size and strength were difficult to overpower and, to the captain's great dismay and to the horror of the passengers, each time he lifted him up he only succeeded in pitching the nose up high into the air. The airspeed dropped dramatically, the aircraft plunged back into a full stall and severe buffeting and shaking of the structure returned.

The effect on the passengers was palpable as the reality of the situation dawned that their short respite was over. Some vomited with the return of the turbulent ride while others called out or wailed their discomfort. One scream from Club World was particularly disturbing and so penetrating it could be heard on the fight deck. Even as Bill battled with Mukonyi this terrible howl pierced his ears and chilled his blood. It was a shriek he would always remember. The man sounded as if he was in great pain and was stopping for breath every 6 or 7 seconds. The wailing sound would start low, rise, then fall again, and it sounded as if he was in enormous pain. Not frightened, but more in pain.

Even in First Class Jemima Khan could hear the outcry and it greatly disturbed her.

'A Kenyan man's mouth emitted a sound I never wish to hear again', she declared later, 'like collective male howling.'

With the aircraft fully stalled all the alerts returned with the 'beep, beep, beep' of the low airspeed warning repeatedly sounding every few seconds and the stall warning stick shaker vibrating and rattling the control column loudly. Extremely disheartened by the outcome, Bill now changed tactics and, rather than pull Mukonyi up, he very harshly tried to tug him horizontally rearwards in an attempt to 'throw' him into the cockpit. Disastrously, his efforts failed for as he pulled the big man as far back as he could Mukonyi still clutched the control column and he tugged it all the way back to the rear stop. The nose pitched up from 10 to 30 degrees in only 2 seconds and it was a massive input which generated an excessive climb and a swift reduction in airspeed before the nose settled back downwards again. The second rearwards tug was just as extreme, but by now the airspeed had dropped considerably lower and the response was more sluggish so the nose pitched up to only 23 degrees. The rapid climb peaked at an altitude of 32,000 feet and as the aircraft stalled it dropped 3,500 feet in 40 seconds, an average vertical descent of 5,250 fpm as later shown from graphs of the incident.

At some point during this sequence of events, Richard, the relief co-pilot, succeeded in returning to the flight deck after fighting against the odds all the way from the rear galley. Considering the toppling, pitching, diving and rolling of the aircraft, it was an amazing achievement. He had scrambled along the floor on his hands and knees, run along the aisle when the wings were level, stepped on chair backs when the wings were vertical, jumped over passengers and crawled up the stairs. Where he could, he took advantage of any let up in the aircraft's tumbling. Eventually he was observed by the upper deck passengers running through the cabin, being jolted upwards and bumping his head on the ceiling, then dashing into the flight deck where he quickly shut the door behind him. On entering the cockpit Richard was shocked when meeting the bizarre sight of his captain in his underwear grappling with a huge man who was firmly clutching the controls. By some sixth sense Phil was immediately conscious of Richard's presence but the captain, with his back to the door and straining with his efforts, did not at first realise that help had arrived. Unknown to Bill, Richard immediately joined the fray and grabbed Mukonyi where he could.

In the captain's head, jumbles of instant thoughts were still flashing through his brain. Although in a full stall and in a very critical situation the aircraft was incredibly stable as it fluttered flatly earthwards and, surprisingly, it brought Bill a degree of comfort. The 747 had been subjected to very violent manoeuvring that had put its great strength to the test and it had remained intact. The stalled 747 continued to plunge towards the ground at a high nose-up attitude with the indicated speed hovering at an alarming 162 knots, almost 70 knots below the stall speed, but the rate of descent was steady at about 8,000 feet per minute and much less rapid than the excessive rates when plummeting in the very steep dives. At a guess there was about three to four minutes to impact but altitude was still available and recovery from the stall was entirely possible.

But despair also raced through Bill's mind for Mukonyi was utterly determined to bring the aircraft down, the Kenyan was too big and strong for him to tackle and he was losing the tug of war to the death. Strangely, however, it hadn't yet dawned on him that he might die. Instead, he felt he was the only one who could save the day but the stopwatch was ticking, he was tiring, his strength was sapping and he suddenly felt an enormous weight of responsibility on his shoulders. The overpowering feeling he felt, however, was one of great shame, for he was totally failing in his task. His feeling of guilt was so intense he would never forget the experience. The ordeal, so far, had totally overwhelmed his concentration and it was only then that he recalled, with shock, that his family were on board. He suddenly felt this sinking, drowning feeling that he was also fighting for the lives of his family in a battle he was not winning. This man was trying to murder his kids and he felt a sickening feeling in the pit of his stomach! But then the thought of his children gave him inspiration for, before his trip, he had been asked by his son what he would do if he was attacked by a shark and he had suggested poking it in the eye. The attacker was now about to be attacked!

Instantly Bill launched his assault by spreading the fingers of his right hand apart and reaching over his head from behind in search of an eye socket. As his little finger brushed past the Kenyan's mouth the big man bit it hard, taking off the fleshy end, but the captain barely felt the pain as he continued to find one of his eyes. Soon he found his right eye and immediately pushed in his middle finger with great force while at the same time curling it into a hook. Captain Hagan knew nothing of the Kenyan and hadn't even seen his face but at that moment he was enraged and his adversary was now nothing more than a monster who was trying to kill everyone on board, including his family, and he would tear him apart if he had to. With his right hand attacking the eye he grabbed the assailant's left ear with the other and was just about to pull with all his might when he feared that if he ripped the big man's ear off it would still leave him attached. Bill quickly adjusted his grip to grasp both the ear and a fistful of hair and then, with both hands, pulled the Kenyan backwards as hard as he could. Unbelievably, this mountain of a man was turning out to be superhuman for he still clutched the controls tightly and the captain had failed again to extricate him. Bill's despair turned to horror. He now straightened his middle finger to thrust it as deep into his eye socket as he could with the thought that, if he could force it in far enough, he might even penetrate his brain and that could finish him off. With determination and no feeling, the captain plunged his finger into the hilt and then, suddenly, something amazing happened. He was letting go!

To Bill's utter and total relief, the pain had forced the Kenyan to defend himself and he started to turn round. As he did so Captain Hagan pulled on both sides of his head to try and drag him well clear but, as he was being hauled backwards, the big man reached out to grasp what he could, found Phil's shirt, and tore off a chunk in his hand as he fell. Bill then swung his head and upper body away from Phil's lap, sideways over the centre pedestal, and both tumbled backwards together into the middle of the cockpit. Bill's body now acted as a barrier between him and the controls but, with renewed aggression and anger, he started to push forwards again, this time aiming for the captain's empty seat. As he fought to block the Kenyan's advance, he suddenly realised that someone else was also pulling the man, and only then was he aware that Richard had managed to get back to the flight deck and had been very actively involved in the fight. Even with the two of them now restraining Mukonyi, however, he was a formidable opponent and he still pressed his attack. The assailant grabbed Bill's head with both his big hands, his fingers outstretched as the captain's had been earlier, and Bill then had to turn his head away quickly for fear the Kenyan was searching out an eye socket to pay him back. In spite of the big man's injuries, he had not lost any of his strength and it was proving very difficult to keep him away from the empty seat. This powerful man was still a substantial danger to the flight and there was still a chance he could overcome them and try to retake the aircraft.

Although Bill had his back to the flight instruments, he could still feel the wild buffeting and could sense the aircraft still descending rapidly in a full stall, but he was confident that Phil, now unrestrained, would be able to execute the stall recovery. The 747 would then soon be back to safe flight and he now sensed that the tide was beginning to turn. As the two pilots battled together to restrain Mukonyi they were managing to keep him away from the controls but the fight had not yet been won against this formidable opponent. The captain thought again about the jemmy and asking Richard to grab it and strike him for he was not sure the two could hold this big man back for much longer. Again, thoughts flashed through Bill's mind and it suddenly struck him that an untapped source of help was available, just outside the flight deck door, and that was the passengers. Instantly he began to call out, or more correctly, holler, as loudly as he could.

'Help, somebody help, …help, help, help, SOMEBODY COME IN AND HELP.'

Chapter 7

Assistance From the Cabin

In Club World on the upper deck the captain's calls for passenger assistance had been clearly heard in the forward seats. Unlike the more muffled sounds of Phil's earlier shouts for help, which had been uttered forwards into Mukonyi's jacket, his pleas had been projected towards the cabin and directly at the cockpit door. The first row of four seats just behind the flight deck, two on each side of the aisle, formed row 60 and were annotated from left to right 60A, 60B and 60J, 60K. They were occupied by a Kenyan family of European background and the father in aisle seat 60J had light blonde hair. In the row behind, in 61A by the left window, sat Gifford Shaw, an American from South Carolina, and next to him in aisle seat 61B was Clarke Bynum, Shaw's friend of many years from the same state and a 'six feet seven' ex-basketball player. The two men were travelling together on a Christian mission to Uganda. In seat 62J, an aisle seat on the right of the next row behind Shaw and Bynum, was Jon Keens who was travelling with his partner, Penny Lester, one of the cabin crew on the flight.

All had been extremely shaken by the ordeal and had been fully alert for some time. They now looked around in confusion.

'I saw a black man carrying a green folder go into the cockpit earlier', cried the blonde-haired father in alarm.

He and the two American fellow passengers had been startled at seeing Richard rush into the cockpit with his entry being followed by 'bumping and banging' noises and now there was Bill's cry for assistance which had clearly penetrated the cabin.

'There's someone in the cockpit,' yelled the Kenyan passenger now alerted to the pilots' plight, 'come on.'

He immediately jumped up, quickly followed by Clarke Bynum and Jon Keens leaping from their aisle seats, and they charged towards the flight deck door. Gifford Shaw took a little longer rushing from his window seat but was close behind. As the door was flung open the men could see the back of a very large man who was on top of another in a wrestling match and he was trying to grapple with his opponent's head. They could also see that the man underneath was in a state of undress and that another man in uniform was also trying to restrain the big guy by pulling him backwards. Mukonyi was caught by surprise by the sudden arrival of reinforcements and he released his grip on the captain. As he did so Bill glimpsed the group of passengers arriving and at that moment, to his enormous relief, he knew that they were finally at the beginning of the end of the ordeal.

The fair-haired Kenyan seized Mukonyi by his waist while Bynum, stretching his long arms over the turmoil, grabbed him by the neck and shoulders and Keens gripped him round his knees. The three men then toppled the attacker over, ripping his black hood in the process, and with Shaw's assistance pulled him feet first to the open door, leaving him half in and half out of the flight deck. Shaw, Bynum and Keens then piled on top and held him firmly on the floor.

Whilst the fracas ensued at the back of the flight deck, Captain Hagan was desperate to return to his flying duties as the 747 was still fully stalled and had remained so throughout the wrestling match and, as soon as Mukonyi was out of his hands, he quickly, according to Phil, appeared to leap 'as if on a spring' straight into his seat. Fortunately, it was not long before the passengers with their force of numbers were able to properly constrain Mukonyi and to safely truss him up.

With Mukonyi now removed from the controls, for the first time in over two minutes Phil had a clear view of his instrument panel, but he still had to face the crucial task of recovering the aircraft from its stalled condition and saving the flight from disaster. As the captain strapped himself in to his seat, both instantly focused on the airspeed that by now had dropped down to a staggering 162 knots, still at an inconceivable 70 knots below the indicated stall speed. The aircraft was now flying at 30,000 feet, well above any African terrain, so, with Bill now monitoring the stall recovery, Phil calmly and gently nudged the controls forward to trade height for speed by pitching the nose down to slightly below the horizon. The autothrottle was still engaged and had advanced automatically but as a check he pushed the thrust levers fully forward to ensure the engines were delivering full power. Phil continued to hold the nose just below the horizon whilst carefully watching the speed increase. At moments the aircraft still descended at an alarming rate of 7,000 feet per minute but Phil was confident he had sufficient altitude to complete the procedure successfully. The increasing speed induced a strong backwards pressure on the control column which was anticipated and which he strongly resisted. Judicious and momentary toggling of the electric trim switch also aided his actions. If the nose was allowed to pitch up the dropping speed would have risked a secondary stall from which he would have been forced to attempt a further recovery. At this stage of the procedure the buffeting was still extreme but, as the speed increased, it progressively became less so. Calmly he waited for the speed to build and, as it eased passed the 230 knots stall speed, to everyone's relief the buffeting eventually ceased. Phil maintained the slight pitch down attitude until the speed had increased by almost 100 knots to 260 knots before he gently began a climb and, as the indicated airspeed settled on 270 knots, he slowly started to turn back on course. During the procedure the aircraft had descended to 28,000 feet, losing only slightly over 2,000 feet, and the return to safe flight had been witnessed by Bill as a textbook recovery! By successfully flying the aircraft from the fully stalled condition to stable flight Phil had just completed a procedure that even Boeing's test pilots avoided.

Both pilots now noticed with satisfaction that Lima Mike was already climbing towards 30,000 feet with a reassuring 270 knots on the airspeed indicator. The autopilot was now engaged with 'command' mode selected and, as it was steadily climbing the aircraft back to the allocated cruising altitude of 37,000 feet, both pilots agreed that regaining the planned 370 flight level was the safest course of action. The pilots also considered that the aircraft may have been overstressed but all the indications were that it was structurally sound and they concurred that the low speeds experienced throughout the incident had prevented excessive stress on the structure.

The assailant was still lying on the floor, half in and half out of the flight deck, as with him struggling in spite of the number of people manhandling him it was difficult to get him out through the open door. The big man, however, was not going to cause any further trouble but, even if he did, all were well prepared, for now there were three pilots on the flight deck, a jemmy in the wardrobe and the safety net of the brave passengers and crew who had responded to the call for help. Without hesitation they had, with great courage, rushed to the rescue aware that a man had entered the flight deck but without knowing anything about the intruder or if he was armed.

BA2069 had by now climbed to just over 30,000 feet in stable flight and but many passengers, still unsure of what to expect next, were still in dire distress. Those on the upper deck with 'ring side' seats had the advantage of knowing their ordeal was over but most were wondering if this was yet another lull before a further deterioration. Captain Hagan desperately wanted to give them an immediate reassurance but his first duty was to the safety of the flight. Phil now steered back towards the next reporting point at El Obeid but, as the aircraft was still not yet on track or at the planned level, there was serious danger of conflict with other traffic.

Bill enquired if Phil was OK, or if he needed any assistance, but the captain was pleased to observe that, in spite of his ordeal, he seemed very well and unscathed by the drama. Up until now there had not been an opportunity to get on the radio to report their predicament so the captain picked up his headset from the floor and mentioned he would transmit a 'Mayday' call, an emergency radio transmission to others in the region that a flight is in dire and imminent danger and in need of assistance. This was not a call that any pilot would wish to make. Phil, however, politely and correctly pointed out that although they were not heading in the right direction, flying at the wrong altitude and had a maniac struggling in the flight deck doorway, the imminent danger was now over and a 'Pan' call – one of urgency rather than of emergency – was more appropriate. It was imperative, of course, that other aircraft in the vicinity should be alerted immediately to the flight's circumstances and to be warned to keep a good lookout for BA2069 re-joining the flight planned route and flight level. It was also a requirement to inform Khartoum Air Traffic Control (ATC) of the situation. Mukonyi's struggling on the floor behind the pilots was now becoming a distraction so before sending the call the captain shouted back to those restraining him to 'get him out of here' and then, without further delay, he pressed the transmit button.

'Pan-Pan, Pan-Pan, Pan-Pan. All stations, this is Speedbird 2069, Speedbird 2069, Speedbird 2069. We have suffered a cockpit intrusion and have lost considerable altitude. Our position is now 30 miles northeast of El Obeid and we are proceeding direct to El Obeid to resume our flight planned track. We are now climbing through flight level 320 for flight level 370.'

Captain Hagan's first call was transmitted on 121.5MHz, a frequency reserved for emergency transmissions, and to which all pilots maintain a listening watch at all times. Flights within a 200 nautical mile radius would have been able to pick up the call. Most routine position reports from remote areas were transmitted to control centres by HF, which was impossible to listen to continuously, so he then repeated the alert on the air-to-air frequency of 126.9MHz which was used for communications between pilots in that region of Africa. BA's northbound flight from Harare at Flight Level 350 had picked up the Pan call so they kept a wary eye on the progress of BA2069 but without disturbing them with contact. Bill then finally radioed Khartoum ATC, thankfully by relaying via the VHF frequency of El Obeid Control Tower, and provided them with the same information.

All stations were now aware of their situation and intentions except, perhaps, Khartoum, as the El Obeid Tower controller had simply replied 'Roger'. The captain had some concern that the controller had not understood the serious nature of his abnormal transmission owing to a lack of fluent English and, perhaps, Bill thought, because of his Ulster accent, but it was also likely that the controller had been keeping a listening watch on 121.5MHz and had already noted the details. Traffic within radio range, however, would now be able to monitor the flight's position and to keep a look out while Bill and Phil also kept their eyes peeled for other traffic and would continue to do so till the 747 re-joined the planned airway and flight level. Now proceeding southbound, BA2069, positioned to the northeast of the airway, also had to regain track offset one mile to the west, or right, of the airway centreline and, to make matters worse, to gain the correct route and level, had to cross the airway from east to west and had to climb though all the levels of the northbound flights with a similar offset to the eastern side of the airway. To warn of conflicting traffic the pilots also closely monitored the Traffic Collision and Avoidance System (TCAS) which displayed other traffic in the vicinity and which would alert of any potential collision with another flight. Other flight crews, having received the 'Pan' call, would undoubtedly have been interested to hear of the incident but refrained from calling in order not to disturb BA2069's recovery.

The captain checked to see what was happening behind him and saw that Mukonyi was in the final stages of being dragged out so, as soon as the big man was completely clear, he went straight onto his cabin address. His delivery was breathless and hesitant but he made sure that all his words were loud and clear.

'Ladies and gentlemen…this is the captain…a madman has broken into the cockpit and tried to kill us all…but we've got him out of the cockpit now…and we're going to be OK. …I'll talk to you again …in about 5 minutes, when I get more time.'

Captain Hagan's words were clear and direct and they brought the passengers instant and enormous relief. It was, as if at the last moment, a death sentence had been reprieved. Many passengers burst into tears. All on board had endured almost three long minutes of mental anguish and throughout the brief period had faced imminent death. Some thought the upset had only lasted 30 seconds while others thought it more like ten minutes, but now they knew it was all over and their deliverance from what seemed like certain death overwhelmed many. His address had felt like floodlights being switched on in a totally dark nightmare and, in reality, the enormity of the contrast had not been much different. The incident had begun in darkness with terror, fear and dread, had lasted for what many thought was an age and, literally from night into day and horror into relief, it had ended abruptly in the light of a new dawn with calmness, assurance and reprieve. The flight was now smooth, the sky was blue and now they were all going to live!

Shortly after Bill's announcement, the resting cabin crew members began to appear back on duty throughout the aircraft. On their breaks during the ordeal some had been in the bunks in the upper rear section and others in rest seats at the back of the aircraft. Being situated at the tail they had experienced the worst and, although aware the upset had been critical, they had known nothing of the circumstances until hearing the captain's cabin address.

This was now the opportunity for Kim to have her injury checked for, on inspection, her ankle had the visible appearance of a break. Fortunately, there were a few amongst the passengers who were medically trained who had come forward to help, one of whom was a Canadian doctor travelling in Club World. She came to the First Class galley to examine Kim and immediately confirmed that the stewardess's ankle had been damaged and that her leg had been broken.

The on-board medical kit was then taken from its storage but, as it contained drugs, permission to open it had to be requested from the captain. Other crew members then removed splints from the kit to strap in place on her leg and ankle. Kim now needed a comfortable place to rest but, with the aircraft full, the only option was to sit in her husband's seat in the cabin and for Chris to sit in a crew rest seat. In a cabin crew where communications had not been at their best, however, misinformation now spread that, owing to the violent upset, the landing would be difficult. Some of the crew found this distressing, and it was thought best that Chris should remain in his seat in the cabin. Kim was then placed in a crew rest seat and was made as comfortable as possible with her leg in splints propped up on a cabin bag. Stewardess Kim was now in a lot of pain and was offered drugs from the medical kit to help ease her discomfort but, as she was sitting in a crew position, she did not want to take these strong painkillers as they would make her drowsy. On arrival, she would need urgent medical attention.

On the upper deck, Mukonyi, while being restrained just outside the flight deck, began to talk, in spite of having neither shouted nor uttered a word throughout the attack, but now, for the first time, Gifford Shaw heard him call out loudly.

'Let me go and I will tell you who the others are', he had proffered.

As far as Gifford was concerned, any thought of a deal was out of the question but this was a further complication. The implications of him alluding to accomplices on board could not be ignored and he needed the captain to know of this latest development.

The Cabin Services Director, Laura, had by now arrived on the upper deck from her rest in the crew bunk area at the rear of the aircraft and was on her way to the cockpit to report to the captain and to check the wellbeing of all the flight crew. She found her way blocked by several passengers who, together with some cabin crew, were pinning down Mukonyi so she had to climb over two rows of seats to gain access.

Having ascertained that all was well on the flight deck Laura retrieved the restraining kit and returned to the upper deck where it was opened to bind Mukonyi. The upper deck Club World Purser and others in the group collectively started applying the restraining straps by handcuffing one hand and then the other, with the hands being bound together in front owing to his position. He was then strapped separately around his feet and elbows and, to secure him further, the two manacles around his hands were banded together with a further strap. A wet towel was also applied to his injured eye.

The purser, Ian, now proceeded to check that the passengers who had helped secure the attacker were unharmed and fortunately none of them were injured. At the same time Richard and two other cabin crew members carried Mukonyi to the rear of the upper deck and secured him to seat 68A in the last row. Those sitting there were moved forward but, as there were insufficient seats for everyone,

Jon Keens, travelling as the companion of a staff member, was obliged to move. So, Jon, who had performed so admirably with the rescue, was rewarded with a downgrade to seat 32H in the World Traveller cabin – the same seat that Mukonyi had been sitting in!

Laura visited the flight deck once more and on her way this time was informed by Gifford Shaw that Mukonyi had claimed to have an accomplice working with him. She promptly conveyed this chilling news to the captain and he immediately ordered that he be moved to the rear of the upper deck, but she was able to assure him that the task had already been accomplished. Bill further instructed that for the rest of the flight a male cabin crew member should remain nearby to guard him and also that, to prevent unauthorised movement from below, another steward should guard the upper deck stairs. He then informed her that as an extra precaution the flight deck door would be locked but, to avoid communication problems, Richard would be appointed to liaise between the flight and cabin crews.

As the flight settled back to normal, Bill spotted two shoes by his seat but soon noticed that one was brown and one was black. As these were all he could find he put them both on but, in spite of the fact he wore a size ten, the brown shoe was much too big! He had no idea who it belonged to or to where his other black shoe had strayed. The captain, however, apart from the footwear, remained in a state of undress but, continuing to feel on edge, he was reluctant to go back and put on his uniform. He knew perfectly well, of course, that he must have looked ridiculous sitting in his underwear with one black shoe and one enormous brown shoe but, for the moment, he felt compelled to remain on duty. After a little while, however, he was sufficiently assured to take a quick break and he went back to the door by the bunks to get dressed.

Captain Hagan was now more confident about the safety of the flight and, being back in uniform, he left the flight deck to look for his other shoe and to thank the passengers who had bravely leapt into the cockpit to assist. He finally retrieved his missing shoe from the aisle, much to the amusement of the nearby passengers, and was caught on video by Lucy Helman, Bryan Ferry's wife. She had found her camera after losing it during the incident and had videoed Mukonyi being dragged out of the flight deck. In the cabin downstairs, however, someone else had started recording earlier and had captured all of the aircraft upset* in that area.

Now wearing both his own shoes, the captain returned to the flight deck, shut and locked the door and went back to his seat. Adrenalin had been pumping through him throughout the upset and was still keeping him going in spite of him feeling in a state of shock. This was not the time to dwell on the event, however, or to waste time and mental energy trying to figure it out, for the flight crew had to move on. They now had to concern themselves with what lay ahead and how they would manage the next two hours to landing.

---

* *An aircraft upset is an event where a flight unintentionally exceeds these parameters – a nose-up pitch greater than 20°, a nose-down pitch greater the 10° and a bank angle greater than 45°.*

Chapter 8

Position Report OBD

Less than ten minutes earlier BA2069 had been cruising quietly on a heading of 150 degrees about 50nm northwest of El Obeid, estimating overhead of 0500, when the flight had been plunged into a roller coaster, corkscrewing, terror ride that had curved the track erratically to a heading of 020 degrees and had deposited the 747 northeast of the desert city. One moment everything was proceeding as planned then, in a few short minutes, the aircraft was miles off track, totally in the wrong place, heading almost due north in completely the wrong direction and flying at 30,000 feet, thousands of feet below their allocated Flight Level 370.

Fortunately, the flight was now under full control, climbing towards 37,000 feet and flying directly to El Obeid. Although the immediate danger was over and other aircraft had been informed of BA2069's predicament, little assistance from Khartoum could be expected and the flight was still at risk. The aircraft was climbing reasonably well but the pilots were unsure as to what flights might be catching up behind or what traffic might be coming towards them. They still had to cross the northbound traffic on the 'wrong side of the road' so they kept a good look out and listening watch for other flights and scrutinised the Traffic Collision and Avoidance System (TCAS) for any conflicting aircraft.

Although these were anxious minutes, the flight crew still had time to appraise the situation. It had already been agreed that the best option was to return to their planned cruising level as soon as possible rather than try to negotiate a new flight level with

Khartoum Air Traffic Control (ATC), that the fuselage structure was sound in spite of the violent encounter and that there had been no mention of any serious injuries having been sustained during the upset. It still had to be considered whether to continue or divert but by now the flight was approaching the desert city of El Obeid and the autopilot was close to capturing Flight Level 370.

On regaining the planned cruising level, the captain notified all aircraft in the vicinity on the same frequencies he had previously used when making the original 'Pan-Pan' call that Speedbird 2069 was now level, and the three pilots then briefly discussed whether a diversion was desirable or necessary. By good fortune there was no need for an immediate landing owing to any medical emergency as none had been reported but a diversion for operational reasons had to be contemplated. The nearest airport, El Obeid, could be seen ahead and Khartoum Airport was only about half an hour's flying time away, but there was doubt about the facilities available at either of these destinations. Also, as far as Khartoum was concerned, flight crews were already aware that the political situation in Sudan was not good, that Osama Bin Laden had lived in the city from 1991 to 1996, that there was a risk of terrorism and that it was BA policy not to divert to Khartoum except in an extreme emergency. Captain Hagan believed that the same should apply to El Obeid and, as the emergency was now over, he dismissed them as diversion airports.

There was also the option to consider destinations outside Sudan and to turn north to Luxor, or even to Cairo where BA had a daily service but, in this remote region without radar control, a re-clearance would have to be obtained over the radio from Khartoum Air Traffic Control (ATC). Such a procedure would have been difficult and time-consuming and could have negated any time advantage of continuing to the original destination. It did not take long to conclude, therefore, that there was little benefit in diverting anywhere, and all concurred with the captain's decision to continue to Nairobi.

Although this was in everyone's best interest, the captain still had to assess the perceived risk of proceeding as planned. As Mukonyi had acted alone it seemed unlikely that he had an accomplice but, even if he had and they were also intent on attacking, the crew were now much better prepared. The flight deck door was locked, the jemmy had been removed from the wardrobe and was by the captain's side and they now had reinforcements in the form of nearby passengers who had demonstrated their willingness to rally to the flight crew's aid if attacked.

Satisfied with the security situation, Bill now turned his thoughts to the passengers who, he had no doubt, would still be very apprehensive in the absence of any further information, but his first duty was to the safety of the flight. He had now recovered his breath after his exertions and was feeling more composed so first he would transmit the upcoming position report, then call London to inform them of the upset and afterwards speak to the passengers.

'Khartoum, this is Speedbird 2069, position El Obeid 0505, flight level 370, estimate Malakal 0548, next Tapos.'

The reply came back instantly.

'Speedbird 2069, roger, call me Tapos.'

The earlier upset may have seemed like an eternity to all on board but, in reality, it had only added an extra five minutes to the flight time. As the aircraft turned over El Obeid Airport, the lateral offset of 1nm right of track was again set up and BA2069 finally settled back on the flight's planned course. At about 0510, Captain Hagan now called British Airways in London using a satellite communications system which had only recently been installed as part of an upgrade to all BA's 747s. Calls could be made just like on a landline, except for the delay in receiving responses, but before providing details, he first stressed the seriousness of the situation.

He told them that BA would need to immediately activate their new Operational Crisis Incident Centre (OCIC), a unit that had recently been set up to handle BA emergencies, but was also available to a number of other airlines who operated out of Heathrow.

The captain then provided information on the flight deck intrusion, emphasising that it had caused a very serious aircraft upset and that 'for a start, we lost over ten thousand feet in a dive'. Although the ten thousand feet loss was an estimate, and only a small part of the event, he felt that the detail was sufficiently dramatic to convince BA of the seriousness of the incident. The recipient, perhaps considering such a drop unbelievable, not surprisingly requested verification.

'Confirm a ONE thousand feet loss of altitude?'

A height loss of 1,000 feet would, in normal circumstances, have been considered significant, with a report being mandatory, but was trivial in comparison to the upset, so for clarification he repeated the height loss.

'Negative. Height loss was TEN thousand feet, ONE ZERO thousand.'

Captain Hagan would admit, himself, that he had often been told he was a master of understatement, and he now lived up to that. There was also an issue with the satellite phones, however, for it was common knowledge that they were not secure and were monitored by others, including the press, so it was good to be brief. He knew that news of the event would break soon anyway, whatever he said, and that BA would be obliged to issue a statement. This would no doubt include the large height loss in the dive he had mentioned and he was aware that, if he enlarged on the seriousness of the incident, the company would have had more on which to work. He did, therefore, consider adding to his confirmation of the ten thousand feet height loss that the dive had not been all, but he refrained from doing so. Crucially, he did not mention that the intruder had fiercely seized the controls, that in doing so the autopilot had disconnected, that in a fight with the co-pilot he had then violently manipulated the controls to try and crash the aircraft and that the severe upset was a result of the attacker's inputs. At the time he didn't deem it necessary to provide further details as he believed that BA would retrieve the information quickly and that it was sufficient just to state it had been an extremely severe incident. This was not the moment for reserve, however, and Captain Hagan was later to regret not providing all the details, for his omissions were to be to his cost and to that of his co-pilots. These details had then been passed to BA's Safety Services who, in turn, would notify the Air Accident Investigation Branch (AAIB) and the AAIB would then establish contact with the International Civil Aviation Organisation (ICAO) in Montreal. On the basis of only the slender information provided, however, BA's own assessment of the aircraft upset underplayed the incident and underrated the violence of the upset.

In the meantime, the captain's call was transferred to the Operational Crisis Incident Centre (OCIC) and he was able to speak the staff there directly. Even with the small amount of information they had been provided they immediately recognised that the incident had been serious. Bill's overriding concern, however, was not what had just happened but what was going to happen later when the flight arrived in Nairobi. The initial questions from the centre also focussed on preserving the continued safe conduct of the flight rather than on the past, specifically on what the crew were doing to ensure Mukonyi had been rendered harmless and on ascertaining any passenger and crew injuries. Fortunately, the captain was able to inform them that there appeared to be no damage to the aircraft, that Mukonyi had now been well secured and that, although there had been some injuries, including his own, so far there had been no report of anything serious.

Captain Hagan, further continuing his satellite call to London, instructed that, before any disembarkation commenced, the Nairobi Airport Police should meet the flight on arrival, board the aircraft and remove Mukonyi. The injured should follow afterwards and be taken immediately to hospital for treatment while the remaining passengers should remain seated until they had left. He also suggested that a doctor should be available at the airport for anyone in need and that, if possible, there should be maximum staff coverage.

The captain then spoke to Dr Sandra Mooney, the head of British Airways Health Services (BAHS), and mentioned his own minor injuries and his personal concerns about AIDS, but he was assured he would be looked after on his return and that, to commence treatment immediately, he should get back to the UK as soon as possible.

After the satellite call, Bill then spoke again to the passengers to reassure them and to inform them that the flight was proceeding to Nairobi and, since they were 'a few hundred miles southwest of Khartoum in the middle of nowhere' continuing to destination was the best option. To help relieve the tension he also mentioned that 'the flying conditions are smooth so the seat belt signs will remain off' and, to finish, he took a cheeky delight, which did not go unnoticed, of assuring the passengers that, in spite of all that had happened, landing at Nairobi should be very close to schedule.

Laura now knocked on the locked cockpit door and Richard opened it to let her on to the flight deck. The Cabin Services Director was anxious to check that the captain's injuries were receiving attention and, if not, she would tend to that herself. She then informed him that the man who had attacked Phil was the same person who the Gatwick Police had escorted to the aircraft and who they had suggested was OK to travel. Clearly that had not been the case. As she washed the captain's wounds in cold water and applied disinfectant, he told her that information was needed about any passenger or cabin crew injuries so he could forward the details to the company. Eventually Laura reported that there were only six in the cabin who had suffered minor injuries, four passengers and two cabin crew members, but, astonishingly, no mention of the stewardess's serious injury. This was in spite of the fact that a qualified doctor on board had confirmed the broken leg and other cabin crew members had also known about it. On this flight it appeared that there had been an absurd breakdown of communications within the cabin, and from the cabin to the cockpit, for it appeared that no one person knew what was going on. As a consequence, however, neither did the captain.

Captain Hagan, having established that the injuries were minor, had again used the sat phone to pass these details to BA. Their Safety Services would then have relayed the information to the AAIB and, on receipt, with a report update of only minor injuries added to the previous information of no aircraft damage, they would have classified the aircraft upset as a 'serious incident'. The International Civil Aviation Organisation (ICAO), however, classified an aviation occurrence in which there is aircraft damage and/or serious injury/death as an 'accident', and a broken leg qualified as a 'serious injury'. The aircraft upset, therefore, had in error been classed as a 'serious incident' when it should have been classed as an 'accident'.

In the UK, a Mandatory Occurrence Reporting (MOR) system operates whereby it is a legal requirement to inform the Civil Aviation Authority (CAA) of any occurrences of a safety nature, no matter how small, and, for more significant events of aircraft serious incidents and accidents, it is a legal requirement to directly inform as soon as possible the Air Accidents Investigation Branch (AAIB) and, if in the UK, the police.

In the AAIB's own publication, 'Guidance for Airline Operators', it states at Part 1 that: 'Those occurrences that fall into the category of Serious Incidents or Accidents to which the regulations apply shall be investigated by an independent Safety Investigation Authority and a subsequent report published. The AAIB is the authority in the UK and its territorial waters.' At Part 6 of the Guide, it states that 'The AAIB is an operationally independent organisation embedded within the Department of the Environment, Transport and the Regions (DETR) and is completely separate from the CAA and the UK judicial system. The AAIB is responsible for the investigation of civil aircraft accidents and serious incidents to aircraft of any state when occurring in the UK, and has the rights of participation in investigation of accidents and serious incidents to aircraft registered in the UK regardless of the location of the occurrence.'

When a serious incident or accident occurs to a UK registered aircraft in a foreign country, however, the 'Guidance for Airline Operators' at Part 17, with the title 'Overseas Investigations', states that, 'The initial response to an accident or serious incident occurring to a UK operator in another State is the accident investigation authority of the State of Occurrence. Operators must report the occurrence in accordance with the local procedures and laws.' It also states at Part 2, entitled 'Who should report the accident or serious incident and how', that: 'It is a legal requirement that when an accident or serious incident occurs in or over the UK or occurs elsewhere to an aircraft registered in the UK, the commander of the aircraft involved at the time of the accident or serious incident, or if he be killed or incapacitated, the operator of the aircraft, should notify the AAIB by the quickest means of communications available.' As recognised by the AAIB, however, airlines function differently and it also stated at Part 2 that, 'In practical terms for commercial air transport operators, it is normal for the operator's safety manager or equivalent to be the reporter.' The AAIB can also relay details to the State of Occurrence if the commander has difficulty making contact and, once informed, the AAIB may have a right to be involved in any subsequent overseas investigation.

Wherever the 'serious incident' or 'accident' occurs, however, if the circumstances of the event change later it is also a legal requirement to report any updates that affect the original report. The UK Government takes the requirement to report very seriously and failure to report, or failure to update a report, is a criminal offence, with (in the year 2000) punishment of fines up to £5,000, of up to two years in prison, or both. Also, if the offence is sufficiently serious to be indictable, there could be no statute of limitation and offenders can be prosecuted at any time.

As BA operated their own flight Safety Services department, as did other airlines, it is they who would receive Mandatory Occurrence Reports (MORs) and would manage the MOR system. If the safety departments assess these reports as not being of a 'mandatory' nature they can be dealt with internally, and the reports are then passed to the relevant company departments. For reports considered mandatory, it is their responsibility to forward them to the CAA and to forward serious incident and accident reports, or updates on reports, directly to the AAIB, both of whom then make their own assessments.

It was acceptable practice, therefore, for Captain Hagan, having immediately informed Sudan by radio, to then inform BA of the incident and, as the upset was obviously of a more serious nature, for BA to immediately telephone the basic facts in order to alert the AAIB as soon as possible. Having assumed all details received, BA had then faxed a written report, and the AAIB would, in turn, have alerted the International Civil Aviation Organisation (ICAO) in Montreal and then either ICAO or the AAIB would have contacted the authorities in the State of Occurrence, Sudan, and then in the State of Landing, Kenya. Soon after notifying the AAIB of the incident, BA had then called the CAA and had submitted a Mandatory Occurrence Report (MOR) by fax. In spite of the violence of the upset, however, with no mention of aircraft damage or serious injury, the AAIB had classified the upset as a 'serious incident' rather than as an 'accident' and that would also have served to support BA's initial assessment, which seemed to have focused on 'air rage'. Stewardess Kim Parker would have her ankle and leg X-rayed in Nairobi, however, and, with broken bones confirmed, BA's Safety Services Department, as they had done with the first report, would relay this update to the AAIB who would then reclassify the incident as an 'accident'. This was important as, under ICAO rules, 'accidents', unlike 'serious incidents', must be investigated and a report must be published. All can then learn from the experiences of others and, with knowledge, reoccurrences can be avoided.

BA then advised the Government's Department of the Environment, Transport and Regions (DETR) who, following receipt of the initial early morning BBC Ceefax bulletin, had already alerted the head of their Threats Office, a gentleman to be known only by his initials, DM. He had been tasked with producing a risk assessment but it would take some time to complete before it could be submitted.

With the upset now behind them, the flight crew still had to endure another two hours or so of flying and they needed to avoid dwelling in their own minds on what had happened and to settle down to the task in hand. What had to be prevented at all costs was each alone being distracted by the upset to the point where the result was another situation of the crew's own making. Chatting together about aspects of the event could be therapeutic.

'By the way,' enquired the co-pilot, 'how on earth did you think of going for his eye to get him off?'

With some amusement Bill told him of a recent question from his son, Aidan, who had asked what he would do if attacked by a shark and he had replied, 'I would poke it in the eye.'

The captain had been abruptly aroused from a very deep sleep during the attack and, trying to waken up, had been hurled from slumber into turmoil so, not surprisingly, he was struggling a little to accept reality. He found that talking to Phil about it helped settle his mind and together they also pondered afresh their survival. They agreed once more that, without doubt, the primary factor that had saved the day was the very low airspeed sustained throughout the upset. Their ten to fifteen-minute exchange had the desired effect as it helped clear the air and they were then able to put the matter out of their minds for the rest of the flight. Captain Hagan had also asked Richard to go through the cabin to reassure the passengers and the cabin crew about the situation and he became the link between them and his fellow pilots. The use of the relief pilot as a cockpit/cabin go-between was very useful and helped overcome communication difficulties with the locking of the flight deck door.

As the flight continued there was some stirring in the cabin as a considerable degree of resentment had grown against Mukonyi amongst the passengers and at one time a particular gentleman in the lower cabin had attempted to round up support to do him some harm. The captain was later to learn that only a few months earlier, on 11 August 2000, a Mr Jonathan Burton, travelling on flight Southwest 1763 within the USA, had charged the cockpit of a Boeing 737 in what had been classified as air rage. He was restrained and subsequently beaten to death by the passengers. Fortunately, any movement against Mukonyi had already been blocked by closing off the steps to the upper deck in order to protect the flight deck from a possible further attack by an accomplice. Only a doctor on board, a Canadian lady passenger, had been permitted upstairs to treat Mukonyi.

Nearing Nairobi, the pilots commenced the before descent checks and briefed thoroughly for the approach and landing at Jomo Kenyatta Airport. Much of East and South Africa is on a high plateau and the airport elevation is 5,500 feet above sea level. At that altitude the air is thinner, the airspeed is higher and so the ground speed is nearly 10% more than at sea level. The descent and approach have to be carefully monitored otherwise the aircraft can get high and fast and if that occurs speed brakes may then have to be used to increase the descent rate. When the speed brakes are extended the 747 vibrates slightly and, with about 400 very nervous passengers on board, the captain felt that was the last thing they needed. A slow, gentle and undisturbed descent and approach was in order so he briefed Phil to commence descent about twenty miles prior to the calculated descent point. The Cabin Services Director, Laura, was then also advised that the descent would be commenced earlier and that the landing time alert would be brought forwards fifteen minutes, so everyone was aware that the plan was for a more relaxed approach.

On cue, Phil carefully commenced descent and the captain switched on the 'seat belt' signs much earlier than usual to give everyone plenty of time to calmly prepare for landing. He then briefly spoke to the passengers over the PA, saying they would be landing soon and that the weather conditions were good. At the end of his passenger address, he advised the cabin crew that they now had twenty-five minutes to landing. After his address he was informed that Mukonyi was so trussed up that the cabin crew could not properly strap him in but, after several attempts, they eventually managed to strap the big Kenyan safely into his seat.

On the final approach in the rarefied atmosphere the airspeed was noticeably faster and the rate of descent slightly increased so, to avoid firm contact with the runway, the captain planned to ease the control column back a little early to flare the aircraft and arrest the rate of descent. The runway at Jomo Kemyatta International Airport in Nairobi is long in order to cope with the conditions so he had also planned to carry out an unhurried deceleration after touchdown which gave him a little extra time to finesse the landing. He flew the final approach as smoothly as he could and, thankfully, to the gentlest of landings onto Runway 06, much to the audible relief of all the passengers. The cheering could even be heard on the flight deck.

Chapter 9

Nairobi

As the aircraft slowed down the runway, the captain let the speed drop to just below 10 knots, the maximum permitted for the sharp right-angled turn required to exit the runway at taxiway Lima. Almost simultaneously, 'Tower' called to exit at taxiway 'Lima' and to call 'Ground'. On entering Lima, Phil contacted 'Ground' who instructed them to taxi from 'Lima' via 'Golf' and 'Juliet' to Gate 2. The time was now 0709 and, as the 747 approached the stand at Gate 2, the captain asked Phil to taxi the aircraft slowly to give him time to talk to the passengers. He then informed them that before they could disembark the police would first remove Mukonyi and afterwards medical staff would board to help those injured who needed hospital treatment. After the PA announcement, Bill retook control, parked the aircraft then shut down the engines and completed the checks.

In the meantime, with the passengers remaining in their seats, Mukonyi had been arrested by the Kenyan police and removed from the aircraft and then, shortly afterwards, he had been followed by the five with minor injuries, four passengers and the other stewardess. Kim, by then, had been sitting in the crew rest seat with her leg in splints propped up on a cabin bag for about two hours and now she was starting to shake with shock and the agony of the pain. Having earlier refrained from taking stronger drugs she now took the offer of some painkillers. As Kim's leg had been strapped with splints, arrangements had been made to take her off the aircraft in a wheelchair to an ambulance that had been dispatched as a precaution by the hospital and it was waiting outside the terminal. Kim's husband, Chris, asked if he could accompany her to the hospital and he would carry both their cabin bags. Kim and her husband also shared a suitcase, but other cabin crew members assured them they would look after it and take it with them on the crew bus to the hotel. On board the ambulance, the couple were joined by two passengers who on the flight had not kept their seat belts fastened and had suffered minor wrist and neck injuries when, after floating in the air, they had fallen back to the floor. The other cabin crew member and the two remaining passengers with only light injuries were escorted by private transport.

The captain had waited for Mukonyi to be removed and for the medical team to board then, with the passengers still seated, he left the flight deck and went down the stairs to the galley below. His children, Alanna and Aidan, were nearby so he checked to see how they were and was pleased to see that they seemed fine. He also felt that the first-class passengers, of which his wife was one, deserved his personal touch so he then quickly walked forward into the cabin to talk to each in turn. Lady Annabel Goldsmith first introduced herself and her family to him and he then spoke to other passengers and his wife, Charmaine. There was a feeling in the group of a common bond in the joy of survival and all were enormously relieved and thankful to be alive.

As Bill walked back through the First Class cabin a few passengers took the opportunity to hand him scribbled notes which he placed in his pocket to share later with Phil and Richard, and he thanked them for their kindness. At the same time a few more notes had been handed to cabin crew members by some other passengers with the request to pass them to the captain. On his return to the flight deck, Bill made a PA announcement to the passengers bound for Dar-es-Salaam. They would be continuing their journey on the same aircraft that had clearly 'exceeded normal flight parameters' and, not surprisingly, the travellers would be more than a little concerned. The captain reassured them that the 747 would undergo the fullest inspection and would have to be thoroughly checked before its next flight but, unfortunately, this would cause a substantial delay. On these normally short transits passengers are expected to remain on board but, after due process, and to the relief of those continuing to Dar es Salaam, Captain Hagan received permission for them to disembark with the Nairobi passengers and to proceed to a comfortable lounge.

Shortly after the disembarkation had started, Laura, the Cabin Services Director, returned to the flight deck to tell the captain that the local staff were having a bit of a confrontation with one particular passenger. Apparently, he had videoed the entire drama of the upset in the cabin and he had been overheard on the walkway talking to Sky News on his mobile phone about selling it to them. Local BA staff members were attempting to persuade him, somewhat insistently, to hand over the recording but he was refusing to do so. The station manager, Laura explained, had considered that the tape recording could be of use in an enquiry and should be securely retained as evidence. Laura had been asked to obtain the captain's opinion as, of course, obtaining the tape by force was out of the question, but Bill did consider that taking the approach of explanation and persuasion was not unreasonable.

As the last of the passengers were disembarking, Bill completed the post-shutdown items and then prepared to record the details of the aircraft upset in the Technical Log. He first discussed with Phil the actions of the autothrottle as they had remained engaged throughout, but he was not sure that the autothrottle system had worked satisfactorily. It had seemed to him that the power demanded by the thrust levers had not at all times been matched by the power from the engines. Phil concurred, stating that after Mukonyi had been removed, the thrust levers had immediately advanced automatically to full power, for he had followed the movement with his left hand, but the engines had taken a considerable time to 'spool up' to the power demanded. Both agreed this was almost certainly owing to the fact that, with the aircraft stalled and the speed nearly 100 knots too low, the airflow to the engine intakes would have been at an obtuse angle and turbulent. Later the flight data recorder (FDR) was to confirm that the thrust had remained low over a period of about 45 seconds when it should have been at full power. Bill's own opinion was that short term stalling of the engines was the more likely reason and that they had been very fortunate that the lack of thrust had only been temporary.

Both pilots also discussed and agreed that it appeared the 747 had not been overstressed, either because any damaging forces had been resisted by Phil's inputs or had occurred with the aircraft being fully stalled. When a control surface moves in flight it deflects the airflow and that exerts a force on the control which is proportional to the square of the speed but, with the aircraft repeatedly at low speed it had essentially stopped flying during these periods, and the forces on the deflected control surfaces had been much reduced. As far as the two were concerned, the aircraft had flown perfectly normally after the incident with no appearance of damage. They then also confirmed their opinions once more that the unbelievably low speeds that had been experienced during the fully developed stalls, although terrifying, had ultimately been the most significant factor in saving the day!

The captain's problem now was that there was no 'post-stalling' check as big aircraft are not expected to stall so, to complete the Technical Log, he simply stuck to the basics and recorded only three entries. The first and third entries were straightforward but the second was just made up as best he could.

1. A mandatory Air Safety Report has been raised due to an intruder attempting to seize control of the aircraft.
2. The aircraft requires both a severe turbulence check and a heavy landing check, plus any other appropriate stress check, as it had been flown outside the normal flight envelope as a result of item 1.
3. De-icing was carried out in Gatwick with the type and mixture strength noted and was completed by 2155.

Captain Hagan would have been forgiven for overlooking this third entry, but to him the act of remembering such an insignificant matter represented a return to the real world, going back to normal and, once again, to the mundane and trivial having a place!

One important person in the capital who would most certainly have been informed immediately of the incident was the President, Daniel Arap Moi, and he would soon have learned of the attacker's background. Mukonyi was not just any young Kenyan man, but was one of Moi's stars, a very bright student with a flair for languages who had graduated from the President's own Moi University with 1st class honours and who had been awarded a scholarship for postgraduate study at Lyon University in France. As one of Moi's brightest and best, Mukonyi's behaviour would not have reflected well on the president or on the educational institutions he had established and he would not have taken this lightly. President Moi, however, had by then been in power for over 20 years and had a tight grip on the country so he was very much in a position to stamp his own authority on procedures.

In the UK, several departments in BA, including Safety Services, Security and the Press Office, were having a very busy morning. A press release, plus reports for the relevant UK aviation agencies, had to be urgently prepared but, before any assessment could begin, BA had to first establish how serious the incident had been. The facts available, however, were limited. The detail from the Flight Data Recorder (FDR) would not be available until after the aircraft arrived back in London and the only primary information the company had received had been from Captain Hagan's sparse satellite call after the upset with the short report that BA2069 had plummeted 10,000 feet in a dive. BA surmised, therefore, that had an intruder induced a steep dive at an estimated rate of descent of about 20,000 feet per minute for a period of 30 seconds that could have accounted for such a drop. This assessment of the dive, in fact, turned out to be accurate. It was also considered, however, that, if it had taken the intruder a few seconds to dive the 747 and the pilot a few seconds to level it, the maximum time of the loss of control would have been about 20 seconds.

BA were aware that the incident would be headline news and that it would be best not to be too detailed about the aircraft upset, but they could not do much more than go with what whatever data they had available. Those BA staff members evaluating the facts would have been at senior level and to them the event seemed to indicate an issue of 'air rage' rather than an attempt to hijack or crash the 747, so this was how the aircraft upset was presented. What was needed most then was to provide a press release, as distributing some basic information would be better than nothing.

Back in Nairobi, all the passengers had now disembarked and, as the cabin crew was about to leave, one of them passed Captain Hagan a few more passengers' handwritten notes which he pocketed with the others. After disembarking, the three pilots proceeded to the airline office and, on crossing the tarmac, bumped into the southbound flight crew, Captain Bob Grimstead and Senior First Officer Graham Mounsey, who were also on their way to the BA office. They would later operate the 747, now being thoroughly checked, on the shuttle down to Dar es Salaam and back again to Nairobi later that evening. Bob Grimstead, as the ongoing captain, clearly had a vested interest in the incident and the state of the airframe of the aircraft he was about to command, and he and Graham Mounsey were provided with as much information as possible. Details of the aircraft upset were discussed and the ongoing crew were left in no doubt about Mukonyi's determined attack to crash the aircraft. After asking many questions, which were answered by the group as best they could, Bob requested if they could attend the debrief in the manager's office and, of course, both were made welcome.

By now, the convoy of Mukonyi in a police van, followed by the injured in the ambulance and the private transport, were arriving at Nairobi Hospital. At A&E the young Kenyan remained under police armed guard while his wounded eye received attention and the cabin crew members and passengers had their injuries treated. On examining Kim Parker's back and broken leg, however, the doctor was concerned by the extent of her injuries and he arranged for her to have X-rays. As it was a private hospital, the doctors required approval from BA for treatment, and the company was informed of the fractures and that the damage had to be X-rayed. BA2069 had arrived at 0715 UTC/1015 Kenyan local time so, by the time Kim had been wheelchaired to the ambulance, driven to the hospital, and examined by the doctors, it would have been about 0845 UTC/ 1145 local when BA would have found out about her broken leg. That must have come as a shock to BA as only about three-and-a-half hours ago they had been informed that there had been only minor injuries, that the aircraft upset had been classified as a 'serious incident', that both Sudan and the UK had declined to investigate and that they would be conducting the investigation themselves. How would they respond to this now? In the meantime, Kim had to wait for a BA representative to approve the expense and, as she sat near the X-ray equipment, Mukonyi, to her extreme distress, was sat next to her as he also waited for BA to approve an X-ray of his eye.

Back at Nairobi's Jomo Kenyatta Airport, the flight crews had arrived at the BA Office where the cabin crew had been waiting patiently for the debrief. Captain Hagan opened the meeting by explaining what had happened to the aircraft and told them they were all very fortunate to have survived. He then cautioned that the press would be seeking any information they could get and reminded everyone that BA had a very strict policy of not talking to the media. Finally, he informed everyone that it was standard practice after a major incident to suspend all crew members and, having done this, he then thanked all the cabin crew for their help. Bill was also aware, however, that BA would be anxious to hear from him so he and his fellow pilots remained in the office to call London. The rest of the crew then made their way to the terminal where the cabin crew transport waited outside to pick them up and drop them at the Nairobi Intercontinental, the BA crew hotel at the time. The flight crew would follow later in their own transport.

By the time the cabin crew reached the terminal building the disembarking passengers had already cleared immigration and customs and, on exiting into the arrivals hall, were being met by a substantial media presence. The press had no doubt been alerted to the incident by monitoring radio emergency frequencies and satellite communication systems, and passengers willing to share their experiences were already being pressed for information by the large number of reporters waiting.

Clarke Bynum and Gifford Shaw, the tall Americans who had helped remove Mukonyi from the flight deck, were easily identifiable in their checked shirts. Photographers snapped them together as Clarke described his version of events to a reporter from the *Daily Nation*, the prominent Kenyan newspaper.

'We could hear hollering and banging from the cockpit,' explained Clarke, 'and I said to Giff we have to do something. I looked out the window and could see we were going straight down so I went into the cockpit. My mind was whirling with what I might find – a hijacker with a gun or knife.

'I just grabbed his neck and shoulder,' added Bynum, 'and just joined in the fight. I was able to pull him off and from there we got him to the ground and the pilot was able to get control of the plane.'

'Everyone was woken up by some screaming,' explained Benjamin Goldsmith as he described his experience, 'then the plane went into a really weird angle, going down to the left and basically very, very steep.

'There was violent shuddering and then the engines cut out altogether. This was the scene of an aeroplane about to crash. The lights went out and the oxygen masks came down and the plane sort of re-gained control after what must have been about 20 or 30 seconds.

'I don't believe there was a single person on that airplane who did not believe we were about to crash. Every single person on that aircraft was absolutely terrified. There were grown men screaming, people praying aloud.'

Rob Adam, an upper deck passenger, described what he had witnessed of the rescue.

'Three passengers in the front row jumped into the cockpit and physically carried out this guy. They were helped by the stewards to tie him up and then two stewards sat him in the row behind.'

Zanne Augur, a 32-year-old graduate student on her way to climb Mount Kilimanjaro, related that 'there was this awful lurching. It felt like turbulence but with this horrible noise. It was like a roller coaster when the pit of your stomach drops out.'

A World Traveller passenger, Todd Engstrom from Portland, Oregon, on the flight with his young daughter, said, 'The aircraft went into a series of very steep dives, three or four in succession and then made a very sharp turn. Everyone was asleep. There was a movie playing when suddenly the plane took deep, steep dives, about three or four in succession. It was like a roller coaster - the fasten seat belt sign did not go on, some people hit their heads.'

A young lady, Zoe McNaughton from Kent, described how 'it sank really quickly. It felt like we were going to crash, you just had no idea what was going to happen. The plane went very quickly up into the air, everyone's stuff went up in the air, people hit their heads on the ceiling, it really did feel like this was going to be it. Passengers were all over the place, lying down.'

'Mukonyi appeared to have a suicide note,' Zoe also mentioned when questioned.

Ms McNaughton was referring to a rumour that had been circulating that one of the notes known to have been handed to Gifford Shaw was a suicide note and the hearsay may have been based on that, but, unfortunately, the notes later disappeared and were never recovered.

Celia Gregory, on her way to celebrate the millennium in Zanzibar, mentioned that she mostly remembered the severe juddering.

> It sounded like it was going to break apart. Not being informed of what was going on was incredibly worrying and I began to take on board the possibilities.
>
> Eventually I had a very strong feeling of letting go, which in a sense was my knowing there was nothing I could do about it. If that's what was going to happen then that's what was going to happen.

The other two gentlemen passengers who had been involved in the cockpit rescue had managed to avoid attention. The fair-haired Kenyan had slipped away with his family without being identified and John Keens, the partner of Stewardess Penny Lester, had simply melted into the background the moment he had been moved from

Club World into Mukonyi's seat downstairs in the World Traveller section. Unnoticed by the press he eventually made his way to the cabin crew transport parked outside and there he waited for the cabin crew to arrive.

By now there were a lot of passengers mingling in the arrivals area of the terminal but, with insufficient BA staff to cope, they did not, unfortunately, receive the support they deserved. The passengers in transit to Dar es Salaam fared a little better as they were all escorted to the BA airside lounge and thereby avoided the crush. For most, however, the lack of company staff made the arrival in Nairobi difficult but this had been the unfortunate result of flight scheduling and staff rostering. In the year 2000, BA had two daily flights operating through Nairobi, the overnight southbound flight from London, as operated by Captain Hagan and his crew, transiting in the early morning on its way to a final destination, and the return of the same aircraft transiting in the early evening for its overnight northbound flight back to London. The morning shift was already on duty but those staff members on the evening shift were off duty and, with few, if any, owning phones, they could not be contacted to assist. The few BA staff members on duty soon became overwhelmed and it was impossible to provide the individual attention required. The sketchy details received by the staff referred to the event as only 'air rage' and, as far as they were aware, their priority was to those passengers requiring medical attention. They knew almost nothing of what the passengers had endured and had no real understanding of how devastating the aircraft upset had been so were unprepared to offer the kind of succour most needed.

Many passengers later complained that there was little or no BA staff and that there were no refreshments, no assistance with luggage, no assistance with immigration formalities, no contact information for counsellors or doctors and no details even of BA's local offices provided. Some passengers asked if they could call home to reassure their families that all was well as they had no other way of doing so but were refused on the grounds of cost. In Kenya then international landline phone calls were very expensive and phone networks were limited. Once again this reflected a lack of understanding by the staff as they had not been properly apprised of the situation and were not aware how close these passengers had come to losing their lives or of how distraught they were feeling. This 'lack of understanding', which was basically a staff misunderstanding, was, however, perceived and commented on by many passengers and BA was later to acknowledge that there had been shortfalls in customer service. They also gave assurances that lessons had been learned from the experience and that if a similar event ever occurred in the future there would be better passenger support and better recognition of their needs.

At this stage Captain Hagan and the co-pilots were still in the BA office and they were unaware of the circumstances prevailing in the terminal. A number of calls from unknown BA staff in London requesting information were received and Bill left them in no doubt that the autopilot had been disconnected when Mukonyi had first grabbed the control column and snatched it to his chest and that, in spite of their best efforts, he had remained clutching the controls for an extended length of time.

Amongst other calls received was one from 'Engineering' asking whether or not the aircraft had at any time experienced an overspeed, i.e. if the maximum speed of the aircraft had been exceeded? Bill was able to reassure the caller that, as the 747 had spent most of the two to three minutes of the aircraft upset in the stall, and, therefore, at low speed, he was certain there had not been any instances of 'overspeed'. With formalities completed, the three pilots said their goodbyes to Bob and Graham and then, finally, made their way to the terminal.

The immigration area was quiet when they arrived so they were quickly processed at the crew desk before going to the baggage hall to collected their suitcases. Phil was travelling light for his short stay with just hand luggage and his golf clubs, and the two bags for Bill and Richard had already been moved from the belt by porters and had been set aside for collection. To the captain's surprise he then spotted his family standing alone in the empty baggage hall as they waited for their luggage by an equally empty and stationary carousel. It was only then that Bill realised he had forgotten to tell his wife that, owing to their late arrival at the aircraft in London, their bags could be not be loaded and would follow twenty-four hours later. From there they all sailed through customs and, to their good fortune, into a deserted arrival hall as the mass of media had by then left to tail the passengers and cabin crew to the hotel. The sightseeing crowds had also evaporated and the building had the appearance of having been evacuated.

The Kenyan police, having 'got their man', didn't take any further interest in proceedings at the airport. They did not make any attempt to interview any of the passengers, including those of most relevance to the attack, such as the two Americans involved in the rescue, or those who had overheard Mukonyi muttering his intentions.

Meanwhile the passengers for Dar es Salaam waiting in the BA lounge were facing an extended delay of at least six hours owing to the additional checks on the aircraft. Those enforced to endure the lengthy stop in Nairobi would have plenty of time to ponder their drama and many would have later departed on the next leg to Dar es Salaam with considerable anxiety and trepidation, and even more so for those continuing onwards with another airline to Zanzibar.

BA issued their first press release entitled 'Nairobi flight lands safely after an in-flight incident' only about ninety minutes after the landing and it is summarised below.

> ...It appears that a male passenger entered the flight deck and attempted to seize the flight controls.
>
> The flight crew struggled with the passenger during which the auto-pilot became disengaged.
>
> A number of passengers are believed to have suffered relatively minor injuries as the aircraft made sudden manoeuvres ....the passenger was restrained...
>
> British Airways staff stationed in Nairobi are also in attendance to cater for the needs of passengers.
>
> The aircraft was carrying 379 passengers, 3 flight crew and 16 cabin crew.
>
> [This was a slight error as the quoted number of passengers on board only included the adult count of 379 adults and omitted the six infants.]

The press release was likely to have been issued at the time Captain Hagan was in BA's airport office and telephoning London with his more detailed report of the incident, for the information in this first release could only have been based on what the captain had relayed by satellite phone to the Operational Crisis Incident Centre (OCIC) during the last part of the flight.

Chapter 10

You Will Passenger Back Tonight

As the pilots exited the terminal building, the group, now six including Bill's family, made their way undisturbed to the waiting flight crew minibus in which they could all travel to town together. Their delayed departure from the airport owing to completing procedures relating to the incident was proving to be very fortunate for, once again, there was no one there, and they were able to board the bus without being bothered by anyone. The driver had been instructed to proceed directly to the hospital to have the captain's wounds treated so the others were obliged to accompany him. The drive into town was not long but, as the group was still in a state of shock, the journey was quiet and everyone was left to their own thoughts. Soon they arrived at the hospital where they all disembarked and waited together in reception for Bill to be called to have his wounds properly dressed. The laceration on his ear needed attention and the small, fleshy end of his little finger was hanging off and required treatment.

The single-storey Nairobi Hospital was small and resembled the kind of cottage hospitals that were common in UK villages until the mid-1950s. The tiny casualty centre was at full capacity although there was only a handful of passengers who were accompanied by some local BA airport staff. All the surrounding treatment cubicles were in use when Bill arrived so he had to wait to be called. In the meantime, the pilots had each received the relevant pre-emptive inoculations and the captain was given tablets sufficient for the first one to two days of his anti–HIV course, based on the AZT retroviral, with four to be taken immediately. He would receive further tablets for his course of treatment when he returned home. Phil was also offered a course of treatment as he had been bitten by Mukonyi but, having considered his risk of infection to be very low, he declined.

The atmosphere in casualty was quite relaxed and the captain went to visit one of their injured passengers, a Canadian teenage girl who had a neck injury and whose mother and father were waiting with her in the cubicle. He presumed she was one of the few unfortunates who had been unstrapped and who had floated upward from their seats until their heads knocked the ceiling. They had then drifted from right to left across the cabin and had fallen in passengers' laps on the opposite side. Bill spent some time with them and, while there, the doctor arrived to let them know that her injury was not serious. She would be released subject to the x-ray examination, which was expected to be satisfactory, and for the time being they were free to wait in reception. The doctor then announced that he would attend to the captain.

The scene had been somewhat less relaxed earlier when Mukonyi had arrived in the police van at the hospital at about 0830/1130 local with the ambulance and the injured group's private transport close behind. Dr Devashish Roy, the registrar in charge of casualty, remarked that 'a few looked terrified while others looked as if they were about to cry'. The hospital's director of nursing, Sue Carr-Hartley, mentioned that Mukonyi was 'very aggressive' when he arrived at the hospital and was struggling with the police. She said he had been sedated to the point of unconsciousness and added that her team would make sure 'it lasted through the night'.

At about 0900/1200 local, Stewardess Kim Parker, who had been obliged to sit uncomfortably close to Mukonyi while both waited for their X-rays to be approved by BA, fortunately had not had to wait too long as she had been taken first for her X-ray.

After the processing of the X-rays of Kim's back and right leg had been completed, it was first revealed that she had suffered a slight fracture to one of her vertebrae. Her lower right limb was much worse, however, for she was informed that not only was her ankle damaged but that she had also sustained a complicated spiral fracture to her right leg which was very serious and which would require surgery. She was given the option of having the surgery in Nairobi or being stretchered home to a hospital in the UK and, not surprisingly, she chose the latter. The doctor had explained she should remain in the hospital under observation for the time being but that she should be stretchered home as soon as possible and BA had been contacted to arrange her return to London that evening.

Following her X-rays, Kim had been taken to a small room at the back of the hospital and had been instructed to rest. That evening she would be driven straight from the hospital to the airport for the flight home. BA had been concerned about the press getting to Kim in the hospital, so a steward, who was scheduled to fly later on the long delayed BA2069 to Dar es Salaam, and who knew her, had been dispatched by BA to sit outside her room and fend off any press approach.

Later, when Captain Hagan was being examined, the group waiting for him had already met up with Chris Parker, Kim's husband, and, when Bill returned, Kim's situation was discussed. Chris was also interested to hear more of the incident and the flight crew told him what had happened. In the meantime, while Kim had protection, Chris took the opportunity to go to the hotel in a taxi and collect their suitcase.

The BA station manager then approached Bill to remind him that in the hospital he must avoid being questioned by the media and that he should also be careful when arriving at the Intercontinental Hotel. The captain, however, thought that the manager was being over-cautious about the level of publicity the event had attracted for he found the hospital corridors empty and the reception area devoid of people.

Well before the small group left the hospital, a number of their passengers had already checked in to the same crew hotel, the Intercontinental. The arrival of Lady Annabel Goldsmith and other family members travelling with her had been captured by photographers and film crews and a few hours later these images formed a major part of UK television reports. Jemima had arranged to meet her husband, Imran Khan, in Nairobi for the family holiday in Kenya and he had already flown in from Pakistan.

When Chris arrived at the Intercontinental Hotel to pick up their suitcase, he found to his dismay that it was quite chaotic for there were reporters, photographers and TV cameras in a large throng at the entrance. Mr Parker had to push his way with some difficulty into the hotel and, in the lobby, he caught up with the cabin crew, who were still in uniform. He told them of Kim's broken leg and that they would be flying back that night with Kim on a stretcher. The crew, of course, wanted to hear more of the incident and he was also able to pass on what he had heard from the pilots. Now he had been seen talking to the cabin crew, however, he was of interest to the press and, with suitcase in hand, he had to force his way back through the scrum outside eager to interview him. Having been traumatised by the incident, still in shock, tired and concerned for his wife, it was the last thing he needed. It was a very relieved Mr Parker who managed to reach his taxi and return with their suitcase to the hospital.

It was not until the early afternoon local time that the pilots' hospital group finally arrived at the hotel and walked into an almost empty lobby. Relieved that the manager's warnings were of no consequence, they were able to proceed unhindered directly to the check-in desk. At the desk the receptionist immediately recognised Captain Hagan's name and she gave him a few more passengers' notes that had been handed in earlier by another stewardess. When added to the notes in his pocket there were no more than a dozen and, as the check-in was somewhat leisurely, he divided them up equally for each to read together while they waited. In that quiet moment it only took a minute or two for all the notes to be read but the words left a profound effect on all of them.

One message from Ann Marie was a moving text on two pages of a small hotel note pad: 'How does one possibly thank someone for their very life? Because of you I will be able to be a mother to my six-year-old daughter, to know the joy of the responsibility of raising her, to finish the job and give her all she deserves and needs to grow. Thank you for your strength and courage, God bless you to know you have saved hundreds of lives this day.'

A gentleman by the name of Sandy, who was waiting in Nairobi for his son, Alexander, wrote: 'We cannot possibly thank you and your crew enough for your courage and skill in that nightmare episode. You will live in our thoughts and prayers forever.'

Flor was a lady of few words: 'Thank you very much for saving our lives. It was traumatising but you got us through it. My life changed forever.'

Ten-year-old Bretta had scribbled in red ink: 'Thank you so much for keeping us safe! I was really scared but I think you guys did a great job of keeping things under control. I think you are all very brave. This is my first trip to Africa and I'm glad we landed safely!!!!!!!!!!!'

After completing check-in, Captain Hagan was handed a note from BA informing him that the Kenyan police would not permit anyone to leave the country without first making a formal statement so, when settled in his room, he began preparing what he would write. This was the captain's opportunity to make it clear in the police statement that the assailant had clutched the control column for a period of minutes and that, in his opinion, there was no doubt the young Kenyan was trying to crash the aircraft.

A short time after the flight crew's arrival in the hotel, the Kenyan police spokesman, Dola Ndidis, issued the police's own press release at about 1100/1400 local, less than four hours after BA2069's arrival in Nairobi.

'A suspected mental patient on board had gone berserk. We do not wish to speculate on whether he will be charged or not and we should not treat him as criminal', declared Mr Ndidis, adding that, 'Investigations might show he was a sick man.'

The statement was released unknown to the crew now ensconced in the hotel, but had they read it they would have found much to challenge in the content. They were aware that the police had not taken any statements or conducted any investigation at the airport and that, according to the hospital's Director of Nursing, Carr-Hartley, Mukonyi was to be kept sedated overnight. At the time of the press release, therefore, he could not possibly have been interviewed by the police or have provided them with a statement. Any medical examinations could also not have been possible so the doctors could not have reported on his physical or mental condition. Later, on 31 December, a report in the *Kenyan Sunday Nation* corroborated these details by revealing that Mukonyi had still been under sedation at lunchtime on the afternoon of Saturday, 30 December, about 22 hours after the police press statement that had been released on the Friday mid-afternoon. Also disclosed in the *Sunday Nation*'s report was a comment from the police at the hospital that Mukonyi had mumbled incoherently through the night of Friday to Saturday.

A proper investigation, of course, may later be able to establish that Mukonyi's behaviour, as a determined attacker intent on crashing the 747, had been a result of mental illness but, at that instant, the police had no evidence whatsoever to reach such a conclusion. Even in the absence of any evidence, however, it was not difficult for the police to consider that the perpetrator of such an outrageous act may not have been of sound mind but, in the light of the seriousness of the incident, they also did not have the medical knowledge or experience to make such a statement. The police press release could only have been conjecture, and its sole purpose seemed to have been to establish from the outset that the police had been directed to investigate the incident and they would be in charge.

In the Intercontinental Hotel, the phone in Bill's room rang almost constantly over the next three hours. He was wary of calls received from various press agencies all over the world, but he also received calls from relatives and friends. BA Engineering called too, and again discussed details of the aircraft upset he had relayed by phone earlier from BA's airport office. Another call was received from BA's Director of Customer Services and Operations, Mike Street, and he asked if after the aircraft upset the captain had told passengers on the PA that 'a madman had broken in to the cockpit and had tried to crash the aircraft'.

'You didn't actually say that, did you?' he questioned, delivered in a tone that seemed to indicate disapproval.

'Yes,' responded Captain Hagan. 'My immediate and overwhelming impression throughout the attack was of a man determined to take his own life by crashing the aircraft and I believed that no one of sound mind would have done such a thing.

'I didn't have long to think about what I was going to say to the passengers,' continued the captain, 'so I told them the truth!'

When Mr Street was asked by Bill what he would have said, there was no reply.

A further call from BA requested permission to release the flight crew's personal details, which they all approved, but, with hindsight, that turned out to be a mistake, for soon the press were searching for anyone who knew them and were pressing them for information and photos, for which they would pay.

In the meantime, in London, BA's Press Office had prepared their next press release after carefully considering Captain Hagan's latest comments and, at 1200/1500 local in Nairobi, the second BA report for the press was released. Entitled 'Nairobi flight incident update', it repeated that 'a male passenger attempted to seize the flight controls'. It then added that there was a 'two-minute struggle between the flight crew and the man' and that 'during the struggle the autopilot was disengaged causing the aircraft to make some sudden manoeuvres'.

The 'disengaging of the autopilot' mentioned in the press release was sufficiently loose to leave it open to interpretation as to whether or not the control column had been seized or how the autopilot had been disconnected and this, of course, appeared to be intentional. That may have been for several reasons, the most obvious being the company's desire to tone down the horrific magnitude of the aircraft upset.

By now BA was well aware of the details provided by Captain Hagan, but the contrast between his report from the aircraft and his more detailed reports from the airport office and the hotel, the lack of aircraft damage and only a few minor injuries, may have led some to consider that the later statements may have been somewhat embellished. Whatever the reason, this background of BA departments discussing and forming opinions without any consultation whatsoever with the captain or his co-pilots was a practice that was to continue.

Shortly after the Friday afternoon release of BA's second press report, BA Operations in London sent a fax to the Intercontinental Hotel in Nairobi and on receipt it was pushed under Bill's door. It was short and direct – 'From BA Operations: you will fly back to London as passengers tonight.' The instruction, of course, was to the entire crew, although Kim Parker and her husband had already requested to do that anyway. A short time later a call from the BA local duty manager confirmed their immediate return and, as they could not leave the country without providing a statement to the police, he had arranged for the Kenyan police to take their statements at 1800 local in the conference room on the ground floor of their hotel.

BA clearly wanted to isolate the pilots from the outside world by whisking them back to London as soon as possible, and they had even downgraded passengers booked in First Class to Club World to accommodate them. The group of six, therefore, comprising the three pilots and the captain's family, would travel back to London together in splendid isolation. The shielding of the pilots from probing reporters, at all costs, seemed to have been a company obsession, perhaps because BA's press releases had contrasted with what the flight crew had reported and they feared that one of the pilots might inadvertently reveal a different version to the press.

The BA instruction to return immediately, however, seemed to be extreme, and BA appeared to have had their own interests at heart. Only the evening before, on 28 December, the crew had all struggled through the snow, some more than others, to get to Gatwick, the flight had departed late, only a short period of rest was possible on the flight, the extremely violent upset had occurred about 0500 UTC on the morning of 29 December, after arrival they had procedures to manage at the airport, an extended visit to the hospital and much to do in the hotel liaising with the company during the afternoon. The entire crew was already exhausted. The pilots would now need to consider their statements for the police at 1800 local, snatch some rest afterwards if they could, find some time for a meal and then pack and prepare to take the bus back to the airport. Even in the comfort of First Class they would get little proper sleep and would arrive in London very early on the morning of Saturday, 30 December with two disrupted nights and only about 24 hours after the upset. They would be totally weary and drained, but there they would be expected to face the music of more interviews.

A captain, of course, has a duty to consider the welfare of his crew and Captain Hagan could have refused on their behalf. Several cabin crew, rostered separately and with a different management structure, refused and spent that night in the hotel before returning the next day. Bill was also concerned about his anti-HIV treatment but he had started treatment well within the timescale and could easily have continued the treatment in Kenya for another day or two. Captain Hagan, perhaps under stress and with a desire to return his family home quickly, accepted BA's instruction and the two co-pilots, ex-RAF officers who may have been more used to accepting orders, also acquiesced. The captain, however, with hindsight, was to regret his decision, for he recognised he should have refused BA's order and should have insisted on spending the night in the hotel before returning the next day.

On another call from the local BA office, this time again asking if the flight had experienced any overspeed, to which the reply, once again, was 'no', Bill had the chance to enquire about the checks on the 747, Lima Mike, which were almost complete. He was told that, externally, only a few rivets had popped, which was not unusual even under normal circumstances and was of no consequence, that internally the damage in the cabins had only been small and on the flight deck only minor. The lack of damage reflected the strength of modern aircraft and Boeing's design, and doubtless BA would be relieved to hear that there was nothing more serious. In some quarters in BA and London, however, the report unfortunately seemed to strengthen a growing opinion that the violent manoeuvres had not been as extreme as Captain Hagan had implied.

Later in the afternoon, Bill went to visit the cabin crew, who had gathered in the 'crew room', a larger room where the crew could meet and which was provided by many hotels. All were keen to talk

Captain Bill Hagan at the controls.

Captain Bill Hagan in BA uniform by the plaque of those who have been awarded the BA Safety Medal. The names of the three BA2069 flight crew are etched at the bottom.

Stewardess Kim Parker in BA uniform.

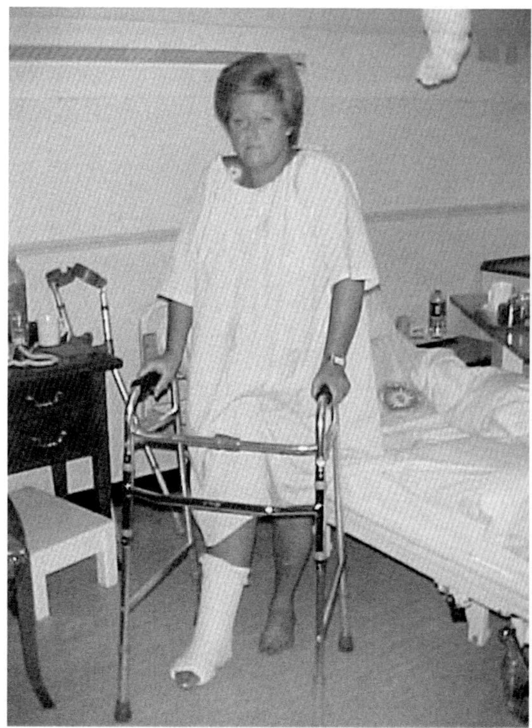

Stewardess Kim Parker in hospital after surgery in January 2001.

BA Boeing 747 G-BNLM, Lima Mike for short.

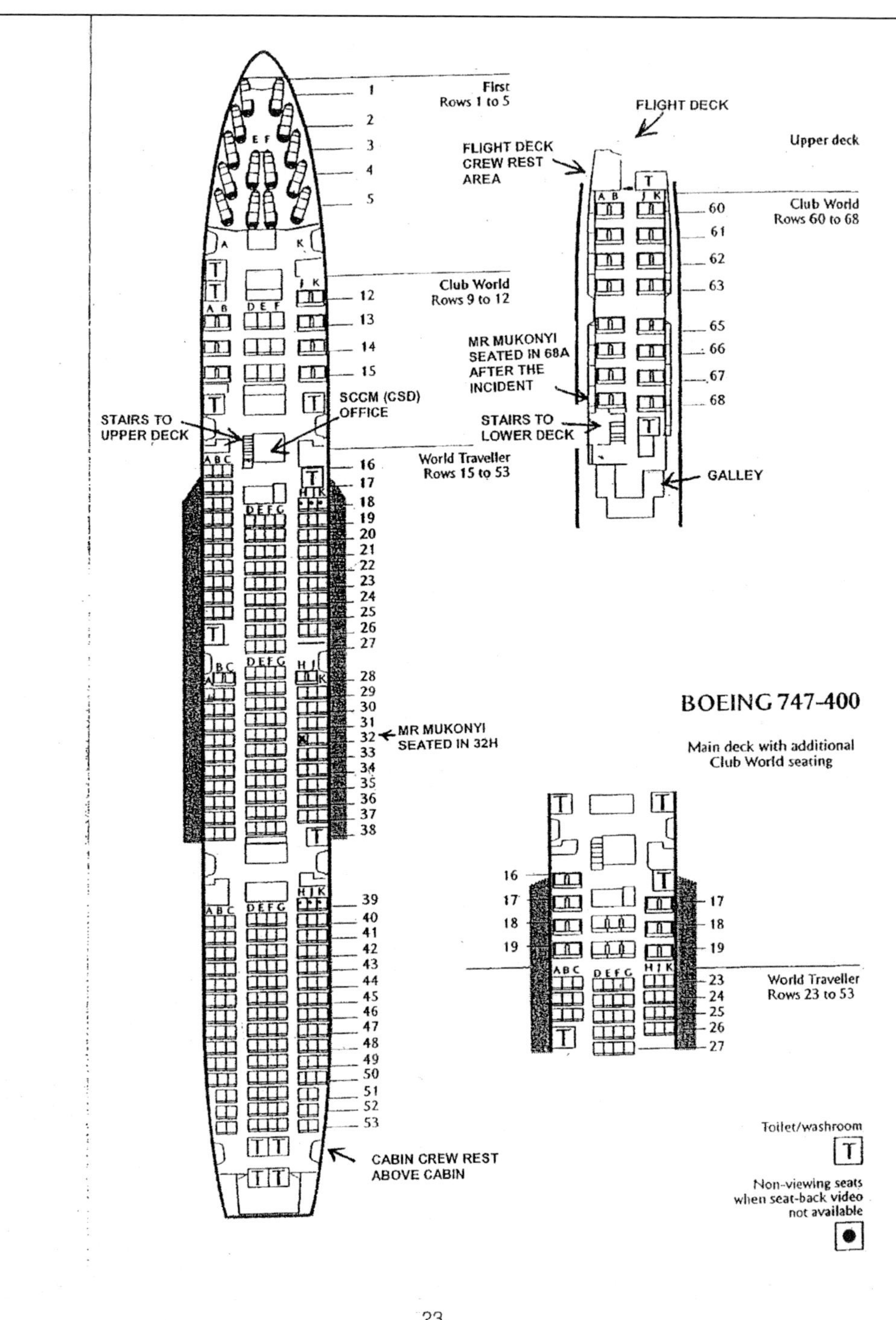

BA Boeing 747-436 layout.

BA2069 during the aircraft upset at the most dramatic point of almost ‘tipping’ over, -35° nose down and 94° left bank.

	ALTITUDE feet	SPEED knots (Stall speed 230)	FLIGHT PHASE	PITCH ANGLE
0	37000	280	Cruise	2
0-0.40	Climb from 37000 to 40255	Reduces to 195	Steep climb A/C becoming fully stalled	Max 27 Nose up
0.40-1.15	Descends to 29500	169min-257max Max descent rate 30,000 feet per minute	Steep dive 94 bank angle Speed increase causes recovery from stall	Max 35 Nose down
1.15-1.25	Levels out into gentle climb	250 +	Feeling of normal flight for 10 seconds	-5 changing to +5
1.25-1.47	Rapid climb to 31500	Decreasing to 170	A/C Stalls once again	Max 30 Nose up
1.47-2.38	Lowest point in stall. 27672	Decreases further to 162 when assailant removed at 2.02 Recovery begins	Recovery from stall is complete at 2.38	

Digital Flight Data Recorder (DFDR) derived data.

A A I B 23/04 '01 15:49 NO.537 01/01

Department of the Environment
Transport & the Regions
Air Accidents Investigation Branch
Bershire Copse Road
Aldershot, Hampshire.
GU11 2HH

FACSIMILE NUMBER: 01293

TO:

ORGANISATION: SRG, CAA

FROM: KEN SMART

DATE: 23 APRIL 2001

NO OF PAGES INCLUDING THIS PAGE - 1

Message:

Mike,

Boeing 747 Incident at Nairobi

When we spoke this morning I promised to let you have a note confirming our reasons for not being involved in the investigation of the above incident.

When the incident was first reported to us by British Airways, we offered assistance to the Kenyan Directorate of Civil Aviation under the provisions of Annex 13 to the Chicago Convention. The Kenyans informed us that they were not able to conduct an investigation as the incident was being treated as a criminal act and was under investigation by the national Police.

In these circumstances the AAIB was unable to appoint an Accredited Representative to participate in the investigation by the State of Occurrence.

Best regards

Ken Smart

Facsimile No: 00 44 1252 (from overseas): 01252 (within UK)

If you do not receive all the pages, please call back.
Telephone No: 00 44 1252 (from overseas): 01252 (within UK)

INTERNET: http://www.open.gov.uk/aaib/aaibhome.htm
E MAIL: aaib-dot@dircon.co.uk

Ken Smart's fax with his reasons for not investigating. This was the only Air Accidents Investigation Branch 'Nairobi Incident' communication that was recovered.

DEPARTMENT FOR TRANSPORT,LOCAL GOVERNMENT AND THE REGIONS

ABBREVIATED VERSION OF CIVIL AVIATION AUTHORITY REVIEW OF THE BRITISH AIRWAYS INVESTIGATION INTO A PASSENGER ENTERING THE FLIGHT DECK OF A BOEING 747-400 AND INTERFERING WITH THE AIRCRAFT CONTROLS ON 29th DECEMBER 2000 EN-ROUTE FROM LONDON GATWICK TO NAIROBI

7th May 2002

Copy of the abridged Civil Aviation Authority Review released from the House of Lords. Note the House of Lords stamp.

DEPARTMENT FOR TRANSPORT,LOCAL GOVERNMENT AND THE REGIONS

ABBREVIATED VERSION OF CIVIL AVIATION AUTHORITY REVIEW OF THE BRITISH AIRWAYS INVESTIGATION INTO A PASSENGER ENTERING THE FLIGHT DECK OF A BOEING 747-400 AND INTERFERING WITH THE AIRCRAFT CONTROLS ON 29th DECEMBER 2000 EN-ROUTE FROM LONDON GATWICK TO NAIROBI

7th May 2002

3.5 Events Immediately after the Incident

3.5.1 The British Airways report states that on regaining control of the aircraft, the flight continued to Nairobi. There appeared to be no structural damage to the aircraft.

3.5.2 The report goes on to state that Captain Hagan suffered injuries to his head, ear and right little finger. Mr Mukonyi received an injury to his right eye and forehead. One cabin crew sustained a broken leg and was hospitalised. One passenger suffered a neck injury whilst three other passengers sustained minor injuries.

3.5.3 The report states that the landing at Nairobi was uneventful and Mr Mukonyi was removed from the aircraft by the Kenyan Police.

3.5.4 The aircraft was inspected at Nairobi for damage prior to return to service, in accordance with the manufacturer's maintenance requirements. No damage was reported and the aircraft was returned to service.

Extract from the BA Report revealed at Cause 3.5.2 in a copy of the abridged Civil Aviation Authority Review – hard copy written evidence.

about their experiences and to shed additional light on Mukonyi's behaviour during the flight. The captain was astonished to hear of the kind of details the young Kenyan had tried to glean from them for what appeared to him be a 'plan of attack'. The cabin crew were, of course, keen to hear the flight crew's side of the story and Bill gave them a brief outline of the fracas on the flight deck. Having talked to Kim at the hospital he passed on the news that she had broken her leg badly and that she was to be stretchered back to London that night. The captain was told, however, that most of the cabin crew would not passenger back immediately and he thought them right to refuse.

After an interesting ten-minute exchange, Bill had to leave to get ready for the meeting with the police but, on the short walk back to his own room, his head was spinning with what he had just heard. Mukonyi's restlessness, his questioning, his timing of the intrusion and his stealthy entrance into the flight deck suggested that his attack had not been spontaneous but had been a premeditated assault.

Chapter 11

Departure from Kenya

At 1800 local on the early evening of Friday, 29 December, the three pilots gathered in the conference room where they were welcomed by the Nairobi Police Commissioner, the Airport Police Commissioner, the BA Kenya Manager and the BA Airport Manager.

Each pilot presented their individual statements outlining the basic details of the incident, including the unanimous opinion of all that the assailant had been trying to crash the aircraft. Regrettably, they were informed that their statements were inadmissible as they could only make statements of facts, not of opinions, and what Bill had prepared earlier in his hotel room had been to no avail. This was not as Captain Hagan had expected, and, at that moment, he had a strong feeling in his gut that this was not going to be the last. In the aftermath of the incident, and by now very tired, the pilots just wanted to be on their way and summoning their strength for a confrontation with the police didn't seem worth it. They could not leave without first having their statements signed and accepted so they did not pursue the matter and, with only a minimal degree of protest, they all reluctantly signed their abbreviated statements which now only recorded the most basic of facts. At the time the matter of the wording seemed unimportant but later the fact that they had signed such scanty reports without a fight became a matter of regret.

The third press release was presented in London only minutes after the pilots had signed their police statements in Nairobi and one can only speculate as to whether this was coordinated or coincidence. The flight crew personal details were provided in the BA release but, in other short statements, all references to the assailant attempting to seize the controls were omitted, never to be mentioned in the public arena again. The Kenyans, in the guise of the Kenya Police, and the British, in the guise of British Airways, seemed to be in accord in downgrading the incident and seemed to concur that Mukonyi had not acted with intent. With similar opinions and purpose, the Kenya Police and BA continued to liaise closely together and appeared to adopt a common stance on the incident.

The BA2069 upset, however, still had to be investigated, and the UK was in a position to get involved, if only in part. International civil air operations are co-ordinated and regulated by the International Civil Aviation Organisation (ICAO), a Montreal-based specialist agency of the United Nations, and the bedrock of ICAO is the Chicago Convention, which is a 131-page tome in four languages. The Chicago Convention consists of almost 100 Articles that define its principles and applications and almost 20 Annexes that set Standards and Recommended Practices with which states are expected to observe. The Annexes have been added to over the years and, of these, Annex 13 is the well-known 'bible' of accident investigation. There are now about 200 hundred states worldwide who are signatories to the Chicago Convention.

ICAO's Tokyo Convention is only eight pages long, is less well known, and regulates the investigation of interference of aircraft and behaviour on board flights. The ICAO website, conveniently, has a potted history of the organisation which explains that in 1944, when the Chicago Convention had been ratified, no one envisaged that acts of hijacking or terrorism against aircraft would be perpetrated and, as a result, there was no Article that defined unlawful interference against international civil aircraft. When the 'take me to Cuba' era began in the late 1950s, ICAO was unprepared and it wasn't until 1963, at a convention in Tokyo, that ICAO finally ratified the Tokyo Convention which 'regulates offences and certain other acts committed on board aircraft on international flights' and which consists of its own 26 Articles that define its own principles and applications in all aspects of aviation security. It then took until 1969 before the Tokyo Convention finally came into force and stood on its own as the 'bible' of investigation of 'unlawful interference of an aircraft'. Annex 17, on security protocol, was later added to the Annexes of the Chicago Convention in 1974.

With reference to safety, the Chicago Convention's Article 26 and Annex 13 regulate investigations of 'serious incidents' and 'accidents'. Article 26, however, relates only to an 'accident' but Annex 13 relates to both 'serious incidents' and 'accidents'. The basic difference between these aviation occurrences is that the former is an 'almost accident' while the latter involves aircraft damage and/or death/serious injury. The ICAO regulations stipulate that these investigations must be conducted by a separate Safety Authority, like the UK's Air Accident Investigation Branch (AAIB), Sudan's Air Accident Investigation Central Directorate (AAICD) or Kenya's Directorate of Aviation (DCA), with the proviso that 'serious incidents' should be investigated but that 'accidents' will be investigated. Such Safety Authorities taking jurisdiction must act independently from their national governments, must conduct the investigation in confidence, must act for the sole purpose of establishing cause to improve safety in order to prevent a reoccurrence and must never apportion blame. What is essential to emphasise, however, is that investigators are not banned from including in their reports acts of error, carelessness or neglect that could be considered blameworthy, for the purpose of a report is to inform other pilots of the details of an incident/accident in order to avoid the event occurring again. Reporting of incidents/accidents is mandatory and failure to do so a criminal offence, but investigations are non-punitive, no names are published and no fingers of blame are pointed.

The initial report submitted by BA to the AAIB had stated that there was no aircraft damage or serious injury so it would have been classed as a 'serious incident' and, in accordance with Annex 13, should be investigated. Annex 13 also sets the order of who would be granted jurisdiction to investigate, and the first in line would be the State of Occurrence, in this case Sudan, with jurisdiction, by agreed rules, being automatically assigned to them. The second in line would be the State of Registration, in this case the UK. If Sudan was going to exercise their right conferred upon them to investigate the 'serious incident' through their Air Accident Investigation Central Directorate (AAICD), they would be required to offer the UK, as the State of Registration, 'the opportunity [for the Air Accident Investigation Branch – AAIB] to appoint a representative to observe and assist and who would be kept informed of the investigation'. As the requirement for a 'serious incident' was only that it 'should be investigated', however, that was only a recommendation and Sudan was not obliged to conduct an investigation and the UK did not have to appoint an observer.

With reference to security, the Tokyo Convention's eight pages and the Chicago Convention's Annex 17 regulate investigations of 'unlawful interference of an aircraft'. In the Tokyo Convention at Chapter 2, entitled 'Jurisdiction', Article 3.1 states that: 'The State of Registration of the aircraft [in this case the UK], is competent to exercise jurisdiction over offences and acts committed on board.' This is somewhat vague for, although it acknowledges that such a state is capable of assuming jurisdiction, 'there is no corresponding duty to exercise jurisdiction' and 'there is no scheme of priority of jurisdiction'. On this matter, however, it does leave an option open in Chapter 5, entitled 'Powers and Duties of States', where at Article 13.4 it states that, 'Any State in whose territory an aircraft lands following the commission of an act [of 'unlawful seizure of an aircraft' – in this case Kenya], shall immediately make a preliminary enquiry into the facts.' Article 13.5 also states that, 'The State which makes the preliminary enquiry shall promptly report its findings.... and shall indicate whether it intends to exercise jurisdiction.' States taking jurisdiction, therefore, are at liberty to criminally investigate such offences in keeping with their own laws and to pursue offenders through their own criminal courts. Unlike the Chicago Convention, the intent of the Tokyo Convention is most certainly to apportion blame and to convict where possible.

In keeping with the Tokyo Convention, the state of Kenya, being the country in which Mukonyi had landed, and the state of the UK, being the country of registration, both had the right to claim jurisdiction to investigate the 'unlawful interference of an aircraft'. As Mukonyi was a Kenyan citizen, Kenya also had the right, in line with their own laws, for their police to conduct a criminal investigation of the offence. UK law also extended to British registered aircraft, no matter where, so they, too, had the right, in keeping with their own laws, to conduct a criminal investigation. If Mukonyi was to face the British court system, however, he would have had to be extradited and it was very doubtful that the Kenyans would have approved. Whichever state did exercise jurisdiction on these grounds, neither the UK's AAIB nor the Kenyan's DCA, in accordance with ICAO regulations, would be allowed to participate.

The ICAO process of allotting claims for jurisdiction had been agreed by signatory states on the premise that, as explained in a UK legal guide to the Chicago and Tokyo Conventions, 'A number of States may be in a position to exercise jurisdiction in respect of a single event and conflicts of jurisdiction may be possible, but what is of far greater consequence is that it ensures that there will be at least one State of competent jurisdiction to conduct an investigation.' If an aircraft 'accident' occurs, Article 26 of the Chicago Convention states that it will be investigated, so one signatory has to take jurisdiction. A single state, therefore, could claim jurisdictions to concurrently investigate both a 'serious incident'/ 'accident' and 'unlawful interference of an aircraft' as long as they were conducted independently and separately. Had BA2069 diverted to Khartoum, for example, Sudan would be both State of Occurrence and State of Landing and could have claimed jurisdiction under both the Chicago Convention and the Tokyo Convention. In the case of a major 'accident' occurring, however, especially if there had been fatalities, many state would likely have an interest in being involved – State of Occurrence, State of Registration, State of Operator, State of Manufacture, State of Design, State of Landing, etc – and many investigations may run concurrently, but, with respect to the confidential nature of the accident investigation, all being conducted for different reasons, different purposes, different intentions, and by different investigators.

In the period immediately after the aircraft upset, Captain Hagan had reported the BA2069 upset to BA by satellite phone from the flight deck early that morning, at about 0510 UTC, and the company's Safety Services had then alerted the UK Air Accident Investigation Branch (AAIB). Soon after that report, the AAIB would have been in contact with ICAO (in Montreal), Sudan (the State of Occurrence), Kenya, (the State of Landing) and the UK, (the State of Registration), including UK organisations such as the Civil Aviation Authority, the UK Government's Department of the Environment, Transport and the Regions (DETR) and, of course, BA. On the morning of the event, therefore, much contact would have been generated between the AAIB and others, but only a few brief exchanges between the UK and Kenya are on record.

At the time of the aircraft upset, Mr Kenneth Smart was the Head of the AAIB and Chief Accident Investigator, with direct responsibility to the Transport Secretary, Lord Macdonald, and he was a highly capable and very experienced investigator. He would have acted on behalf of the AAIB in consulting with the others involved, including ICAO. The UK, as the State of Registration, had the right for the AAIB to appoint a representative to observe and assist with the investigation of the serious incident and Ken Smart had planned to get involved. Soon after the aircraft upset, Mr. Smart then decided that he would get in touch with the equivalent of the AAIB in Kenya, their Directorate of Civil Aviation (DCA), to offer the AAIB's assistance, but this was strange. The BA2069 incident had happened in Sudanese airspace and, under ICAO rules, Sudan, as the State of Occurrence, would have had jurisdiction automatically conferred, without request or choice, to investigate the serious incident under Annex 13. If Ken Smart had been informed that the Sudanese equivalent of the AAIB, their Air Accident Investigation Central Directorate (AAICD), was proceeding with the investigation, he would have offered assistance to them. So, what was going on?

The only explanation was that, by the time Mr Smart had contacted ICAO, Sudan had declined to investigate the serious incident, as was their right, and that the Kenyans had acquired jurisdiction, otherwise he wouldn't have decided to contact them. He would, however, also have been aware that Kenya had no first right to jurisdiction under the Chicago Convention so he must also have assumed that, with Sudan declining to investigate, the Kenyans, in keeping with the rules, had obtained jurisdiction from Sudan by mutual consent to investigate the incident. These misguided assumptions provided the only creditable reason why Mr. Smart had felt compelled, with conviction, to offer assistance to the Kenyan DCA. However, although what he had learned from ICAO was correct in that Sudan had declined and Kenya had taken jurisdiction, the Kenyans had *not,* as he had thought, taken jurisdiction to investigate the serious incident under the Chicago Convention but had taken jurisdiction to criminally investigate the 'unlawful interference of an aircraft' under the Tokyo Convention. Mr. Smart had got it completely mixed up!

Unknown to Ken Smart, and to others, Captain Hagan's report to the El Obeid Tower controller, in spite of his concerns, had been relayed directly to Khartoum, who had then immediately informed Nairobi. Only a few minutes after the aircraft upset, therefore, both had been in early contact with ICAO, but it is likely that neither Sudan nor Kenya would have had any interest in being burdened by investigating an essentially British incident. As Sudan was the State of Occurrence, they were first in line to investigate and, if the event had been an 'accident', they would have had no choice, but otherwise they could have indicated that they did not wish to get involved. As Kenya was the State of Landing in which the aircraft with the culprit on board had landed, they had the right under the provisions of the Tokyo Convention to claim jurisdiction to conduct a criminal investigation by their police. Since Mukonyi was a Kenyan citizen, they also had the right to prosecute him through their own courts and ICAO had granted their claim. The Tokyo Convention and its purpose would have been familiar to accident investigators, and there would have been an awareness that it did not in any way apply to accident investigation, but the Kenyan state's early seizure of jurisdiction under its provision could have been a rare event and that seemed to have sown confusion. Since the Kenyans had known exactly what they were doing it was surprising, however, that it appeared the UK did not. Kenya had no interest in investigating the serious incident and had not requested Sudan to delegate, so, in spite of Sudan withdrawing, the jurisdiction to investigate the serious incident would still remain in limbo with their Air Accident Investigation Central Directorate (AAICD) but they wouldn't act upon it.

Mr Smart, unaware of his misunderstanding, then contacted his counterpart in Kenya's Directorate of Civil Aviation (DCA) to offer assistance with the investigation of the serious incident, so his intention to help was clear. At exactly what time he did call is not known as the AAIB had destroyed all their records, but it was likely to have been very early in the morning, about 0515–20 UTC, when there was a lot of other communication activity. In response, however, the DCA, to Ken Smart's surprise, had said that they could not accept the AAIB's gesture. 'A decision had been taken to treat the incident as a criminal act,' explained the Kenyan director, 'which was to be investigated by their national police so they, themselves, were not able to carry out an investigation.' This information would have immediately alerted Mr Smart to his mistake regarding jurisdictions. That excluded the Kenyan DCA and the UK AAIB from any involvement and it would now be up to the Kenyan police to decide if Mukonyi was to be charged or, if he was innocent, or not able to stand trial, to release him.

Ken Smart now had to reconsider the position of the AAIB for, with Sudan declining, there was no investigation to which he could appoint an observer. As the aircraft upset had been classified as a 'serious incident', the AAIB, of course, was not under any obligation to do anything, but his misplaced offer of assistance to Kenya did indicate Ken Smart's interest in getting involved. The UK, as the 'State of Registration', was second in line to take jurisdiction to investigate the serious incident, but, with Sudan out of the running, the UK was now first in line to claim. The one option that was now readily available to Mr Smart was just to ask ICAO to delegate jurisdiction to the UK. Sudan would have been very happy and ICAO would have been delighted to approve. In the AAIB's 'Guidance to Airline Operators' it states that 'every reported aircraft accident or serious incident, to which the regulations apply, shall be the subject of an AAIB investigation'. Investigating the serious incident under the auspices of Annex 13 and in keeping with UK law would most certainly have applied.

This was the perfect opportunity for the AAIB to get involved in what was essentially a UK incident and they would have produced an excellent report.

As far as Mr Smart was concerned, however, far from this being an opportunity, for him it seemed to have been more of a dilemma, for soon after his call to the Kenyan DCA he made the staggering decision not to investigate the serious incident. The UK, like Sudan, was not obliged to investigate and, as ICAO protocol applied in this case, there was no breach of regulations or of UK law, so Ken Smart was perfectly entitled to decline. This was a startling outcome, however, difficult to believe and an act that could possibly be considered as suspect. The AAIB's own mission statement was 'To improve aviation safety by determining the causes of accidents and serious incidents and making safety recommendations intended to prevent a recurrence.' It would have been thought that he and the AAIB would have been eager to investigate such a significant event and his 'about turn' from his earlier misplaced offer of assistance to Kenya was astonishing. Mr Smart, after all, was Head of the AAIB and he had refused to investigate a very British incident that had occurred in a foreign state. It was also an opportunity lost, so what had changed Ken Smart's mind?

With Kenya now doing their own thing and Sudan not doing anything, Mr Smart's declining to investigate was significant, for the AAIB, at a stroke, had washed their hands of any BA2069 serious incident investigation. This was a very British event involving a British registered aircraft with a British airline and a British crew having had a British serious incident (in reality an accident) occur in the back yard of another sovereign state and no one, not even the AAIB, was prepared to investigate it. This was not the behaviour expected of a country like the UK that was internationally recognised as a leading aviation authority, so what was Ken Smart doing? No reason had been given for his change of mind, but questions would be asked and, in due course, he could be compelled to provide an explanation.

By contrast, the Kenyan state had acted to the letter of the Tokyo Convention and had seemed more interested in treating Mukonyi's unlawful act as an internal affair to be dealt by them exclusively. The Kenyan police in their press release had nailed their flag to the mast without any proper investigation or justification, and, with the enquiry classified as a criminal investigation, it placed responsibility firmly with the police and, by default, with President Moi. It was now clear that the Kenyan state was going to conduct matters in their own way and that they did not wish assistance. Checkmate to the Kenyans on that account!

In only a short period after the BA2069 upset had occurred early in the morning, perhaps no later than 0525 UTC, it now appeared that the lines had been drawn in the sand. With Kenya conducting a criminal investigation and Sudan and the UK abandoning any serious incident investigation, the only remaining organisation with the ability to investigate along similar lines was BA. In the absence of anyone else, the airline then, out of the blue, offered to take on the task, and BA's senior management must have had difficulty in believing their luck when ICAO accepted. This had all been happening about two hours or so before BA2069's landing at Nairobi and about three hours before BA would learn from the Nairobi Hospital that a stewardess had badly broken her leg. Unknown to BA's senior management at that time, they were about to face their own roller coaster! At a very early stage in procedures, therefore, the airline had been left to investigate their own serious incident that had occurred overseas to one of their own aircraft with their own crew. The problem with these scenarios was that the state of Kenya had a vested interest in its own image and the Kenyan police would now internally be criminally investigating a very serious offence involving a Kenyan citizen who was of interest to both the nation and their president, and BA also had a vested interest in its own image and would now internally be investigating a 'serious incident' involving its own aircraft which was of international interest. It was a big ask to expect either investigation to be unbiased or to reveal the whole truth.

In London, in the late afternoon of the 29th, BA was by now providing information on the incident more liberally to the media, who were hungry for news. As quickly as updates were released the details were rapidly reproduced and posted in various accounts on the internet. Once again Mike Street, who had earlier questioned the captain about his PA address, praised the crew involved in flattering terms. 'Our crew are trained to deal with every situation, however rare, and it was this training and their professionalism that ensured a quick resolution of the incident.'

The 'catch all' phrase of 'trained to deal with every situation' was misunderstood and widely misreported for most had taken it to mean that BA flight crews were trained to fight intruders, which was most certainly not the case. The only advice imparted by the airline to flight crews in that respect was to leave any disruptive passenger handling entirely to the cabin crew and, for obvious reasons, never to get physically involved!

By now Captain Hagan had spoken several times with BA and they were able to select and release his quotes gathered from their conversations.

> 'In the struggle the intruder bit my finger and ear, but Richard and I got him out of the cockpit while Phil flew the aircraft.'

> 'With the help of some passengers we managed to restrain the intruder and the incident was brought to a swift conclusion.'

> 'I am very proud of my two first officers and cabin crew and I'm very grateful for the assistance from our passengers.'

Back in the Intercontinental Hotel in Nairobi, as the time now approached for the small group to be picked up at the hotel for the BA2068 return flight to London, Bill went down to the lobby to check out himself and his family. At the BA travel desk in the foyer were Clarke Bynum and Gifford Shaw, and they were organising their onward travel to Uganda. On spotting a very smartly dressed Captain Hagan in suit and tie at the hotel desk, they went over to say hello, and Bill thanked them for their valued help in preventing Mukonyi from launching another attack. If Bill and Richard had not been able to restrain the Kenyan, without their assistance the ending may have been very different.

The crew bus drive from the hotel to Jomo Kenyatta International Airport was in total darkness owing to the lack of road lighting, and once again everyone travelled in silence. In the meantime, Kim and Chris were being picked up by a BA car at the hospital to transport them to the airport. It had not been possible in the time available to plan for a stretcher but, as an alternative, Kim and her husband were to join the others in First Class as in flight the seats could be adjusted flat for her comfort. BA had arranged for Kim to be taken straight to hospital on arrival in the UK and her line manager, Janet Newton, would meet her at Gatwick. At Jomo Kenyata Airport the flight crew bus was met by the BA manager and, to avoid unnecessary encounters, they were escorted without delay to the VIP lounge. At the last moment before departure, they were accompanied to the side of the aircraft and, on boarding, were joined by Kimberley, nursing her damaged ankle and shattered leg, and her husband Chris. Such was BA's determination to keep them all as isolated as possible that the operating cabin crew had been instructed not to let anyone in to First Class under any circumstances.

Chapter 12

Arrival in the UK

As BA2068 climbed out of Jomo Kenyatta Airport just after midnight Kenya time, CNN published an online article, presumably precipitated by the Nairobi Incident, entitled 'Airlines vary in cockpit door safety policy'. It noted that 'outside of the USA (where airlines must adhere to the Federal Aviation Administration (FAA) policy of a locked cockpit door at all times), other airlines, including Air France, Aeromexico, KLM, South African Airways and TAP Portugal, had locked door policies but BA had not.' The article mentioned that on BA flights passengers are sometimes invited to visit the flight deck at the discretion of the captain and that it was 'BA policy that the doors were only locked for take-off and landing.' This statement was incorrect as the doors were only required to be closed for take-off and landing and it transpired that someone in the BA Press office was the source of the error. The inference of the CNN article, however, was that, irrespective of whether the flight deck doors were required to be only closed or locked during take-off and landing, some other airlines did require them to be locked at all times and, had that been the case on BA2069, the incident may not have occurred. In BA, at that time, it was not a requirement to close cockpit doors in flight, although they usually were, but if closed they were to be left unlocked as a locked door was considered to be detrimental to crew communications in the event of an emergency. BA policy then did not require them to be locked at any time and this was also the policy of many other airlines for the same reasons.

During the flight, all in the small group in First Class struggled to get some rest but it was difficult to sleep, and that wasn't helped by the fact that they were flying back on Lima Mike on its way home to Gatwick, the same 747 on which they had experienced the upset. Like the others, Phil was also having a restless journey and, on noticing in the early hours of the morning that Bill was also awake, he went over and pointed to the time on his watch. It was exactly 0453 – precisely twenty-four hours after their violent aircraft upset! An hour later they were back on UK soil.

On disembarking at about 0600 in the early morning of Saturday, 30 December at Gatwick's North Terminal, they found that BA had obtained authority for them all, including the captain's family, to bypass customs and immigration, and immediately Bill, Phil and Richard were taken aside and ushered directly into a debriefing room. Ian Seymour was there, the flight crew manager from Gatwick who had been so helpful in getting the captain's family on board the flight to Nairobi, also Steve Wright, a flight crew manager from Heathrow, and two people from the BA Press Office.

Kim and Chris, on exiting at Door 2 Left, were met on the airbridge by Janet, Kim's line manager, who escorted the couple to a waiting ambulance. While Kim and husband were taken to Redhill Hospital in Surrey, Janet followed in her own car and, on arrival, they went together to A&E reception. Kim was informed, however, that it was pointless her being admitted there as her complicated right leg fracture would require surgery and physiotherapy with a stay in hospital of about six days, so she would better off going straight to her local hospital. Janet arranged for a BA car to pick them up and then, after Kim had taken some strong painkillers, the three set off for Hillingdon.

Back at Gatwick Airport, by the time the debriefing began the pilots had had little or no sleep for two nights, 28 and 29 December, and now on the early morning of the third day, 30 December, they all struggled to answer questions about what had occurred during the event. This was the first face-to-face encounter with the BA Press Office for the pilots but over the next two years, especially for the captain, who was naturally the centre of interest for the media, BA's press office and legal department were to control many aspects of their lives. They began by discussing a few suitable quotes for the press that BA would later release as the captain's comments, especially remarks that he wished to make in praise of his crew and Phil's flying, and Phil and Richard also gave their perceptions of the incident. They then had to face the assembled press on their way to their transport, with Bill being the target, but, too tired to think of the correct thing to say, he said what he thought appropriate.

'I'm awfully tired because I have been unable to sleep,' the captain explained to the extended microphones as they ran the gauntlet. 'I've tried to sleep but the events have been.... quite difficult.'

'What can you tell us about what happened?' asked a voice that seemed to come from nowhere in the throng.

'I did what I had to do. I removed the assailant from the controls and Phil Watson, my first officer, did what he had to do. He controlled and recovered the aircraft and he did it very well.'

Unprepared his remarks may have been, but they concisely summarised the parts played in the incident, and they also pleased the press officers for, as far as they were concerned, he had given nothing away. What he had imparted, however, was that Mukonyi had actually been handling the controls, a fact that BA had been, and would continue to be, reluctant to admit. Fortunately, that seemed to pass unnoticed, and BA later released suitable parts of their debriefing. They then clambered into the transport to be driven away and most were soon asleep.

About the same time the group were snatching sleep on their journey to Heathrow, Kim and the others had arrived at Hillingdon

Hospital's A&E reception and Kim was admitted for a medical examination. Astonishingly, Janet had told reception that during Kim's presence in hospital she had to be registered in an assumed name but, not surprisingly, the receptionist was unhappy with that. After further explanation and Janet's insistence she was registered with a pseudonym. This was not normal practice for a BA line manager and it appeared to have come from a senior level. Kim, of course, would be of interest to other parties in more ways than one for she was BA staff, she had endured the upset and had primary experience of the event, she was the only one on board to have received a serious injury, for which she would most certainly be seeking compensation, she had suffered a broken bone which was not only a serious medical injury but was also classified by ICAO as 'serious injury', and one that would elevate the serious incident to the status of an accident. Although Kim would not have known at the time, any inadvertent leak could have resulted in serious damage to BA's attempts to play down the incident and could have provided information to prospective litigants. It also appeared to confirm that BA had been aware of Kim's broken leg from the outset, from the afternoon of the day of the upset when her injury had been confirmed by X-ray, for Janet Newton had been informed before the group departed Nairobi that the stewardess's right leg had suffered a complicated fracture and that Kim would be off work for some time. BA's Safety Services office was responsible for keeping the AAIB informed and it was now their legal duty to submit the update of Kimberley's broken leg to the AAIB. Although there was still no evidence they had done so, they were obliged to report it as soon as possible, and, when they did, the situation would change dramatically.

Kim had arrived at Hillingdon Hospital carrying her medical report and X-rays from the Nairobi Hospital and was examined by a Mr Bodey, a consultant orthopaedic surgeon. As the X-rays she had been given in Nairobi were poor quality her back and leg were X-rayed again. These new X-rays clearly confirmed a complicated spiral fracture of her right leg and a wedge compression of a vertebra in the 12th thoracic region. The vertebra would heal itself with time but the leg required some delicate surgery. Owing to the time between the injury and Mr Bodey's examination, however, the leg had become too swollen for surgery so Kim was to be sent home with strong pain killers to be re-admitted when it had improved. By now the trauma of the event was catching up with her and her husband, and Kim began to feel anxious and emotional. The nursing staff were also concerned about Chris's condition so they were both very relieved when they were discharged and the BA car could take them home. Subsequently, Kim was medically certified to be unfit for work, initially for ten months, so it would be a long time before she was fit and well again.

After a journey round the M25, the group of pilots and family were woken by the driver announcing they had arrived at their first stop, the BA medical centre at Heathrow. There the pilots received a thorough examination. Bill, in spite of it being reconfirmed that the risk of HIV infection was low, decided to continue with his antiretroviral course and to accept the unpleasant, but inevitable, side effects which would follow. His bitten fingertip was recovering well and the wound on his ear was less severe than thought as it appeared it may have been caused by switches on the overhead panel rather than a bite. Medical checks over, the co-pilots returned home while Bill and his family were driven to the Edwardian Hotel near Heathrow to rest overnight before flying home the next morning.

Back in the Intercontinental Hotel in Nairobi early that Saturday morning, the two tall American passengers, Clarke Bynum and Gifford Shaw, who had had helped restrain Mukonyi, watched the local news in their hotel room. With some trepidation they saw photos of themselves appear in the clothes they were still wearing accompanied by a reporter saying that they had removed the intruder from the controls as well as the flight deck and they were now resting in the Intercontinental. On disembarking the two men had spoken to reporters at the airport and were being portrayed as 'stars' of the show, but that was the last thing they wanted. From listening to Mukonyi's murmurings they had considered him to be a terrorist who may have had accomplices onboard who had not interfered at the time. Any fellow terrorists could be in Nairobi, however, with the two as targets, and not only could they now identify the Americans but they would know where to find them. It didn't help that they had noticed an armed guard patrolling the corridor outside their room overnight, but they were not to know that the extra hotel security had not been just for them. Fearing for their safety, they now decided not to continue to Entebbe, and they called BA asking that they be removed from the hotel as soon as possible and returned to the States. Without delay a car was despatched and they were driven straight to the airport, where they would spend the day in the BA lounge waiting to be flown back over the Saturday night to arrive in Gatwick early Sunday morning.

By now BA was well aware of Captain Hagan's account of the aircraft upset but the company was still playing down the incident and sticking to their own story. It was not surprising, then, that senior management would attempt to protect the company's image and BA's press releases and reports had all been carefully crafted, but they needed to be managed with care.

The airline's press releases were brief and vague so they could not be considered in any way untruthful but, by omission, it could be suggested they were not telling the whole truth.

The image BA presented obviously suited the company and, although there could be no accusation of collusion, it was also convenient that BA and the Kenyan police, perhaps not surprisingly and for similar reasons, were singing from the same hymn sheet and thereby backing up each other.

Also, in London that Saturday morning, the Department of the Environment, Transport and the Regions (DETR) was now expecting to receive from their Threats Office a completed risk assessment of the event. The DETR was, at that time, a multi-functioned part of the government that administered all three divisions, with 'Transport' being responsible for security and safety over all the key transport sectors, both nationally and internationally, of land, sea and air. Within the DETR there were also many other offices, groups, units, sections and subdivisions, of which one was the Transport Security Directorate (TRANSEC) headed by Ian Devlin. Their aim was to protect the public and retain security. There was also a Threats Office, a separate unit within TRANSEC, whose task was to gather information, collate incidents and accidents affecting UK transport and to evaluate threats by producing risk assessments. A further section within the DETR was the Multilateral Division (MLD) whose role, amongst other matters, was to ensure that transport in general was safe and to oversee the compliance of safety standards. A separate unit within the MLD was the Multilateral Division Aviation Group (MLD A/G), whose head was Michael Smethers. With TRANSEC responsible for security and the MLD Aviation Group responsible for safety, both had an interest in the BA2069 upset and both would have their own input on the incident.

The International Civil Aviation Organisation (ICAO), in addition to setting standards and procedures, also produces an Aviation Security Manual and obliges individual states to produce their own specific security manual based on the ICAO model and appoint a committee to supervise its content. In keeping with ICAO, in 1982 the UK authorities published their own restricted manual entitled the National Aviation Security Programme (NASP) that was aimed at safeguarding UK civil aviation operations against acts of unlawful interference. To oversee the manual and keep it continually updated, they also formed a National Aviation Security Committee (NASC) that consisted of various groups, including the Civil Aviation Authority (CAA), police authorities, airlines, airport authorities, and some trade unions. The NASC was also part of the government's antiterrorism initiative and met every six months, as well as on demand, to review procedures and threats.

The risk assessment's author, known only by the initials DM, had been very busy since early the previous morning when it had fallen upon him to produce an assessment of the upset. Throughout Friday he had spent a hectic day making numerous detailed enquiries and contacting as many people as necessary to collect what information he could. Having been informed by BA that the flight had been out of control for only about 20 seconds, he had contacted Security Manager Gaynor MacLaughlin, who had been called in immediately after the crisis centre had been activated, and she was able to provide some details of the fracas on the flight deck. He also approached the BA Duty Operations Security Manager who had been called into the incident centre after Captain Hagan's satellite phone call and he reported that the attacker had been unarmed, that he had 'disengaged some controls' during the struggle and he repeated that 'the aircraft was reportedly out of control for some twenty seconds'. Unfortunately, this misguided detail had been accepted as fact by DM in the Threats Office, the DETR and BA Security Services. Mr M had also heard from the British High Commission in Nairobi that the Kenyan police had established that Mukonyi had no political or criminal affiliations but that in their opinion he was mentally deranged and possibly a paranoid schizophrenic. Other opinions, however, offered by UK police sources at Heathrow and Gatwick, and by Davis Lewis of the Air Accidents Investigation Branch (AAIB), did indicate that they considered a hijack or suicide attempt to be possible motives. BA, of course, discounted these proposals as they considered it a case of air rage by a deranged passenger, and the Kenyan police, having already expressed their opinion on the assailant's mental state, did also not consider 'hijack' or 'attempted suicide' as motives. After discussing all the available information with his team, it was surmised that 'because no demands were apparent and, as the passenger had been forcibly constrained, this appeared to be no more than an "air-rage" incident'. On the Saturday morning, DM made his final touches to the 'risk assessment' then discussed with his Threats Office staff the official line to take with the press.

In the process of preparing the Threat Office's risk assessment, it was also understandable that any author would not have had full knowledge of the facts or full understanding of the circumstances, and would have been obliged to collate information from others, but it did appear that Mr M was just gleaning details from lots of other departments and sources who also did not have full knowledge or full understanding of the substance of the upset and was blindly accepting what BA had told him. Compiling a very influential document without first bothering to engage the assistance of someone who did understand, or who did know the facts, is more than a bit surprising. Someone, like, for example, Captain Hagan, who was a primary witness of the incident and who could have made a hugely valuable contribution to any report. The captain, like all BA staff, was not permitted by company regulations to disclose information to the press without permission, but that did not prevent him from talking to a Threats Office official who was researching and compiling an important document for his government department. If the Air Accident Investigation Branch

(AAIB) was to investigate the aircraft upset as a serious incident/ accident they would have questioned the flight crew at length, and there appeared to be no reason why Mr M, as part of his risk assessment research, could not have asked the captain to give his account of the event or, at the very least, to have just talked to him about it.

Chapter 13

The Final Days of 2000

Later in Saturday, as Captain Hagan rested, the Threats Office risk assessment composed by DM was submitted to the Department of the Environment, Transport and Regions (DETR). The document was dated 30 December 2000 and was entitled 'AIR RAGE INCIDENT/ATTEMPTED SEIZURE?' It stated that it had sourced its information from BBC Ceefax, the Air Accident investigation Branch (AAIB), various news broadcasts and from the internet, but mostly from BA. All available information had been collated, except details from the Digital Flight Data Recorder (DFDR), which was still being processed, and a decision had been made as to the nature of the incident. As there had appeared to be no substantial contact with the controls and therefore no apparent breach of the National Aviation Security Programme (NASP) protocols, the risk assessment summary concluded that, 'Unless directed otherwise, this incident will be recorded under the 'Miscellaneous' category until the next meeting of the National Aviation Security Committee (NASC).' The next scheduled meeting of the NASC, however, was not until May 2001!

It could be understood that there was some urgency to produce a risk assessment but to do so without first obtaining details from the 747's Flight Data Recorder seriously risked submitting a risk assessment that was seriously inadequate, and that was exactly what had happened in this case. If a risk assessment had to be submitted it should have been as an interim assessment to be updated after the flight details from the FDR had been obtained but, instead, this inaccurate document, even with some later amendments, became accepted as the defining account of the aircraft upset.

In the Saturday afternoon at the Edwardian Hotel, Bill awoke from his nap and immediately went down to the lobby to buy as many morning papers as had remained unsold. He was soon to find out that although the headlines reflected the high drama of the aircraft upset, the vital details that he had provided BA had all been withheld.

The front page headlines of some UK broadsheets were:

'Battle for life at 35000 feet' – *The Daily Telegraph.*

'A nasty man tried to kill us all' – *The Times.*

'Two minutes fight for BA2069' – *The Guardian.*

'Pilot in life-or-death battle with jumbo jet intruder' – *The Glasgow Herald.*

Although the horror of the violent intrusion was evident in the headlines, the articles mostly contained references to 'a 10,000 feet dive or plunge' that had lasted two minutes, but that timing was excessive. Such a drop would have been equivalent to a rate of 5,000 feet per minute, and any airline pilot could have told them that was a target rate for an emergency descent in the event of a sudden decompression. Although steep, therefore, it was not excessive. The entire duration of the incident had been only two to three minutes, including two climbs and two stalls, so the 10,000 feet drop could only have lasted about 30 seconds. That was, however, equivalent to a horrifying descent rate of at least 20,000 feet per minute and the dive had, in fact, been an extremely rapid, stomach-churning plunge.

The UK newspapers, devoid of the significant facts of the event, had tried to enlarge on BA's vague press releases, but the unfortunate result was a wide circulation of an inadequate account that gained credence in government circles. By comparison, some international newspapers seemed to have been able to glean a more realistic view of the event. *The Herald Tribune* international edition reported 'terror after cockpit attack' and 'violent, violent dive'. The *Windsor Star* included that 'He grabbed the controls sending the plane on a wild ride of dips and dives' and The Kenyan *Daily Nation*, with the headline 'Kenyan storms jet cockpit', stated that, 'He had rushed into the cockpit, grabbed the controls and was pushing the Boeing 747-400 into a series of nosedives as he struggled with the co-pilot for the control of the plane.' Another Kenyan daily had also referred to Mukonyi's behaviour and had asked 'how he could have done such a thing and how could this young Kenyan have brought so much shame upon the nation?' That would not have pleased President Moi.

On Saturday evening, the UK TV channels aired the 747 aircraft upset as the leading news item, as did international news broadcasts from Sky, CNN and Fox. It may not have been surprising that the newspapers' headlines had been dramatic while their published copy was much less so, but what was said on the evening BBC News by BA's Michael Blunt, their Head of Corporate Communications, was more than a little surprising. On being interviewed he stated in response to questions that,

'At no time was the aircraft out of control.'

'It is BA policy to lock cockpit doors during take-off and landing.'

That first statement, having been issued before any flight recorder data had become available, appeared to be based on no more than wishful thinking, perhaps on the basis that only minor damage to the 747 had been reported. At that time, apart from the details provided by Captain Hagan, BA had no knowledge whatsoever of the extreme loss of control that had actually occurred. The second statement simply repeated the earlier error made by the press office. These assertions, however, inaccurate as they might have been, generated a lot of very valid questions which demanded answers. Why was someone who appeared to be disturbed allowed to board the flight? What was BA's policy on cockpit doors? Why was that policy not more robust? What had actually happened on the flight deck? Did the intruder succeed in grabbing the controls, or did he only attempt to do so? What had been the aircraft's actual flight path and how close had it been to seconds from crashing?

In the UK, inconsistencies in reports of the aircraft upset in newspaper articles, media broadcasts, BA press releases and other company statements remained unexplained owing, in general, to a lack of aerodynamic knowledge about the stalling of an aircraft. The public tend to relate this to a vehicle engine stalling but, in aerodynamic terms, it has nothing to do with engines and has all to do with airspeed and lift from the wings. When an aircraft speed drops excessively low, lift from the wings is lost, flight cannot be sustained and a full aerodynamic stall occurs with the aircraft plummeting vertically from the sky.

All aviators, piloting no matter how small or big an aircraft, are familiar with the shaking of the airframe that occurs when approaching a stall. Big aircraft, like the 747 with all its safety devices, are not expected to stall but, on an extremely rare occasion like this incident, airline pilots are well aware of the recovery procedure. The one big difference between small and large aircraft, however, is the degree of turbulence close to the stall, from the light shaking of a little plane to the horrendous cacophony of noise and the violent jarring and jolting of a giant airliner. Any airline pilot in the world experiencing these unmistakeable characteristics would instantly recognise this as a big jet in the process of stalling.

The very steep dive of the 747, however, having been relayed to London from the outset, had by now become the dominant topic. In spite of the fact that the violent, frightening shuddering and shaking of the airframe during the aircraft upset had been widely disseminated, it was just not understood by laypeople that these distinct characteristics had clearly indicated the stalling of the aircraft, not only once but twice, and that these stalls, not the dive, were the devastating features of the upset. As the two antagonists had wrestled on the flight deck for control, the rearward tugging of the yoke had resulted in the first stall and, as the nose dropped sharply, the 747 had plunged at a huge rate. Further tugging aided stall recovery by pulling the aircraft out of the dive but, as the big jet climbed, continued pulling had resulted in the speed dropping again and the 747 entering a second stall. Owing to a lack of aerodynamic knowledge amongst those disseminating the information, however, this vital link between the stalls and the plunging dive was never recognised and, as a result, these details were left unreported. The main risk to the 747, therefore, was structural break up in the air if the aircraft upset overstressed the aircraft, not impact with the ground as some had suggested, and this was another example of the facts being distorted owing to lack of aerodynamic knowledge.

If, at the time, BA had acknowledged Captain Hagan's account, had made more of an effort to fully understand the upset, to properly recognise the risks and to appreciate the seriousness of the incident, the statements they released may have proved to be less misleading. The passengers on the fateful BA2069 flight were fully aware of what had happened and, as most on the flight had submitted their testimonies, these provided BA with valuable information. Their passengers, however, also wanted further details for, apart from what had been stated about the dive, BA had said nothing about what had happened during the rest of the time of the aircraft upset.

The decision was then taken to release the passengers' accounts and, with primary evidence now being made available to all, including the press, interested parties were better able to appreciate the passengers' experiences and the circumstances of the event.

What everyone was also now waiting for was release of the detail on the Flight Data Recorder (FDR), but there was a problem. Shortly after the arrival of the pilots at Gatwick early on Saturday morning on Lima Mike, the 747 involved in the upset, BA had attempted to gain access to the aircraft's FDR but, on first play, the tape was found to be distorted at the extremes of the operating envelope. The company then sought help from the Air Accident Investigation Branch (AAIB) to extract meaningful data but, with it being a weekend and Monday being the New Year Bank Holiday, it was going to be a while before the detail could be made available.

In the meantime, the perception of the incident as one of air rage predominated, as did BA's argument that the flight had only been out of control for 10 or 20 seconds. As a consequence, opinions of government departments became crystallised along the lines of misguided assumptions and it would take time for these to assuage.

Early on Sunday morning, 31 December 2000, Clarke Bynum and Gifford Shaw landed at Gatwick Airport in transit to the United States and later, in the Edwardian Hotel, the Hagan family awoke refreshed after a good night's rest. Bill read the *Sunday Times* with interest for it was ending the year with a reasonably accurate account of the aircraft plunging down in its dive. Inexplicably, an internal BA statement attributed to Phil, the co-pilot, had appeared to have been leaked to the newspaper and it had reported what Phil had stated.

> This huge guy suddenly appeared on the flight deck. He was at least six foot and he seemed to be wearing at least six layers of clothing. He seemed so bulky. He had this determined look

> in his eyes. He leaned right over me and grabbed the yoke (the control column) and rolled it to put the aircraft down to kill us all. I hit him and tried to put him in an armlock and yelled for help. He was all over the place, leaning across the instrument panel and between me and the windscreen so I couldn't see anything outside. It was difficult to get the aircraft properly under control from what had been some quite violent manoeuvres but that is what our training is all about.

It was never established how the *Sunday Times* had managed to obtain what was known to be Phil's description of events.

Later that Sunday morning, 31 December, the captain and his family were picked up from their hotel by a BA car and taken to the VIP lounge at Heathrow, where they were held till the last moment before boarding. In Glasgow, like royalty, they were met at the side of the aircraft by a private car and driven straight home where, fortunately, there were no journalists waiting.

As the Hagan family had been flying up from London and settling back in their own home, other events of interest were happening elsewhere. At the small Nairobi Hospital on Sunday afternoon Kenya time, Mukonyi had recovered from his heavy sedation and the opportunity had been taken to review his physical and mental condition. Two doctors, Dr Dan Gikonyo and Dr Frank Njenga, had been appointed to conduct medical and psychiatric examinations and, on completion of their preliminary assessment, they called a press conference for the next day, Monday, 1 January 2001, with the announcement that they would then report their diagnosis.

On the far side of the Atlantic on New Year's Eve UK time, but afternoon North Carolina local time, Clarke Bynum and Gifford Shaw landed at Charlotte Douglas Airport. Their local Sunday papers had covered the incident with an American bias and reported that 'it was an American who saved a British Airways jumbo jet... from disaster...Despite being sure he was about to die, he leaped from his business class seat and rushed into the cockpit to find a tall Kenyan man trying to crash the plane and the pilots trying in vain to stop him.' Needless to say, their return was eagerly awaited and on disembarking they were met with flashing cameras and a crush of reporters. Over the next few days, they appeared on many TV shows as heroes, in their home city of Sumter, South Carolina, a day of prayer for missions was proclaimed in their honour and Clarke Bynum was awarded the Order of Palmetto, the highest civilian honour in the state. The two men preferred to acknowledge that their actions were the answer to the prayers of many, rather than their heroism. 'We consider ourselves ordinary men whom God did extraordinary things through. We thought our mission trip was to Uganda, but God has given us another mission to thousands here in the States.' The local press, however, continued to bestow an American slant on the story by portraying their timely assistance as having completely saved the aircraft from disaster, but Clarke Bynum graciously emailed Bill to say that was not of their doing. Had Richard and the captain been unable to restrain Mukonyi without their help, however, the American version of events could have turned out to be true.

On the Sunday, New Year's Eve, at midnight local time, wherever in the world any of these fellow travellers on the BA2069 flight fateful might have been, they would all have had similar thoughts. To welcome the New Year, of course, but more especially just to celebrate that they were there, that by skill, determination and good fortune they had faced death and survived, and that they were still alive.

END OF PART 1

PART 2

THE COVER-UP

When BA was asked about this, they denied the suggestion made to them that there had been a cover up.

Chapter 14

The Psychiatrists' Press Conference

Much had happened over the last few days with positions being taken and opinions being formed. In the UK, the relevant units within the Department of the Environment, Transport and Regions (DETR) and the Civil Aviation Authority (CAA), having now assumed the incident to be nothing more sinister than air rage, were quite happy to quietly monitor the BA investigation of the event. By the holiday Monday, with the previous evening's New Year celebrations over, world interest in the upset was waning and there was reduced press coverage in the UK. For the crew and passengers on board BA2069, however, the ordeal was still very much uppermost in everyone's mind.

In Nairobi, the Kenyan police had by now taken over the handling of the affair and had met the BA investigators the previous day. Then they had confirmed their similar opinions that had been expressed earlier when they had downgraded the incident and had agreed that Mukonyi had not acted with intent. Now on New Year's Day, Monday, 1 January, the psychiatrists who had examined Mukonyi, Dr Gikonyo and Dr Njenga, held their press conference at the Nairobi Hospital accompanied by Isaac Litani, the hospital's acting chief executive. Their medical opinion embraced that of the police and BA, and the doctors publicly announced that Mukonyi was indeed suffering from acute paranoia. They were now in the process of investigating how long Mr. Mukonyi had suffered the condition but Dr Njenga believed that he may have been affected by the illness for over a month. They also stated that all, including the

Kenyan police and BA, concurred that he had not been attempting to crash the aircraft.

'We are of the very firm belief from his story,' Dr Njenga added, 'that at no point did our patient contemplate the hijacking or doing harm to anyone.'

'When everyone was settling down on the flight he felt completely crowded,' the doctor continued, 'and he said that people in front and behind were threatening him. He ran towards the front of the airplane believing people were in hot pursuit of him. All he remembers is that somebody hit him on the back and put a finger in his eye. When he came to, he was frightened. To him, he was the one who was in danger.

'Since November,' the doctor further explained, 'Mukonyi had believed he was being followed and spied upon by a group of people, mostly of North African Arab origin, in the university campus in Lyon where he had been studying tourism since September 1999. His illness could have been brought on by the stress of exams. He kept a diary of his fears and on at least three occasions he had reported his concerns to the French police. They had said that with no proof he was being followed they were unable to help. As his fears increased, he felt it was imperative to escape to Kenya.

'In the weeks and days preceding this incident,' Dr Njenga concluded, 'there were many opportunities when an alert security person could have said there is something wrong with this person and not let him board.'

Dr Gikonyo added to his colleague's last comment by saying that 'people who had suffered physical illnesses like malaria, high fever and uncontrollable diabetes, although not the case with Mukonyi, were particularly vulnerable to paranoia so the condition was not uncommon and was easily recognisable'. Finally, both psychiatrists agreed that if in his current state any charges were to be brought, he was not fit to stand trial.

Mukonyi's story, as recounted by the doctors, bore no resemblance whatsoever to the facts as understood by the flight crew but the clinicians' conclusions had been as expected and it was easy to pick holes in their statements. Their claim that 'Mukonyi had not been attempting to crash the aircraft' came as no surprise, but the fact that it had been concluded from questioning him was difficult to reconcile with their comment that 'all he had remembered was being hit on the back and poked in the eye'. If that's all he recalled, how did he remember he hadn't been attempting to crash the aircraft? The doctors' opening statement that Mukonyi had been suffering from acute paranoia could have explained their claim that 'He ran towards the front of the airplane believing people were in hot pursuit of him', but that could easily be challenged for it simply wasn't true. The young Kenyan was a giant of a man and had he been running forwards in a still cabin he would not only have been noticed by the few passengers who were awake but he would also have woken those in deep sleep. His movement forward had gone unnoticed because, as witnessed, he had been so stealthy. Also, it is a well-documented fact that the condition of acute paranoia can lead to violence – 'Sometimes it happens that an individual suffering from intense paranoia and genuinely believing themselves to be under threat of physical harm will decide to strike first to eliminate what they see as the threat and this may result in violence. Research has indicated that people who experience paranoia, hallucinations, or delusions are more likely to become violent than people with mental illness who do not have these symptoms.'

The medical evidence, therefore, did seem to indicate that Mukonyi, if a victim of acute paranoia, could have been driven to violence by his intense condition, which would have exonerated him from intent. The psychiatrists would have been well aware of this possibility, but it appeared by their statement that they were in agreement with the opposite: 'We are of the very firm belief from his story that at no point did our patient contemplate the hijacking or doing harm to anyone.' Instead of explaining that Mukonyi's violent behaviour had occurred as a result of his serious illness, however, they completely denied everything by issuing a totally contrary statement that 'all had concurred that he had not been attempting to crash the aircraft'. That had implied that he had not been driven by his illness to do anything and seemed to contradict their claim of acute paranoia. Mukonyi had certainly been of unsound mind, but his condition of paranoia may not have been anywhere near as acute as the doctors had intimated. In fact, on no occasion during the period of his illness leading up to the BA2069 incident had Mukonyi been violent owing to his paranoia, for on the previous occasions he had felt trapped and threatened by his persecutors he had always found a way to avoid confrontation. But on the flight deck he had attacked violently, and if he had not been driven by acute paranoia then the only other option was that he had been driven by intent.

It was not difficult to accept that on Mukonyi's journey from Lyon to the time of the attack he had been displaying signs of some kind of paranoia, but the pilots had no doubt from Mukonyi's violent behaviour, from evidence that was circumstantial, factual and of primary source, that his intrusion had been premeditated, that he had planned a window of opportunity, that he had waited for the right moment, that he had, perhaps, got lucky seeing Richard depart thinking, as others had done, that he was the captain, and that it was then that he had taken his chance to enter the cockpit, seize control and crash the aircraft. All of this had been indicative of intent and, although Mukonyi's mental state would have been unsound, with his mind more lucid than had been admitted he could then have acted as any individual would have done had they been bent on suicide and had been as determined as he had to accomplish their aim. In these circumstances, therefore, it could be considered that he was responsible for his violent actions.

Some of the doctors' comments were also uncomfortable for BA for the company was walking on a tightrope. The clinicians' explanation of acute paranoia for his behaviour, and the admission that Mukonyi had felt threatened and had run from those in hot pursuit, although inaccurate, had weakened BA's claim of 'air rage'. The doctor's remark that his 'condition was not uncommon and was easily recognisable' also did not help BA's explanation as to how he had been allowed to board, but not all of that, of course, had been down to BA. It did seem, however, in what appeared to be a recurring feature of this event, that although the clinicians may have been telling some of the truth, they were not telling the whole truth. Otherwise, what they had said was possibly what they had been told to say by the police, and it was no surprise that they had found Mukonyi not fit to stand trial on any account.

In the UK, Captain Hagan and his colleagues were less than impressed with the news from Kenya and were concerned that there appeared to be a concerted effort by the police, the psychiatrists and BA to play down the severity and significance of the incident, claiming that the upset had been short, that Mukonyi had not acted with intent, that he was not trying to crash the aircraft and that the event had been one of 'air rage'. The flight crew were more than dismayed by the manner in which the version of the event they had told was being ignored and that, without consultation, an inadequate account of the upset was being perpetrated in spite of the amount of available evidence to the contrary. The statements only seemed to suit the purposes of those telling the story and the group seemed to be ganging up against them.

It was not surprising, however, that others were peddling their own version of events, for the Kenyan police, having conducted little or no investigation, would have been saying and doing what they were told to say and do by those at the top. The clinicians, also in regard to Mukonyi's behaviour, would have been saying and doing what they were told to say and do by the police and BA would have been saying and doing what they had to say and do to soften the blow on BA's reputation and to protect the company as best they could against a possible multimillion-pound claim for damages. Some might say that in these circumstances not telling the whole truth was not unreasonable, but that could only be up to a point. There was also the issue, however, of BA's intransigence and their focus on 'air rage', for suspicions were already being raised that BA was deliberately trying to cover up the intensity of the incident.

The Kenyan daily paper *The Nation* reported that over the New Year the team of BA investigators, having completed their investigations in Nairobi, had left for France where it was expected they would follow up on Mukonyi's source of paranoia. The BA team went to Lyon Airport via London to speak to the police who had been on duty at the airport on the day of Mukonyi's departure and they were able to confirm that he had reported his concerns to the Lyon police on three occasions. They also spoke to local airline staff and, in town, to the university authorities, and references were made to his recent beliefs that he was being followed and threatened. Otherwise, nothing of significance was unearthed concerning the Kenyan's behaviour and mental state but what they did learn was that there appeared to have been no diagnosis recorded of any pre-existing mental condition.

Back in the UK, attention was beginning to focus on what had actually occurred to the aircraft during the incident. The Digital Flight Data Recorder (DFDR), a sophisticated quick-access recorder, had only just been returned to BA as they had requested assistance from the Air Accidents Investigation Board (AAIB) to decode it. It was three days since the aircraft had arrived back in the UK and the DFDR data had now been retrieved so the company was naturally very eager to see the details of what the analysis produced, as was the British Airline Pilots Association (BALPA).

Chapter 15

The Digital Flight Data Recorder

On modern aircraft there are two so-called 'black boxes,' both of which are, in fact, bright orange to aid recovery in the event of a crash. The Flight Data Recorder (FDR) records up to 25 hours of data on a continuous loop and the Cockpit Voice Recorder (CVR) records for two hours in a similar manner, both providing information analysis following an accident.

Modern aircraft also incorporate a separate recorder designated the Digital Flight Data Recorder (DFDR). It records a significant amount of detail from numerous aircraft sources that is easily retrievable whenever required and BA had spent many years pioneering the development of this very useful alternative source of information. In the late 1960s British European Airways (BEA), later to merge with the British Overseas Airways Corporation (BOAC) in 1974 to form British Airways, commenced the world's first automatic landing programme on the Trident aircraft. When the system was enhanced to operate automatic landings in very low visibility, referred to as Category 2, and later, for landings in even lower visibility, to Category 3, the CAA required BEA to record the data as part of that procedure. In the pre-digital age this was achieved by use of an easily accessible cassette recorder that provided information similar to the FDR 'orange box' but tailored to record specific data during the approach and landing phases.

This process prompted BA eventually to develop and to more fully extend the use of flight digital data that could be downloaded electronically from an aircraft into a monitoring programme called the Special Event Search and Master Analysis (SESMA). SESMA soon became an effective tool in managing the safety culture of complete airline fleets worldwide by identifying trends outside the standard in day-to-day operations. This allowed action to be taken to prevent these identifiable non-standard operating procedures from developing into an incident. When the Nairobi aircraft upset occurred, SESMA was a mature, in-house system that helped make BA a world leader in air safety, but it would be a further six years before the International Civil Aviation Organisation (ICAO) required airlines worldwide to set up similar data monitoring programmes on all commercial flights.

The SESMA recordings were of particular use for analysis of individual incidents and two months prior to the BA2069 event an enhancement was introduced in the form of a computer simulation. A monitor displayed a basic flight instrument panel at the base with, in its centre, a computer-generated image (CGI) of a small aircraft that flew in sympathy with the instrument indications. The upgraded Digital Flight Data Recorder (DFDR) with the visual enhancement of the Flight Data Simulation (FDS) could now display an accurate visual image of exactly what had happened during the almost three minutes of the upset and the DFDR detail was expected to reveal the prolonged extent of the stalls. An explanation would, thereby, be provided as to why the passengers had reported the aircraft shuddering and shaking over such lengthy periods.

On 2 January 2001 the viewing of the Flight Data Simulation (FDS) and the release of the Digital Flight Data Recorder (DFDR) information took place inside the Flight Safety Office on the ground floor of the Compass Centre on the north side of Heathrow Airport. Ian Hibberd, who as the chairman of the BALPA security committee had a seat on the National Aviation Security Committee (NASC), joined the members of the technical team who had been working on the project for several days and also a number of flight managers who had been able to attend. All present would have been totally familiar with the defining parameters to be observed to prevent 'Loss of Control' (LOC) – max nose pitch up of 20 degrees, max nose pitch down of 10 degrees, max bank angle of 45 degrees and, within these parameters, an inappropriate airspeed – so would have been aware of the yardstick by which to measure the severity of the incident. If such conditions are exceeded it may not be possible to sustain safe flight and all pilots are aware that an approach to these boundaries demands prompt, preventative action to contain the aircraft within limits. An event where these parameters are unintentionally exceeded is defined as an 'upset', or 'aircraft upset', and in these circumstances the flight could be in great danger. The aircraft must then be flown immediately to within these parameters.

As the group viewed the simulation there was initially silence as the computer-generated aircraft image soared upwards and, with the airspeed dropping off rapidly, entered the first full stall. It then rolled to the right and all noticed the pitch up limit of 20 degrees being exceeded when the nose-up pitch reached 25 degrees. When the nose eventually dropped, the aircraft began rolling sharply to the left and the roll rate increased rapidly as the bank angle approached the 45 degrees. Ian waited breathlessly to see if this limit would also be exceeded but he did not have long to wait for the bank angle swiftly more than doubled to 94 degrees. Gasps were now heard as the nose-down pitch parameter of 10 degrees was violated excessively with the nose dropping down to 35 degrees and the group watched in astonishment as the reality of the aircraft upset dawned on them. All then noticed with relief that the aircraft gradually returned to normal flight, the wings levelled, the nose-down angle reduced in a series of pitch ups and the airspeed became more normal as the cruising attitude was approached. Ian was then about to say how unbelievable the simulation had been but, to his disbelief, he realised that the aircraft upset was not yet over. Once again, the nose reared up, this time to 32 degrees, settled back then pitched up again several times with the airspeed dropping further at each jolt. Everyone now watched with shock as the aircraft quickly entered a second full stall. Alarming as the simulation was, however, it could not reproduce any of the buffeting and violent shaking that had so puzzled and frightened the passengers and it was a stunned group of viewers that now fully understood what a horrendous experience it had been for them.

Almost immediately after viewing the simulation, Ian called Captain Hagan in Glasgow expressing surprise and concern about what he had witnessed and stated that the incident was clearly much more serious than he had been led to believe. He said that he now found it extremely unlikely that this was a case of air rage and added that he believed Mukonyi should have been intercepted and refused permission to travel long before he reached BA2069. He told the captain about Mukonyi's behaviour on the flight from Lyon and it was then that Bill learned for the first time about the Kenyan's previous extremely suspicious conduct.

It was also explained by Ian that the Digital Flight Data Recording (DFDR) had taken longer than expected to decipher because data had been corrupted during the period when some input data had been outside recording parameters. The DFDR had been calibrated to record descent rates up to 20,000 feet per minute (fpm) but, as the descent had exceeded 30,000 fpm, the data had been distorted at the extreme points and the replay by BA had failed to produce valid results. As BA had been at pains to downgrade the incident, it was somewhat ironic that the upset had been so serious it was now found to be outside the ability of the DFDR to properly record it! A new method of optical decoding of the recording had been used by the AAIB, however, and that proved to be successful, so BA was able to receive the complete data.

Ian, with the viewing of the DFDR and its simulation now foremost in his mind, also firmly expressed his view that the aircraft had been unbelievably close to disaster. The captain was not in the slightest bit surprised to hear this, of course, for he knew that already. Since arriving back in the UK, however, it seemed the perception of the seriousness of the incident had been diluted, and there were even suggestions circulating that the press, who were then not always highly regarded in aviation for their accurate reporting of aircraft incidents, had been guilty of exaggeration. By contrast, it could now be clearly seen that the incident was actually worse than portrayed by the press. It was the captain's assumption, therefore, that in the light of the truth being out, although only partly, and with a fresh analysis of the upset now being available, events would move forward and governmental departments would revise their options. He couldn't have been more incorrect.

The total altitude plummet in 2 minutes 38 seconds, comprising two climbs and two descents, was 19,083 feet. The upset had previously been compared to a giant roller coaster and the highest roller coaster in the world is at the Six Flags Great Adventure Park in Jackson, New Jersey, USA. The ride has a drop of 456 feet with a maximum vertical speed rate of 12,600 feet per minute and the inadequacy of the comparison with the BA2069 incident is obvious.

	Loss of control (LOC) parameters	Maximum angles experienced during upset
Bank Angle	45°	94°
Nose up	20°	32°
Nose down	10°	35°
Stall		Occurred twice lasting about 1 minute each time

Seven 'loss of control' events can be identified throughout and it can be seen by all criteria that the aircraft was significantly out of control for most of the 2 minutes 38 seconds of the aircraft upset. The group who had viewed the simulation in the Flight Safety Office at Heathrow knew that perfectly well.

The British High Commission in Nairobi appeared to be very much better informed of the seriousness of the incident at this early stage of the proceedings than any of the aviation bodies in the UK. The High Commissioner was on vacation and so it was his deputy who, on the morning of 2 January, the day of the first showing of the Flight Data Simulation, transmitted an unregistered telegram for restricted circulation to certain recipients, including the Department of the Environment, Transport and Regions (DETR).

In the telegram the High Commission had disclosed that a male passenger had filmed the incident and had been offered a substantial sum for his footage by Sky News but had instead handed it to BA. A staff member had then told them in confidence that the film 'had been mislaid' while in BA hands. 'Mislaid', euphemism or not, was the exact word used, but the film had been lost without trace and had never been found. It was in the interest of both BA and the Kenyan Police, for their own reasons, to play down the incident so neither would have been concerned by its loss.

The telegram also stated that the Deputy High Commissioner had been in close contact with a member of the UK team who was working to retrieve data from the Digital Flight Data Recorder (DFDR) and in paragraph 6 of the telegram he had further divulged that, 'weekend press reports have made much of the incident and it could have been disastrous. Privately BA technicians admit that the plane lost significant altitude and was only seconds away from flipping (on its back). That it did not was due to the actions of the pilot. A very close call which should prompt a review of cockpit security procedures.'

A copy of the telegram showed that the unknown person in the DETR who had received it had scribbled in the margin, 'Para 6 is clearly worrying. Are there any plans to re-visit cockpit security procedures?' The telegram and its details, however, were never forwarded to the Transport Security Directorate (TRANSEC), to Mr DM at their Threats Office or to Mr Smethers at the Multilateral Division Aviation Group and they were left unaware of this vital information. As a result, those who would have found these contrary details to be of importance could only accept as fact what BA had passed to TRANSEC.

On the same day Captain Mike Jeffery, the BA Director of Flight Operations, wrote a personal letter thanking the captain for his 'decisive action in a very significant event which had prevented what could have been a catastrophe'. It appeared he had earlier studied the flight data simulation on 2 January and it was rewarding for Bill to receive such a sincere letter the next day from the head of Flight Operations.

By now, 3 January 2001, most of the crew, the two co-pilots, Phil and Richard, and cabin crew members, had reported fit for duty, while two remained off sick, Kim, the stewardess with the broken leg, and Bill, who had been painstakingly following his anti-retroviral course. As he was undergoing treatment his flying licence had automatically been revoked and he would now have to wait until the course was competed before resuming flying duties. In the afternoon Captain Hagan then received a call from BA Safety Services saying they had opened a BASI-4 (BA Standing Instruction No. 4) incident investigation. Most big organisations have standing instructions relating to codes of conduct and in BA 'Standing Instruction No. 4' addressed their safety and security policy. Safety Services would like to meet the flight crew to discuss the incident as soon as possible so the captain arranged to fly down the next morning and to join the meeting later that day.

Chapter 16

BA's Investigation Begins

On the morning of 4 January Captain Hagan received another welcome letter, this time from Bill's immediate boss, Captain John Leahy, Chief Pilot Boeing 747-400 fleet. Both the responses from Captains Jeffrey and Leahy made Captain Hagan feel a lot better about himself and about how the incident was now being understood, at least by Flight Operations.

After reading the letter he left to fly to London and arrived with plenty of time for his appointment at BA's Compass Centre, the building where air crews checked in and which housed flight-related offices such as flight operations, rostering and flight management. With time to spare he first visited the Flight Safety Office on the ground floor where he met Captain Roger Whitefield, Head of Safety, and Roger invited him to view the Flight Data Simulation (FDS) which visually displayed the BA2069 upset flight path. This was the first time Bill had had a chance to observe the video with the new format and, as he followed the image of the model tracing the flight path, a deep chill ran through his body. He was taken aback when, on seeing how close they had been to the edge, he felt like he was reliving it and, for a brief moment, he was quite shaken by the experience. Roger asked if he would like a copy of the flight simulation on disc 'to show his grandchildren' and he gladly accepted. The co-pilots were not to be given a copy but later Captain Hagan made sure Phil received a copy from his own. Bill and Roger then moved to a first-floor office where they joined the co-pilots, Phil and Richard, and Ian Hibberd, the British Airline

Pilots Association (BALPA) representative. Captain Whitefield then explained to the group that the purpose of the BASI-4 investigation was to establish the facts and causes, not to apportion blame or liability but to implement changes to prevent a repeat occurrence. These terms and conditions, although relative to BA's internal investigation, were also in keeping with the International Civil Aviation Organisation's (ICAO) Annexe 13 of the Chicago Convention which applied internationally to investigations by independent safety authorities like the UK's Air Accident Investigation Branch (AAIB). BA's investigation, therefore, would be conducted in compliance with international standards. A final BA report would also contain other aspects of the BA2069 event, but the substantial content would be the Safety Services BASI-4 investigation, so the BA report and the BASI-4 investigation report would mostly be the same document.

The three flight crew were quizzed in depth about the pre-departure circumstances of the flight, commencing with the conversation that took place on the flight deck when Laura reported to Bill whilst Mukonyi was still outside the aircraft accompanied by the police and the aircraft dispatcher. They were then asked about communications from the cabin crew thereafter right up to the occurrence of the incident, specifically if there had been any further reports to the flight deck and whether they had been informed about details of the cabin crew rest periods. It was confirmed that there had been no further reference to Mukonyi and that Laura had called before Bill had commenced his bunk rest to inform him that she was commencing her rest period and who would be taking charge in her absence.

Other questions relevant to who did what and at what time in the hours preceding the incident were answered and then each of them was given the opportunity to relate in their own time what had occurred during the two to three minutes of the attack. Phil described the difficulties he had trying to fight off the intruder yet had managed to apply sufficient input to the controls to recover safe flight in spite of Mukonyi's attempts to 'put it on its back'. Richard told of his immediate and difficult return to the flight deck and this prompted the question of how Richard and Bill had both managed to get back there in spite of the aircraft's violent manoeuvres. Richard had been compelled from the beginning to battle his way through the most extreme of upsets, yet astonishingly had overcome the difficulties and had fought his way back. He then referred to the struggle with Mukonyi, saying that he was a heavy, tough guy and that, after they had him under control, he was so big one of the major problems they had was getting him out of the flight deck. Richard felt it was a pretty scary experience and that they were all keen to put it behind them now.

The captain was not able to recall exactly when he exited from the bunk area into the forward flight deck, but felt he had done the right thing waiting in the bunk for the best moment. Just after the most extreme bank angle had been reached, Phil's herculean effort to reduce the bank had allowed him to enter the forward flight deck without too much difficulty. This was consistent with his memories of being in the bunk whilst the aircraft stalled, first to one side, then the other, and was entirely consistent with Phil's recollection of him first becoming aware of his presence behind him as he levelled the wings. Bill also mentioned that having assumed there were two capable pilots strapped in on the flight deck he had been uncertain of what benefit he could have been in the extreme turbulence. If he had been tossed about, he could even have been a hindrance.

Bill then recounted his entry into the fracas when he quickly struggled to remove Mukonyi from the controls with blows to his head but, at that point, Roger stopped him, saying that details of his attack would not be included in the report. All Captain Whitefield needed to know was that he had successfully removed Mukonyi from the controls but the manner in which that had been achieved would not go on record. Roger then explained that by omitting the details BA were trying to protect him and the company but, when Bill naively asked from whom he was being protected, to his astonishment Roger informed him that it could be Mukonyi. If a record of his belligerent efforts to remove the attacker were leaked, Mukonyi might conceivably be able to sue him for assault and BA might face legal action. Roger also reminded them that the details of the rescue on the flight deck were irrelevant to the purpose of the air safety inquiry, which was all about learning from the incident in order to prevent a similar attack in the future.

Captain Hagan then recounted Mukonyi's talk of 'others', in an apparent claim that he had accomplices on board, and the captain had immediately implemented a locked door policy using Richard as the go-between with the cabin crew. Bill's further comment that this had somewhat restricted communications between the flight deck and the cabin crew was viewed with particular interest. He also raised another issue about the upper deck Club World cabin seat in row 60, just outside the flight deck, which had been used by pilots for flight crew rest on longer flights. Upper deck seats were known to be popular with passengers and, during the previous year, BA's commercial department had insisted on the crew rest seat being moved to near the galley on the main deck Club World, in spite of opposition from pilots who considered this a safety issue. Captain Hagan was now at pains to point out that one important aspect of their survival was that he had been resting in the bunk within the flight deck area and that, even with ear plugs in, he had been able to respond. He stressed that he had no doubt whatsoever that, had he been in the flight crew rest seat on the main deck, the outcome would have been totally different and later he wrote a letter to the company to inform them of his opinion.

Overall, the flight crew gained the impression that BA wanted little more than answers to their prepared questions and that these mostly concerned the information the captain had received about Mukonyi when he boarded the aircraft and during the flight. The pilots felt that there was still much to be discussed about the upset and its aftermath but as these matters were, presumably, outside the remit of the BASI-4 enquiry, there was no more questioning and the meeting ended abruptly. Captain Whitefield thanked the three for their help and stressed that as BA Safety Services had targeted a completion date within two months, their investigation should be concluded quickly. Before the group broke up, Roger also told Bill that it was normal procedure for the operating captain to attend the preliminary meeting of an incident review and that he should expect to be invited.

By now the update of Stewardess Kim Parker's broken leg should have been passed by BA's Safety Services Department to the Air Accident Investigation Branch (AAIB) as it was a legal requirement for BA to inform of any changes to their first report as soon as possible. Unfortunately, that had still not happened. Some BA managers would certainly have been aware of the broken leg as the Nairobi Hospital had informed them and a cabin crew manager had arranged to meet Kim at Gatwick to take her straight to hospital. Others, like the BA2069 crew, would also have known of her serious injury, but almost everyone outside this relatively small group of people would not have heard of the broken leg. Almost anyone who did know, apart from a few specialists, would have thought of it as an unfortunate injury but would not have been aware of its importance. At that time, therefore, it was still possible, in spite of the fact that Safety Services were now involved in compiling BA's report, that they had not been informed and didn't yet know of the broken leg. The insistence on registering Kim at hospital under a false name had seemed to be very strange, and that instruction was likely to have come from senior management. BA's overriding fear, however, seemed to be crew members inadvertently releasing details of the aircraft upset to reporters, so that may just have been to protect Kim from the press in the same way the flight crew had been protected by flying them back to Gatwick in isolation.

Or was something more sinister going on? Could it be alleged that BA were contriving to take advantage of the mix up with injuries? The aircraft upset had been classified in error as a 'serious incident' instead of an 'accident', both Sudan and the UK had declined to investigate the serious incident, as was their right in these circumstances, and BA was now investigating their own incident. If, at this point, Safety Services were to be informed of the broken leg, they would have had a legal duty to report it to the AAIB and that would have changed everything. The AAIB would then have been obliged to upgrade the classification of 'serious incident' to 'accident', someone would have been compelled to investigate the accident and would have had to produce and publish a report. A damaging report in the hands of passengers intent on litigation could end up with BA having to pay out millions of pounds in settlement of compensation claims. If BA did the same as Mr Smart, and that was allegedly to just do nothing, that would cement the status quo and, if they allegedly carefully covered up the broken leg by just ignoring it, they could very likely get away with it. That would be some coup if it worked, but it would be taking a huge risk!

Elsewhere a degree of uncertainty about the incident also began to grow within government departments in regard to how matters were progressing at BA. On the same day as the BASI-4 investigation meeting, 4 January, the Department of the Environment, Transport and Regions (DETR) replied to the chairman of the British Airline Pilots Association (BALPA) Security Committee to say that their offer of assistance had been passed to the Safety

Regulation Group (SRG) of the Civil Aviation Authority (CAA) 'should a review of cockpit security, in addition to the safety review, be launched'. The SRG, the DETR explained, would wait for the BA investigation report to become available 'before considering whether the incident has more general lessons requiring a review'. On a copy of that reply, a handwritten note stated that, 'The incident on 29 December has given rise to suggestion that a review of cockpit security be launched.....you will want to keep an eye on this one.' These comments seemed to indicate a suspicion that there was more to the incident than mere 'air rage', but any possible security review would have to be kept on hold until the BA report was competed.

When Captain Hagan arrived home that evening a large official looking, A4 sized, brown envelope awaited him and on opening it with interest he found that it contained a note from the DETR and a copy of Mr M's risk assessment. What was crystal clear, however, was that this was the DETR's way of notifying Bill that the Department had classified the incident as 'air rage'.

The enclosure consisted of two parts, the first of which was a single sheet entitled:

> 'AIR RAGE INCIDENT INVOLVING BRITISH AIRWAYS BOEING 747-400 FLIGHT NO BA2069'.

The second part was the four-page risk assessment with a subtly different title:

> 'AIR RAGE INCIDENT/ATTEMPTED SEIZURE? OF BRITISH AIRAYS BOEING 747-400 FLIGHT NO BA 2069 – 29 DECEMBER 2000'.

The risk assessment document listed the names of several other recipients and presumably they received the first part as well.

On the same day, 4 January, the weekly publication of 'BA News', the company's in-house newspaper, featured an article on the front page with the headline 'Calm crew praised after mid-air drama'. It acknowledged that certain departments, presumably including Flight Operations, had commented on the extreme aircraft manoeuvres during the incident. A photograph also showed one of the members of the flight data team holding a Boeing 747 model in the most extreme attitude with the comment that the group had been working on the playback over the last few days. The article continued that the flight and cabin crew of BA2069 had been praised for their quick thinking and professionalism. Mike Street, Director of Customer Service and Operations, was the first to express his gratitude to the crew for tackling the man when he entered the flight deck. The article stated that Mukonyi 'had lunged across the control panel disengaging the autopilot' and that Phil had been 'unable to properly take control of the aircraft', but it stopped short of singling him out for praise or recognising that he had saved the day. His huge individual efforts remained unreported. It was also acknowledged, however, that once all the factors had been reviewed the company would examine any opportunities for improving safety and security and would make changes if appropriate. The article was entirely consistent with the theory of 'air rage' linked to an accidental disconnect of the autopilot as the cause of the significant flight disturbance.

Chapter 17

Differences of Opinion

Within the Flight Operations department, however, the emphasis was singularly different. Bill's immediate managers, who as fellow captains were all very familiar with aircraft operations, had all viewed the Flight Data Simulation (FDS). They were aware of all the circumstances of the incident and had commended both Phil and Bill for their actions for they knew that the aircraft had almost been lost.

The head of the Department of Environment, Transport and Regions (DETR) at the time was John Prescott, with the title of Secretary of State for Environment, Transport and Regions. He was also deputy leader of the Blair Government and the post had been specially created for him.

The Transport Security Directorate (TRANSEC) of the DETR reported directly to the Minister of State for Transport, Lord MacDonald of Tradeston, who acted as deputy to the Secretary of State on transport issues. A copy of the risk assessment was, therefore, first sent for analysis to TRANSEC, then to John Prescott's Department and, in turn, to Lord MacDonald's desk in Transport before, on 4 January, being distributed to restricted groups.

TRANSEC had initially taken a very keen interest in what had appeared to be a security incident but that had rapidly dissipated on receipt of the risk assessment. No violation of security protocols had been indicated, the upset had been downgraded to 'air rage' and, as such, the event was now considered to be a safety matter rather than one of security. The DETR then made the decision to allocate all issues involving the incident to the unit responsible for aviation safety, the Multilateral Division (MLD) Aviation Group (AG).

All of this had, of course, been as a consequence of the risk assessment, but the problem was that the assessment had been produced in London by Mr DM on 30 December, only a day after the early morning incident on the 29th, and only with the details that he had been able to glean at the time. Since then, however, rumours had been emerging from those in the know, particularly about the leaked information from the Nairobi telegram which by now had spread, and from the results of the video of the Flight Data Simulation (FMS), that the situation was much worse than revealed. All these factors caused something of a stir which generated a considerable number of discussions of the incident, some of them a bit heated, and a greatly increased circulation of internal documents.

On 5 January, the International Civil Aviation Organisation (ICAO) in Montreal contacted the UK's ICAO delegation representative there mentioning that they had faxed the Kenyan Government and had declared that they expected Mukonyi to be brought to justice for involvement in 'unlawful interference of an aircraft'. It had also disclosed that they had requested an update on the proceedings from the Kenyans and had asked them to forward a report on both the circumstances of the offence and on the result of the legal proceedings. The UK ICAO representative was also asked to brief the UK authorities in London and to forward a request that they submit their own report.

On 6 January, Kimberley Parker was admitted to Hillingdon Hospital for surgery to have the serious spiral fracture to her right leg repaired with screws and a plate. She remained in hospital until her leg had healed sufficiently for her to return home and she was discharged six days later. During her stay in hospital, it became apparent that she was suffering from Post Traumatic

Stress Disorder (PTSD) and on examination her condition was medically verified.

Amid discussions of the incident, an article in the highly respected weekly aviation magazine, *Flight International*, published on 9 January 2001, reported that they had been able to obtain some flight data recorder detail, although not all of it was completely accurate. The next day's edition of *The Daily Telegraph* on 10 January repeated the same information under the heading of 'Black box shows how pilots averted disaster.' A realistic illustration displayed only the first half of the flight profile from the simulation as it had terminated with Phil's recovery from the first stall but also included was a quote from BA admitting that he 'displayed quite a feat of flying skill' by safely recovering from the correctly quoted bank angle of 94 degrees. This was qualified by the comment that all flight crew practiced recovery from extreme attitudes in the simulator. Uniquely, the newspaper article acknowledged that the aircraft had stalled and, furthermore, accurately quoted the loss of 10,000 feet in 30 seconds in the dive.

Further documentation showed that, on the day this article was written, others were beginning to feel the need to reopen security issues by bringing the Transport Security Directorate (TRANSEC) back into the discussions. The Minister of State responsible for Transport, Lord Macdonald, now expressed concern by stating that he was seeking 'an urgent review of aviation security following the Nairobi Incident'. It appeared that the 'urgent review' had been influenced by both the press reports and the flight data simulation to which he would have been privy. The Multilateral Division/Aviation Group (MLD/AG), it seemed, had a different opinion, for a further document originating from them discussed 'putting a note to Lord M'.

Also, on 10 January, the ICAO UK representative in Montreal sent a fax requesting a report from the MLD/AG about the incident but, in response, the MLD/AG stated that they were still considering the position. On 11 January, the MLD/Aviation Group (AG) dispatched the 'note to Lord M' discarding the existence of any significant aviation security element and stating that: 'The incident is being treated primarily as an operational safety issue rather than a security matter.' The Aviation Group had been resolutely stuck on the concern being safety, not security, and, as far as they were concerned, it was them who were going to be in charge. TRANSEC, however, was not to be dismissed, for it stated they would be contacted at some time in the future to see if they have any other input. The note then concluded by saying that 'the SRG (the CAA Safety Regulation Group) are close to finalising their initial review….and the target output I foresee is a note from SRG setting out the result of their review, including proposed action.' To this end, the heads of TRANSEC, the MLD/Aviation Group and the CAA Safety Regulation Group (SRG) made arrangements to meet the following week.

On 15 January, the UK was now in a position to reply to ICAO and the agreed response was phoned through to the UK representative in Montreal. 'We are not treating this as an Annex 17 (safeguarding protocols) security issue and it is unlikely that there will be any report of the incident.'

In Kenya, the Attorney General and Director of Public Prosecutions (DPP), a Mr Amos Wako, was the person who would make the final decision whether or not to prosecute Mukonyi, but he had gone on holiday and proceedings had to wait. He had returned on the same date as the UK response to ICAO had been sent, but there was now a further delay while he examined the documents and completed his review before announcing his verdict.

All of this activity had been going on without the knowledge of the BA2069 pilots and, apart from their short interview with BA

Safety Services, astonishingly no one thought to ask any of them what had actually happened on the flight deck. The pilots had been convinced from the beginning that the incident had been a suicide attempt and it now seemed obvious that, with the worldwide publicity of their aircraft upset, this could happen again. Within Europe alone there was likely to be a sizeable group of acute paranoid schizophrenics from which only one with suicidal tendencies was needed to improve on Mukonyi's attempt and achieve notoriety. There were also other groups at large that would have observed the incident with interest and it seemed inevitable that another flight deck intrusion might be attempted, and maybe sooner rather than later, but no one imaged how right these thoughts would be.

The BA2069 flight crew still felt that, during their interview with Captain Whitefield at the Compass Centre for BA's Safety Services investigation, they should have been allowed, for the record, to explain in full their side of the story. The investigation had concentrated on how the incident had occurred and how it could be prevented from happening again, but a careful examination of the process of the aircraft upset could also have been useful to another crew if it ever did reoccur.

The pilots, not surprisingly, were less than happy with the lack of any discussion about the event, for there was much of the BA2069 aircraft upset that could have been analysed had the AAIB conducted a professional and independent investigation. The flight crew members were never properly questioned by anyone about their actions and Mukonyi's behaviour was never fully examined. BA had classed this as 'air rage', but this was some 'air rage'. No 'air rage' attacker, no matter how angry, was going to place his or her life at great risk in this manner just because he or she was more than a little annoyed about something, and it was never considered at any time what could possibly have upset the Kenyan so much that he would have retaliated with such an explosive response. This, in fact, did not have the appearance of 'air rage', but, as the circumstantial, factual and video evidence had demonstrated, it seemed more like a premeditated and determined suicidal act by a very disturbed man. Following his demons he had, in a final desperate attempt to escape his tormentors, ferociously fought to crash the aircraft in order to take his own life and the lives of those pursuing him. Anyone viewing the Flight Data Simulation (FDS) with its images of wild control demands and erratic flight trajectory would have concluded the same.

Another example was the possible use of rudder during the upset as that should have been analysed. In the air, the rudder on a big jet is only applied by the pilot on rare occasions such as when an engine fails and a manual rudder input is required to maintain balanced flight. In the scenario of the aircraft upset, however, it should not be applied and, if a wing drops on a big jet in a stall, it should be lifted by aileron, not rudder. The rudder on a big jet is a very large control surface and rapid or large deflections could overstress the tail fin with catastrophic results. During the aircraft upset, however, the co-pilot's feet were free so he could have moved the rudder. Boeing responded by conducting their own research and revealed that in these circumstances judicious use of the rudder would have helped Phil better control the aircraft. This is the kind of information that should have been disseminated just in case such an event occurred again for, in spite of the locking of cockpit doors being required for some time in the United States and elsewhere, attempted unlawful entries to the flight deck still continued.

Potential hijackers always try to find a weak spot and the obvious one is that sometimes the locked flight deck door needs to be unlocked and opened in flight. If an intruder launched an attack when the door was opened with one pilot taking a break, someone the size of Mukonyi could have disabled the departing pilot in the doorway and could have pushed through the open door to the flight deck. There may then be a repeat of the same, and lessons learned from the Nairobi Incident might just have proved useful. These issues, amongst others, could have been fully deliberated by a professional AAIB investigation and the lack of any proper analysis was a loss to aviation safety.

Chapter 18

Mukonyi's Fate Decided

At Heathrow Airport in BA's Waterside headquarters, CEO Rod Eddington had taken a different stance after the incident to the proposal that cockpit doors should be locked in flight at all times. His attitude reflected the then current policy in BA, in other UK airlines and in many other international airlines, that the doors should not be locked in flight. BA had, in fact, already announced through its press office immediately following the incident that the airline would reconsider its locked door policy as a part of its investigation but, in spite of that, it now appeared that Eddington was dictating the outcome. When speaking to the *Daily Telegraph*, the CEO had stated 'we will not be locking the door because it does not make sense. If some crazy guy holds a knife to a steward's throat and shouts 'open the door' we would open it rather than put the steward's life at risk.' Mr Eddington also repeated that BA crews were trained to deal with any incident and added that it was highly unlikely passenger visits to the flight deck would be stopped. Pilots were also concerned that a locked door in an emergency could cause crew communication problems.

In Nairobi other issues were being aired. The Kenyan daily newspaper, *The Nation*, questioned who had been responsible for allowing Mukonyi to board the flight in London and reported what it referred to as 'buck-passing' between BA, the UK police, and the captain. It was also reported that the Attorney General's Office had stated that consideration was being given to charging Mukonyi with one or more of four crimes including attempted hijacking, attempted kidnapping of the captain, creating a disturbance and endangering public life. In another contrasting report it mentioned that the Kenyan psychiatrists tending Mukonyi had said he did not remember his actions and should not be charged with criminal behaviour.

On 15 January, Captain Hagan had received a pleasant surprise in the post from the Deputy Prime Minister, John Prescott, who had written to him in his additional capacity as Secretary of State with responsibility for the DETR. Mr Prescott stated in his letter that 'a catastrophic accident had been averted' and said that he had asked BA's CEO Rod Eddington to single out Phil and Bill for special thanks. Up till then the only other document the captain had received from the DETR was the one on 'air rage', but now he felt this was a significant change for the Prescott letter was the first official recognition that the incident had been extremely severe. What Bill remained unaware of, unfortunately, was that only very senior personnel within the DETR had been informed of these details and that the majority remained none the wiser. At the same time, however, he also received letters from some of the BA board members expressing their gratitude and he began to feel valued. The captain also received more good news that Mukonyi had tested negative for HIV but, in spite of the discomfort, he decided he would stay on the safe side by continuing the course until completion in a further two weeks.

In the UK, progress had been halted while waiting on the BA investigation report but, by contrast, in Kenya quite a lot had been happening during the month of January. Only a short time after the incident on the Friday, 29 December 2000, just after about 0500 UTC, the Kenyan Government had contacted ICAO in Montreal to seize jurisdiction under the provisions of the Tokyo Convention to criminally investigate by their own police the 'unlawful interference of an aircraft'. The incident had occurred just before about 0455

UTC/0755 Kenyan time and BA2069 had arrived at about 1015 local time, too late for the morning papers, but, on Saturday, 30 December 2000, the day after the incident, news of the event had been splashed over the front pages of the Saturday morning newspapers. Amongst the main news items were remarks about Mukonyi's behaviour and the effect of his international notoriety on the nation, and this would not have gone down well in certain quarters.

By Monday morning, 1 January 2001, the tone of the Kenyan newspapers had changed and Mukonyi was now being presented as a mentally sick man who needed help, not censure. This generated a spate of opinions on the matter and, throughout the entire month of January, discussions of the incident dominated the Kenyan press, Mukonyi's fate was debated widely in public as well as in the media and the public's sympathy began to turn away from British Airways in favour of Mukonyi.

In London, the BBC had planned to air a special news broadcast about Mukonyi in the last week of January and in the meantime had sent a BBC documentary film team to Nairobi to investigate and to interview Mukonyi and the medical staff in the small Nairobi Hospital. By coincidence, about the same time, Captain Roger Whitefield, BA's Head of Safety, had also flown to Kenya on behalf of BA to conduct his own investigation and to talk to some of those involved in the incident, including also the medical staff and Mukonyi, but fortunately the BBC's and Captain Whitefield's paths didn't cross. On Roger's visit to the Nairobi Hospital, it is not known if he met Mukonyi but he was told by his doctor that Mukonyi would eventually regain the sight of his right eye. In response, Captain Whitefield reasserted that BA would not pay his hospital costs and would neither carry him back to France nor refund the return part of his ticket.

In about the middle of January, the BA delivery manager, Kola Olayinka, announced publicly that the airline would not service

Mukonyi's mounting hospital bill. This infuriated the Nairobi Hospital officials because the airline had already settled the injured passenger and crew accounts. Paul Mukonyi's father, Bernard, commented that his son had been taken to Nairobi Hospital on the instructions of British Airways and his family was unable to raise funds to settle the bill. A public collection to assist with the payment, however, was soon started by Soita Shitamda, MP for Mukonyi's home constituency of Malavato.

The Kenyan Government, shortly after the aircraft upset, had acted quickly and cleverly to manage the situation internally and the obvious path then was to present Mukonyi as a sick man who was mentally ill. From the outset, however, it was apparent that the police had been more than a little too quick to comment about Mukonyi's condition before any enquiry, medical examination or investigation and it was not difficult, therefore, to be distrustful of their reports. There was also the evidence provided by the psychiatrists, which did not exactly inspire confidence in the truth of their diagnosis. It was also suspected that when the Moi regime acted, others, in this case the media, the doctors and the police, would all be expected to fall into line accordingly.

After twenty or so years as the president of Kenya, Daniel Arap Moi, although from humble beginnings, had enabled his family, through his position of influence, to become the richest, not only in Kenya, but in the whole of east and central Africa. In terms of land ownership, he was placed second only to the Kenyatta family. At the time, corruption had permeated the fabric of the nation at all levels of Kenyan society and it was suspected that had also included Moi and his family. In 2000, a report about the need for reform of the Kenyan legal system published by an advisory panel of legal experts from four countries, Uganda, Tanzania, South Africa and Canada, had stated that, 'Bribery and political pressure are widespread in the Kenyan courts,' and that 'the air is full of allegations of corruption, incompetence and inefficiency'. And that was only the judicial system!

In contrast to these suspicions of corruption, however, Moi had a benevolent side and he had generously invested in his favoured educational projects, Moi High School in Kabarak and Moi University in Eldoret, although it was also rumoured that he had used some government funds in support. Paul Mukonyi's background, it had now been revealed, was not so distant to President Moi's upbringing as both were from the western region of Kenya. Moi, not surprisingly, had his enemies, and the last thing he needed was to be tarnished by an outrage that had been perpetrated by a star student from his own heartland. He had his reputation at home and overseas to protect from unwelcome attention and he had his educational establishments to uphold. As January progressed, however, it also seemed that the Kenyan public did not relish the thought of an educated Moi graduate rotting in an insanitary Kenyan prison and sympathy for Mukonyi grew with each passing day. With the president and the public now on the same side it would not be difficult to guess how this might turn out, but it would be the Attorney General who would make the final decision whether or not to prosecute Mukonyi on a range of charges, including creating a disturbance in flight, assaulting a pilot on the flight deck and hijacking an aircraft. Not long back from holiday, however, everyone had to wait until he had completed his review before he would announce his decision on Mukonyi's fate.

In the meantime, BA had been liaising with the Kenyan authorities and was already anticipating the possibility of no charges being raised, but BA had stated in the Nairobi press that, if Mukonyi was to be released, they would ban him from flying with them. The French Embassy had already invalidated his student visa, effectively barring him from returning to France, but at the same time BA announced their ban, the French reversed their earlier decision and revalidated his student visa.

Back in the UK, BA's CEO Rod Eddington had made his comments about the locking, or not locking, of flight deck doors, but that seemed to have sparked off further discussion. There had been much debate in the media about the rationale of the UK authorities permitting cockpit doors to be unlocked in flight. Comments in the press, both from passengers and aviation personnel, expressed surprise that the authorities in the UK were not insisting on the doors being locked as a security measure. In Japan a flight deck intrusion had recently occurred to All Nippon Airways (ANA) and the airline had quickly introduced a locked cockpit door policy.

In the USA, locked flight deck doors had been the policy for decades owing to a spate of hijackings on internal flights in the early sixties and some airlines in Europe had had already adopted this standard practice. In the UK, however, although easyJet locked doors in flight, the opinion was still largely against such a policy. Within the DETR, only Ian Devlin, the head of the Transport Security Directorate (TRANSEC), had expressed an opinion in favour of locking flight deck doors but the incident was no longer their responsibility.

Aviation expert David Learmount of *Flight International* stated that, 'I doubt if anything will change because of this particular incident'. Learmount went on to outline his argument against the locking of flight deck doors in UK aircraft and he was not alone, for BALPA and most BA pilots were not in favour of such a change. In the present environment this may now seem strange, but locking cockpit doors can be counterproductive to good communication between the flight deck and cabin crews and this can be particularly disruptive in emergency situations when accurate information exchange is essential. Although the majority in the UK were in favour of not locking doors, opinions did vary, and not even all three of the pilots on the BA2069 crew were agreed on the subject.

The analysis of the digital flight data recorder and the showing of the simulation to Flight Operations had now resulted in the seriousness of the incident leaking to almost all BA departments. Media interest in the incident had now revived and it could no longer be dismissed as a simple case of 'air rage'. It was also likely that the legal department had been made aware of the upset's severity and that this could raise further claims. BA needed to reassure the passengers, many of whom had now been in direct contact with the airline, by providing a plausible explanation. Without exception they had all been terrified by the almost three minutes of violent contortions of the aircraft upset and they all thought they were going to die, so how would BA confront those involved? What, and how, would they tell the passengers? Fortunately for the airline a possible solution began to emerge.

Flight Operations knew they had been incredibly fortunate not to have lost the aircraft and, from the outset, had been proud of the performance of their pilots 'saving the day', so they proposed that should be stated publicly. They successfully argued that the publicity would be beneficial to the airline and during the second week in January they began to make arrangements for the flight crew to appear on *Tonight with Trevor McDonald*, the flagship ITN current affairs programme. For the airline, the prestigious *Tonight* slot was also the opportunity to address any earlier misunderstandings, set the record straight and emerge with an image of a caring airline with experienced and skilful crews trained to deal with any emergency. Phil was reluctant and Richard seemed OK, but Bill was still suffering quite badly from the antiretroviral side effects and he asked for a delay until early February by which time his course of treatment would be completed.

A mutually agreed date of 12 February was finally arranged for the three pilots to meet Mr Trevor McDonald in the BA Compass Centre at Heathrow with an ITV camera crew. The pilots were all keen to tell their side of the story, but also apprehensive, for they knew that the BA Press Office would question, as would other departments, the wisdom of letting the pilots go on camera to divulge their version of the aircraft upset. The cockpit crew were also aware that the Press Office would be left looking more than a little uncomfortable when the pilots' revelations were found to be inconsistent with BA's press releases. On the other hand, BA now realised that they had to be more open with the passengers, although putting the flight crew in front of the cameras was indeed a bold move, but on this occasion Flight Operations had prevailed and the ITV interview was scheduled to go ahead in just a few weeks. BA, in contrast to being suspected of covering up, was now going to be incredibly honest and candid, and the pilots were keen to help.

On Monday, 23 January, the BBC had decided to air on their *10 o'clock News* a special news bulletin about Mukonyi, having recently produced it on their visit to Nairobi, and about his likely upcoming release. The article included a film of Mukonyi being interviewed in Nairobi Hospital with the mention that considerable debate in Kenya had generated sympathy for him and that it was increasingly unlikely he would be prosecuted.

Andrew Harding, the presenter of the BBC feature, seemed mostly to take Mukonyi's side in opposition to BA's approach of refusing to refund him or fly him again. Throughout the piece Harding extended an obvious display of sympathy by frequently referring to him as 'Paul' and 'this young man'. In the hospital interview, with Mukonyi's physician by his bedside discussing his condition, the attacker said that he was 'very, very sorry' about the situation. When asked if he meant to down the jet he looked straight at the camera and replied, 'No...No.' Told that he had nearly caused a major disaster he replied, 'Sir, I am shocked about that!'

The feature, however, did at the end include comment from one of the passengers, a Mr. Martin Young, who stated, 'By all reports the police (at Gatwick) handed him over to British Airways and told them to keep him well supervised. Now the question is, why didn't they?' This was the first real public sign that passengers wanted to know a lot more about the background to the violent aircraft upset.

The next day the BBC received many comments of complaint and criticism about the content of Mukonyi's feature and about the over compassionate tone of the presenter. One letter to the *Daily Telegraph* from someone who had experienced the ordeal voiced considerable disgust with the presentation, stating that it would have been more appropriate to give sympathy to the passengers he had nearly killed and who had been totally terrified by what he had done.

In Kenya the response was different, and the Kenya Human Rights Commission targeted the British Embassy and BA to protest about the airline blacklisting Mukonyi from flying on their aircraft. The French Embassy, in spite of them reversing their ban on him resuming his studies in France, also came in for criticism. The Human Rights Commission's consultant, Caleb Atemi, said: 'BA, the French Embassy and the Western media in general had treated Mukonyi badly as they regarded him as a dangerous man contrary to respected medical experts who say his condition is non-life threatening.'

Nearing the end of January, it had now been two weeks since the Attorney General, Mr Amos Wako, had returned from his vacation, but his final decision on Mukonyi had still not been taken. On his desk lay files from the police, the two doctors and the Human Rights Commission along with letters, mostly supporting Mukonyi. The file from the police had been completed two weeks earlier and mentioned taking statements 'from Mukonyi, the pilots, the cabin crew, passengers and other people who handled the matter'. The reports from the two doctors stated that, in their opinion, if Mukonyi was prosecuted his condition would worsen.

On Wednesday, 31 January, finally, just over one month after the aircraft upset incident, the Attorney General, having taken into account the reports and all legal considerations, at last issued his judgement. 'Under our laws, a person is not criminally responsible for an act…if at any time doing an act, he was, through a disease affecting his mind, incapable of understanding what he was doing.'

Now free to go, Mukonyi's condition was deemed to have improved sufficiently for him to be discharged from hospital and his bill of 800,000 Kenyan Shillings (approx. £6,000) was settled by his family with assistance from public donations. He then walked free in Nairobi, becoming a well-known figure and was admired as one of the country's brightest students. The public regarded him with a mixture of hero and victim and the Kenyan daily newspaper, *The Nation*, received a considerable number of letters of support. He was also seen daily on television or in the newspapers as the media monitored his repeated trips to the BA office in an attempt to obtain a refund for the unused portion of his return ticket. BA stood firm, however, and steadfastly refused either to refund him or to carry him back to Lyon.

Other airlines, including Air France, were approached, but they, too, refused to carry him. Eventually Emirates, one of the Gulf airlines, agreed to take him, so he purchased a ticket to return to France four months later, at the beginning of June, when he would fly via Dubai to Charles de Gaulle Airport in Paris then on to Lyon to resume his studies.

Chapter 19

BA's Report to be Completed by March 9th

Captain Hagan had by now completed his HIV antiretroviral course and had finally received the 'all clear'. He then arranged an appointment at the BA Health Services (BAHS) centre in the Compass Centre at Heathrow for a medical check-up as it was them who would declare him fit to fly if they were happy with his examination. On his visit to BAHS he found the atmosphere very relaxed and, after the doctor had chatted to him about the incident during his check-up, she soon declared that his suspension from duty was no longer relevant and that he could return to work.

Although Bill Hagan had now been declared fit to fly, he had to undergo refresher training before flying as captain again as he had been off duty for a prolonged period. To ease him back, the decision had been taken to roster him for some 'supernumerary' trips in the latter part of February, after his 12 February ITV interview with Trevor McDonald. In early March he could then complete his simulator training and checks and would hope to be operating again in command sometime in March.

BA also wanted Bill to attend counselling sessions and suggested that should also include his family, so he had to organise lots of return tickets to London for them all. The pilots had also shot to international fame in the aviation world and a number of invitations to award ceremonies had been received which the company had given them permission to accept. That meant co-ordinating with the Press Office plus regular visits to the BA headquarters at Waterside so, with counselling sessions, supernumerary trips, award ceremonies and simulator checks, it was going to be a busy period. Bill, however, in spite of enquiries, had not yet heard anything of BA's Safety Services preliminary incident review, which Captain Whitefield had mentioned he would be invited to attend, and he was becoming frustrated by the lack of progress. He was also despondent at the hardening attitude against the locking of cockpit doors in flight, which, after his experience, he felt was essential.

In the meantime, one proposition Captain Hagan was able to promote was the repositioning of the lower deck flight crew rest seat back to behind the cockpit on the upper deck and, on 28 January, he emailed a letter to Safety Services on this matter. He voiced his disappointment at not yet having heard from them and reiterated his strong concern about the distant positioning of the flight crew rest seat with the conclusion that 'it is my firm belief that, if I had been resting in the lower deck crew seat, the aircraft would have been lost and I do not have any doubt about this'. His timing proved to have been perfect for a few days later a package arrived at his home containing the minutes of a second Safety Services sub-group meeting. They had been reviewing safety recommendations prior to a further meeting of a larger Safety Services group who would first present a draft before producing the final report. There had, therefore, been more progress than Captain Hagan had thought, but he had been shocked to learn that on yet another occasion he and his crew had been kept in the dark. Once again, this had the appearance of some kind of unspoken ban on talking to any of the BA2069 flight crew, like the ban the crew had on talking to the press, for there seemed something about the inner workings of BA that made anyone associated with the incident wary of just doing the sensible thing of asking the flight crew what had really happened.

On examining the minutes, Bill read, not surprisingly, that several areas relevant to preventing a repetition of the incident had been identified and that the additional information the flight crew had submitted had been assessed. Much detail in the minutes explored a wider arena where some proposals had already been implemented. Amongst those were passenger handling prior to boarding, procedures to improve information transfer to the captain, use of the flight deck door, alerting systems and communications, the desirability of continuing with flight deck visits, cabin crew awareness of problem passengers, composition of cabin and flight crews, self-defence training and the position of the flight crew rest seat. Most topics had already provoked discussions within the media following the upset and all were now being examined by the company to identify, refine and agree recommendations. Few of the statements and recommendations were surprising but some were found to be of particular interest.

Firstly, it was agreed that information available from the flight from Lyon to Gatwick should have been passed on to Captain Hagan.

Secondly, concern was expressed that the company procedures had not been followed in respect to the release of the misleading BA Press Office statement on locked cockpit door policy issued following the incident.

Thirdly, the comment was made that the operating crew felt very strongly about the position of the crew rest seat and it was stated that Captain Hagan had written a letter to that effect.

Fourthly, a paragraph entitled 'Post incident announcements to passengers- should we give more/better guidance?' contained the comment 'Reaction to the Captain's announcement was very positive.' Bill was interested to read this company observation for the only other comment he had received had been: 'You didn't actually say that, did you?'

Finally, swayed perhaps by media pressure in one direction and by the recent comments from BA's CEO in the other, the sub-group felt that extensive discussion about future policy on the locking of flight deck doors should take place elsewhere. It suggested both the BA Flight Technical Safety Group (FTSG) and Operating Standards Group (OSG) should be involved in making the decision and mentioned that the BA policy at the time could be contrary to that recently expressed by ICAO.

The next day, however, BA Safety Services narrowly avoided the embarrassing prospect of having to ask the Press Office to prepare another statement for release to explain how a further flight deck intrusion had occurred on another BA service. On 30 January, during the evening flight from Hong Kong, a passenger had entered the cockpit and had refused to leave. Fortunately, it seemed, he was merely 'trying to make a point' and had no other intention. The Civil Aviation Authority (CAA) were informed of this intrusion and they stated that, as an obvious parallel had to be drawn with the Nairobi incident, they had also prepared a press release in case the intrusion was reported. Fortunately, for BA, this intrusion had not been picked up by the press and there was no mention of it anywhere in the media.

This appears to have been a catalyst for the CAA to become more involved in flight deck security for during the first week in February the CAA had taken the unusual step of writing individually to all operators of larger commercial aircraft. As the matter was sensitive, mailing letters avoided the normal Flight Operations Department Communication (FODCOM) route that was available for all to see. It stated that, 'in the light of a recent incident', although it is uncertain whether this referred to the Nairobi incident (five weeks earlier) or the recent unreported Hong Kong incident, all operators were asked 'to review their preventative procedures to prevent unauthorised [passenger] access [to the flight deck]'. This was to be 'an interim measure pending further analysis and possible additional safeguards.' In another document the CAA stated that it will continue to investigate the options available, together with the 'industry.' This opened discussions between the airlines and the CAA on issues regarding flight deck security.

It also appeared from other CAA documentary evidence that their Safety Regulation Group (SRG) had by then been given a copy of the Flight Data Simulation (FDS) of the upset and that, during the same week in February, members of both the Transport Security Directorate (TRANSEC) and the Multi-Lateral Division (MLD) had been shown it for the first time. That should have immediately altered their perception of the event and its significance and no one within the TRANSEC and MLD offices could now have continued to regard the incident as 10–20 seconds of an 'air rage' event. Although BA was under no legal obligation to share the simulation with any of these departments it would have been more helpful if they had done so earlier.

On Saturday, 10 February, just two days before the flight crew we were due to meet the ITV cameras in the Compass Centre for the *Tonight* interviews, Bill was notified that the event had been cancelled and that the legal department had felt that passenger groups might use this opportunity to take legal action. The legal department would have been aware that the 747 upset had almost been the third biggest aviation disaster in the world and openly admitted that such a possibility might be raised which could be detrimental to the company. It was obviously in the airline's interest to play down the event and have it perceived as less severe than it was and that it had been handled well by everyone involved. As far as the legal department was concerned, therefore, there had to be better ways to be honest with the passengers than letting the pilots tell their full story, hence the cancelling of the programme. What would now be best for BA would be to refrain from releasing any further information, even if it was seen as a cover-up.

Other internal decisions were made which shaped the future company attitude to the incident, with more of an emphasis on the customer service that was provided in the aftermath and how that could be improved. As part of the new strategy, the role perceived to have been played by the flight crew was also reappraised to give a better understanding of the incident. No information from these post-incident discussions, however, were to be shared with the pilots, but with Captain Hagan in particular, presumably as he had been the main press target. He was instructed, if contacted, not to speak to anyone about anything to do with BA, or flying, and to insist that any queries or invitations were immediately referred directly to the Press Office. BA now wrote to all passengers they could contact offering sympathy, understanding and support with, as part compensation, either a full refund of the Nairobi trip or a free return ticket to anywhere on the BA network.

Captain Roger Whitefield had previously stressed that BA Safety Services was in a hurry to complete their report and this was reconfirmed the following week when Captain Hagan received another package with a very short letter. Dated 20 February, it asked him to review the enclosed draft report of BA's Safety Services BASI-4 investigation and to ensure that any amendments or comments were submitted within the next seven days. Finally, and somewhat surprisingly, it said that if he had any major changes they should be discussed in person, either on the 26th or the 27th, so that the report could be issued the following week. At this point the captain did wonder if this instruction was related to his strongly held views on the position of the flight crew rest seat being submitted in writing. The letter that had accompanied the BASI-4 report did seem to target Friday, 9 March for release so, although placed under a tight schedule, Bill was happy that the final hurdle was now in view and that the report would soon be available.

The BASI-4 draft report Bill had received made numerous recommendations, mostly aimed at usefully addressing the problems which had been highlighted by the incident and all of which had been referred to in the earlier documentation sent to him. Aware of attitudes within the company, it came as no surprise to the captain that an opinion on the locking of cockpit doors had not progressed to a recommendation and was still left as an open subject. He was pleased to read, however, that one recommendation to be considered was the use of seats adjacent to the flight deck for 'technical crew' (i.e. pilots) rest seats. What until now he had felt was only his personal crusade was now being addressed and, in spite of what he considered as other shortcomings in the report, at least this vital issue was being taken seriously and he felt reasonably content.

Of those others invited to submit amendments, in addition to the flight crew, were the Operations Director, Flight Technical and Training Management, Heads of Security and Safety, an Engineering Director and the Business Continuity Manager whose task was to conduct risk assessments of future policies and procedures. Captain Hagan, having noted his points of disagreement, then took a flight to London where he went straight to the BA Safety Services office to voice his concerns. He asserted that the report's account of his pre-departure conversation with the Cabin Services Director (CSD) was inaccurate as it did not fully acknowledge that relevant information had not been passed to him. He had been told by the police that Mukonyi was fit to travel, which he understood as their approval for the Kenyan to fly, and was unaware that the police were waiting on his approval for boarding.

Captain Hagan also repeated his views regarding the report's lack of information about what had actually happened on the flight deck during the upset. The primary purpose of the investigation was to learn lessons in order to prevent a similar event recurring and the details of the cause and the flight profile of the violent upset should have been on record. In spite of Bill's argument, however, he was told these details would not be included, and he had to be content with the references of the upset he had identified in the draft report as well as the visual presentation of the Digital Flight Data Recording (DFDR) which were compatible with his first-hand knowledge of the event. Out of interest, he also enquired about the number of cabin crew on duty at the precise time of the incident but was told this too would not become part of the investigation. It seemed that anything sensitive that might be of interest to a litigant was not to be recorded and this could be viewed either as a cover-up or a sensible precaution, depending on opinions. After almost two months since the event, however, there had been no evidence whatsoever of the broken leg update being reported to the Air Accident Investigation Branch (AAIB), or of any accident investigation being conducted by Sudan or the UK as required by ICAO, so it would be interesting to see if the broken leg would be mentioned in BA's report.

Captain Hagan now had to face a frustrating wait for the BA report to be completed by 9 March but, with health checks and counselling sessions behind him, he could look forward to returning to flying on supernumerary trips, albeit in the position of observer to allow him to re-acclimatise to long haul operations. After these flights, he would then have to complete simulator retraining and a route check with a suitably qualified captain. A few days later, therefore, he checked in for the BA005 service to Tokyo, which was a long flight requiring a relief pilot. For take-off and landing he would sit as fourth pilot in the second 'jump' seat, only being legal to observe, while the third, relief pilot, would sit in the first jump seat. BA was also still concerned about Bill's vulnerability and they sent a security 'minder' with him on this trip, with a seat just outside the flight deck, so he could ward off any unwelcome approaches. The airline was taking no chances! After Bill's return to London, he was soon off on his second supernumerary trip, this time to Bangkok without a 'bodyguard', and, when getting back to Heathrow on 4 March, he was able to report to BA that these trips had been of benefit and that he was now ready to resume his duties. A few days later Bill completed the necessary mandatory simulator exercises, followed by a short return flight on which the route check captain passed him ready to operate in command once again. With his licence medical, simulator refresher and route check all satisfactory, his flying licence was revalidated and he was finally cleared to return to normal flying duties as captain.

When 9 March came and went, to Captain Hagan's disappointment, the BA/Safety Services report had still not been released. Instead, on the same day, the company had posted a second, personal letter to every passenger on board whose details they had available. A first letter that had been posted about the beginning of March had emphasized BA's distress at the truly horrific incident the passengers had experienced and offered them sympathy, understanding and the company's full support. Also offered was either a free return ticket to anywhere on the BA network or a full refund. The second follow-up letter acknowledged that many passengers would like answers to their questions and BA invited them to join a series of forums. The captain's wife and family had, of course, been on the BA2069 flight with him and it would have been excepted that his wife as a passenger would also have received the letters too but, for some reason, she did not, so Bill knew nothing of the forums that BA had planned.

A Passenger Action Group (PAG) had already formed which had no doubt been coaxed into action by getting nowhere with BA and by a question posed by passenger Martin Young in relation to the earlier recently broadcast BBC interview with Mukonyi in Nairobi.

Why, he had asked, if BA had been told to keep an eye on him, did they fail to do so? A fellow passenger, Nick Reid, soon became the spokesperson for the group as he continued to pursue the same question, and it was not long before the group had set up their own website, www.nairobiflight2069.com, as an information gathering medium. That opened the flood gates, and questions and comments from passengers began to pour into the site.

Chapter 20

The Customer Forums

In all, four meetings that BA referred to as 'customer forums' had been held with travel and accommodation expenses paid. The strategy seemed to be to open the meetings by reassuring the passengers that flying was exceptionally safe and then, by extension, to argue that the aircraft had not been nearly as close to disaster as many had thought. Management pilots took the stage having first liaised with other interested departments within the company as to what particular facts and details of which the group should be informed.

Before taking questions, a substantial amount of information was provided about the background to the BA 2069 flight. It commenced with Mukonyi's check-in at Lyon Airport, his strange behaviour in the terminal and that, on boarding in Lyon, he had been seated at the rear of the aircraft. They were also informed that, before departing from Lyon to Gatwick, the cabin crew had been told to 'keep an eye on him'. Mukonyi's strange manner during the flight to Gatwick was also reported, including him asking a flight attendant 'How easy is it to enter the cockpit?' and 'How easy is it to hijack the aeroplane?' He was also nervous and restless and he had removed his life jacket from under his seat to check it, and he had gone to the galley and had tried to use the interphone there to call the police in Gatwick.

It seemed that very little information, if any, had been withheld from the passengers about this initial phase of the incident and that the details seemed to have been comprehensively covered. Diane

Attenborough, one of those attending, was very surprised not only to hear what BA had to say, but also how open they had been about the behaviour of Mukonyi, both on the ground and in flight, while on his way to Gatwick from Lyon.

The narrative then continued with his progress through Gatwick Airport up to the time when the police delivered him to the forward door of the BA2069 aircraft where the captain accepted him for the flight to Nairobi. Many were surprised by the frankness of this description but also had been given the impression that he had been brought to the aircraft side where Captain Hagan, in spite of being aware of these facts, had allowed him to board. Mrs Attenborough was also very surprised to hear that the captain had accepted Mukonyi for the flight and, in view of what she had just heard, had assumed that the captain must have had had the same knowledge.

The information then disclosed Mukonyi's behaviour after BA2069's departure from Gatwick up to just before the intrusion, with the implication that his actions suggested a degree of planning. All of this was also very open. BA told the passengers that the duration of the incident had been 2 minutes and 32 seconds, a time obtained directly from the Digital Flight Data Recorder (DFDR). The maximum bank angle reached of 94 degrees and the reassuring figure of 27,672 feet, the lowest level to which the aircraft had tumbled during the upset, had both also been accurately extracted from the DFDR and discussed. In spite of the bank angle of 94 degrees having been very extreme in these circumstances, there seemed to have been an attempt to play this down for the passengers as not being as dangerous as first appeared by relaying the story of the US test pilot who, when demonstrating the prototype Boeing 707, had deliberately flown a barrel roll. This astonishing manoeuvre in such a large aircraft involved the 707 following one corkscrew path all the way round 360 degrees, not just a simple roll, but like rolling the aircraft round a very large barrel from level flight, to upside down and back to level flight again.

The event had occurred in 1955 when aviation engineers were holding their annual convention in Seattle and the plan was to show off the 707 to all the assembled airline executives as it flew over Lake Washington. Tex Johnstone, Boeing's chief test pilot, knew the 707 to be a lively aircraft and, to attract attention, he decided to astound everyone by flying a barrel roll. To further impress, he then flew a second barrel roll on the return pass. To get their message across, BA had shown a video of the 707 performing the aerobatic display to those attending at least one meeting.

If BA had intended to reassure those at the meetings of their experience, the difference in circumstances between their 747 incident and that of the 707 barrel roll could not have been more striking. The 707 had very few on board and, as Captain Johnstone had explained, the barrel roll, although more than a little unconventional in a four-engine commercial jet, to say the least, had been flown as a non-hazardous 1g manoeuvre and not even the aircraft would have known it was upside down. A cup of tea on a seat table, for example, would not have spilled a drop. By comparison, the BA2069 747 at the maximum bank angle of 94 degrees was fully stalled with airspeed dangerously low, gravity zero and the passengers being shaken and jolted violently.

It seemed that BA had been trying to imply that the BA2069 747 could have rolled all the way round and recovered to safe flight, but they would have had a problem proving it because it was more than likely that the 747 would have dropped upside down from the sky with recovery being impossible. A former test pilot explained that: 'Rolling any non-aerobatic jet aircraft is a balanced, skilful manoeuvre which is required to be flown at the correct altitude because flying the roll too high risks damage from excessive speed and too low risks impact with the ground. The correct speed is also absolutely vital – the B707 barrel roll had been flown at a fast 425 knots – for, if the speed was too low to complete the manoeuvre, the aircraft will fall out of the roll before it has been completed and dropping upside down is not a survivable option.' The implication seemed to be that if the BA2069 747 had continued to roll it could have rolled all the way round and recovered, but that would have been stretching the truth too far.

The meetings continued with passengers seeking more details about exactly what had happened during the two to three minutes of the upset and about what had caused the shaking and vibrating that had been so noticeable throughout that period. BA's responses avoided use of the word 'stall', which is not generally understood by the lay person but which could have been easily explained. Instead, a rather ridiculous term, 'switch-back manoeuvre,' was used, but no pilot anywhere would have heard the stall described as such. Those attending were told that 'during the recovery phase the plane adopted something of a switch-back manoeuvre with severe rattling and juddering, apparently normal for those experienced in these things but rather frightening for passengers'. Airline pilots of large jet passenger aircraft, however, never get anywhere near stalling them, except in a very exceptional situation like the BA2069 aircraft upset, and, if they ever inadvertently, for any other very exceptional reason, flew near to stalling the aircraft, the severe rattling and juddering, which on a big jet is extreme, would have frightened the pants off the pilots too. This constant attempt at playing down the upset by pretending it was not as serious as first thought by telling the truth but not the whole truth was not doing the company's reputation any good.

Add to that the fact that there was still no mention of BA having reported the broken leg to the AAIB, a legal requirement, there had been no mention of the ICAO requirement that an accident will be investigated by an independent authority and, if the broken leg had been reported, there was still no mention of what the AAIB were doing about it, or if they had passed it on to the Sudanese to leave them to deal with it. Everyone was aware that BA's behaviour was an attempt to prevent a multi-million pound claim for damages but some might say that, with what appeared to have been a failure to report an accident, they had now crossed a red line. After more than three months since the aircraft upset, an accident investigation had still not been instituted, and it now allegedly appeared that BA were deliberately dismissing the broken leg as if it wasn't there. With no serious incident investigation, BA could just continue with their own investigation as if nothing had changed. If so, this was a criminal offence with a possible jail sentence for non-compliance and, if indictable, there could be no time bar.

While the passenger groups did learn a lot, not everyone was entirely satisfied with the information provided. Some wanted to know how many cabin crew members were on duty and what their locations were, but BA repeatedly avoided answering questions on this matter. There was also an interest in when the BA report might be available but the company had already produced a draft and it had been assumed that they were also keen to progress to completion and to publish the report. At one of the meetings, however, a BA spokesperson suggested that owing to security reasons the report may not be published, for, as part of the investigation, flight deck door policy regarding the locking, or not, of cockpit doors was being reviewed and this could prove to be confidential. BA would also have had the concern that, if sensitive information did get into the hands of potential litigants, it might be very damaging. Captain Hagan, however, completely ignorant of events, continued to push for and await the publication of the report.

The Civil Aviation Authority (CAA) was now doing more than just monitoring the progress of the BA report, for documents revealed that discussions had taken place between the CAA and the Department of Environment, Transport and Regions (DETR). On 23 March 2001, the CAA had faxed the DETR questioning if it had been right for Kenya to have taken jurisdiction of the incident. This appeared to have been further evidence of a lack of knowledge or understanding of the Tokyo Convention, of what role it had played and what jurisdiction the Kenyan state had claimed. The CAA had also queried the initial Kenyan police investigation of Mukonyi and had enquired if his subsequent release had been owing to the police's failure to prove intent? It was also noted that, after Kenya had taken jurisdiction, no feedback whatsoever had been received from them.

Captain Hagan and the co-pilots were in line to receive many awards for their actions but the first award in late March was only for the captain on the grounds of age. He had been awarded the British Gold Hero Medal from the Association of Retired and Persons over 50 (ARPO50), an organisation dedicated to honouring acts of bravery in that age group, and he had received it in a ceremony at the Café Royal together with his wife and family. Other awards were to follow, but for the company this presented a dilemma. BA, on the one hand, could take pride in awards for their pilots but, on the other hand, they were trying to minimise, or even eliminate, any discussion of the incident. The pilots would be attending ceremonies with some involving a high media presence, and possibly a press conference, and these would inevitably generate questions and demands for answers.

It took a while to ease Captain Hagan back into the roster system again after having been approved to fly but, in the last week of March, he set off to Los Angeles. Now back in harness, flying normal routes as a normal line captain, Bill Hagan found it very rewarding. On his return to Heathrow, there was, of course, still no BA report, and it would now be April 2001 before it would finally surface. The BA2069 incident, Bill noticed, was still generating occasional references in the papers and, during the first weekend in April, a lengthy piece in the *Observer* caught his attention. The article was entitled 'Passengers in Kenya terror flight threaten to sue BA', which, at first, did not surprise him, as he had assumed BA had cancelled the ITV *Tonight* programme over such concerns. On reading further, however, he learned of BA's forums and was dumfounded to read that a series of meetings with passengers, that he knew nothing about, had already been held during the last four weeks. Captain Hagan's wife had been a passenger but had not been invited and, at first, he felt she should have been, but then on second thought he wasn't surprised.

It appeared that BA had introduced this new corporate strategy to more effectively control what information was being imparted to the passengers and, perhaps, to help downplay the risks by providing their own version of the aircraft upset. The airline may have considered, with possibly millions of pounds of compensation payments at stake, that the cost and effort was worthwhile, and, with completion of the BA report imminent, it did seem that they had finally sealed any further airline information cracks. The Passenger Action Group (PAG), now devoid of any further information except what BA was willing to provide, began pressing the airline to release their report on completion, but it is possible this may have had the opposite effect of strengthening BA's resolve to maintain the moratorium. One advantage that BA had gained from the forums was feedback from the passengers and they had now learned that many were suffering considerably from Post-Traumatic Stress Disorder (PTSD). BA's original offer of compensation had been a full refund of their ticket to Nairobi or a free return ticket to anywhere on their network, but the airline had discovered that a lot of passengers at that time were not prepared to go anywhere near an aeroplane. BA then decided to improve the level of compensation by also offering a separate cash payment of £2,000 on top of a full refund, but in return for a signed release and discharge form, and a further letter was also sent later offering counselling to anyone who felt the need for support.

The period from March and into April had proved to be quiet regarding mention of the BA2069 Nairobi Incident in the newspapers and all involved in the aircraft upset had now been compelled to wait further for BA's report to be published.

On Friday, 20 April, however, a large event had been organised at BA's Waterside Theatre by CEO Rod Eddington and Flight Operations Director Captain Mike Jeffrey, to 'honour the heroes of the BA2069' with 'all friends and colleagues being welcome', and for this occasion Bill's wife had also been invited. BA had promised a surprise that would only be revealed on the day and had arranged for all air crew invited to be 'allocated' ground duty for the event. The ceremony was to be very inclusive and the entire crews of both the BA2069 flight into Nairobi and of the continued BA2069 flight from Nairobi to Dar Es Salaam had been invited and, along with some staff passengers, including Bill's wife, they were all to receive 'Awards for Excellence.' Rod Eddington welcomed everyone to Waterside and Mike Jeffrey followed with a speech saying how serious the event had been and how good a job the pilots had done. The thirty-nine 'Awards for Excellence' were now personally presented by Rod Eddington and the three flight crew, Bill, Phil and Richard, were the last to receive theirs. The surprise event turned out to be a wonderful day trip on the Orient Express from Victoria Station with a silver service lunch being served and everyone thoroughly enjoyed the day.

The next edition of 'British Airways News' reported that the lunch onboard had been BA's way of saying 'thank you' to the staff involved in the incident, referred to as 'the company's heroes and heroines', for their 'superb customer service recovery'. On the front page was a photograph of Cabin Services Director Laura Boyd and Captain Bill Hagan boarding the Orient Express, but Bill was disappointed at the lack of a photograph of Phil who, if anyone, was undoubtably the hero of the incident. The showcase event, of course, had been all about the 'entire crew' being heroes but, if it hadn't been for Phil, no one would have been there to celebrate, and the captain felt that Phil had deserved more recognition than that. Bill might also have said to himself that, if it hadn't been for his stroke of genius to drive his finger into the attacker's eye to remove him, Phil might not have had sufficient time to fly a skilled recovery of the aircraft. And Richard might have also said to himself that if it had not been for his heroic feat of fighting through the upset to arrive at the right moment to assist, Bill might not have been able to hold back the big Kenyan. Phil had been the star of the performance, but it had also been a superb crew effort! The turning point of the attack, however, from Mukonyi being glued to the controls to the others pinning him down while Phil flew the recovery, was all down to the captain's son, who had asked his dad if confronted by a shark what he would do, to which Bill had replied that he would fend off the shark by jabbing a finger in its eye. It has been said that life can 'turn on a sixpence', but the lives of over 400 people on BA2069 that morning had turned on the poke of an eye.

A few days later, a half page feature appeared in *The Wall Street Journal* discussing both sides of the locked door argument. It focussed on the fact that the views of the Air Line Pilots Association (ALPA) in the United States, who originally opposed, but who now supported, the locking of cockpit doors in flight, were at total variance to the views of the British Airline Pilots Association (BALPA) in the UK, who strongly opposed the locking of cockpit doors in flight. The British pilots felt they had valid concerns that locked flight deck doors could result in one pilot being locked out, a rapid depressurisation could be dangerous and, in a major emergency, could seriously hamper flight deck cabin/cabin crew communications. The *Wall Street Journal* article had been prompted by a major debate about flight deck security at the International Federation of Airline Pilots Associations (IFALPA) annual conference, which had just opened in Jamaica for a week and had included a summary of several notable cockpit assaults over the previous two decades. The feature then finished with the comment that 'the UK CAA is monitoring what BA is doing following its near-disaster in December'.

Chapter 21

The Head of the AAIB questioned

Information revealed in documentation that, unusually, if not uniquely in UK aviation history, in April 2001 the AAIB had been asked by the Safety Regulation Group (SRG) of the CAA to explain why they had not taken part in the investigation of the 'serious incident' as the aircraft had been registered in the UK, as it was owned and operated by a British company, and as the expectation had been that the AAIB would assist with Sudan's investigation. This, of course, was the big question! The Air Accident Investigation Branch (AAIB) had not given any explanation whatsoever as to why they had declined to investigate the BA2069 'serious incident' and only now, almost four months after the aircraft upset and at the behest of the Civil Aviation Authority Safety Regulation Group (CAA SRG), was the AAIB providing a reason. The fax sent by the AAIB to the SRG had been obtained by a Freedom of Information (FOI) request to the CAA because a FOI request to the AAIB for copies of communication traffic at that time was met with the response that they had no records on file. All AAIB exchanges that had any content relating to the BA2069 event had been deliberately erased and that, in itself, had the appearance of a deliberate attempt to hide something.

In response to the Safety Regulation Group's (SRG) request, on 23 April 2001, Ken Smart, Head and Chief Investigator of the AAIB, sent a fax to Mike Smethers, Head of the Multilateral Division Aviation Group (MLD/AG), with a request to copy to the SRG.

After Mr Smart's first sentence of introduction, the sentences following provided his reasons for not being involved in the investigation of the incident.

> Mike,
>
> Boeing 747 Incident at Nairobi
>
> When we spoke this morning, I promised to let you have a note confirming our reasons for not being involved in the investigation of the above incident.
>
> When the incident was first reported to us by British Airways, we offered assistance to the Kenyan Directorate of Civil Aviation under the provisions of Annex 13 to the Chicago Convention.
>
> The Kenyans informed us that they were not able to conduct an investigation as the incident was being treated as a criminal act and was under investigation by the national Police.
>
> In these circumstances the AAIB was unable to appoint an Accredited Representative to participate in the investigation by the State of Occurrence.
>
> Best regards,
> Ken Smart

Far from Mr Smart's fax being an off the cuff, casual reply, his text had the appearance of a carefully crafted and precisely constructed response that had been cut to the bone. The three reasons he gave for not investigating the serious incident were not devoid of the truth, but were most certainly not telling the whole truth. It is alleged that his response seemed to be a jumble of facts intended to 'baffle by science', and it had appeared that his 'reasons' had not in any way explained why he had not investigated the serious incident.

In answer 1, Mr Smart had said that he had offered help to the Kenyans with the serious incident, but what he had not said, perhaps because he had thought it too embarrassing to mention, was that he had only done so in error owing to his own misunderstanding of the jurisdiction the Kenyans had claimed.

In answer 2, when he had been told by the Kenyans that they could not investigate the serious incident because their police were conducting a criminal investigation, he would have known immediately that he had got it wrong.

In answer 3, he had said he had been 'unable to appoint an Accredited Representative to participate in the investigation by the State of Occurrence', i.e. Sudan, but that was, quite simply, not true. There was no investigation by Sudan because they had declined and, therefore, there was no investigation to which he could have appointed a representative.

What can be gleaned from his fax, however, is that at the time Ken Smart was making his decision to decline, he was aware that the Kenyans were criminally investigating, that the Sudanese were not investigating and that now, with Sudan out of the way, the UK was first in line to investigate. With the UK now in pole position, however, all Ken Smart had to do was to tell ICAO that the AAIB wished to investigate and it would have been his for the taking. He would have known that, so why didn't he?

One can speculate, but the situation that Mr Smart would have found himself in at that time becomes clearer if the facts are examined, and they help explain his action. First of all, as there was no ICAO requirement to investigate a serious incident, there was no compulsion for him to act and no rules, regulations or law requiring him to do anything. Whether he chose, or not, to investigate would be entirely down to him, but, of course, it wasn't that simple. If he had chosen to investigate, he would have acted in keeping with the 'mission' of the AAIB, it would have been considered that he had done the right thing and the AAIB would have produced an excellent report. But he had decided not to investigate, and in doing so he would have been aware that he was acting contrary to the principles of the AAIB, that there would be criticism, perhaps even suspicion, of his conduct, and that one day he could be under pressure to explain his somewhat bizarre behaviour.

At that time, Mr Smart would also have known the background of the aircraft upset from the details provided by BA and, with his extensive experience, he would have been aware that an event of this nature, with an intruder entering the cockpit, snatching the controls and terrifying and almost killing all the passengers, could have the potential to generate a multi-million pound passenger compensation claim against BA. He would have been in touch with BA, probably several times, which was to be expected, and he could even have discussed the situation with them. It can, however, be deduced that, soon after Mr Smart's communication with Kenya and his decision not to investigate, he had been in touch with BA with further information. The result was that, almost immediately after he had been speaking with BA, the airline had contacted ICAO with an offer to conduct an investigation of the aircraft upset. BA, of course, was at liberty to conduct their own investigation if they wished, but they would not have sought ICAO's approval for a serious incident investigation without knowing that both Sudan and the UK had decided not to investigate, otherwise there would have been no point in doing so. Ken Smart was also at liberty to consult with BA on these matters, but there was only one person who knew both these details at that time and who could have informed BA, and that was Mr Smart, for he had known earlier that Sudan had declined, and that the UK had just declined, for he, himself, had made the decision on behalf of the AAIB not to investigate. With no safety authority being prepared to take on the task, BA's offer was accepted, but that left the airline in the very advantageous position of investigating their own serious incident. Although, in these circumstances, Ken Smart's alleged behaviour could be considered suspect, it can be acknowledged that he had not done anything to which he had not been entitled.

Had Ken Smart decided to investigate the BA serious incident, however, he would have been obliged to complete a final report for publication and that could have revealed damning evidence against BA that their passengers could have used to litigate against the airline. Mr Smart could then have found himself solely responsible for substantially damaging BA's finances and no one would have wanted that on their shoulders, especially if, like Ken Smart, there was no compulsion to make that choice in the first place. Some of Mr Smart's actions can only be deduced and alleged, of course, but the above does present a valid scenario of the dilemma he would have faced and there could even have been some sympathy for the situation in which he found himself. In this case, although he had done nothing wrong, it could be alleged that he deliberately colluded with BA to avoid the airline paying out large sums in compensation by acting contrary to AAIB principles and by providing BA with the opportunity to investigate their own incident. If Mr Smart had done anything wrong, it could be alleged that it was not revealing his true reasons for declining to investigate, for none of this detail had been mentioned in his fax, but, in his situation, telling the whole truth, it could be suggested, would not have been an option. It can be alleged, however, that his comments in his fax were more like facts than reasons, that they did not explain why he had declined to investigate, as requested, and that his intention seemed to have been to 'baffle by science'. That appeared to have worked, for he never heard from the CAA again!

The above, of course, had nothing to do with the broken leg, for Mr Smart's declining had occurred soon after the aircraft upset, when the aircraft was still in the air with about two hours or so flying still to go to Nairobi. At that time, only the stewardess whose leg had been broken, the Canadian doctor who had examined her and a few other cabin crew members were aware of her broken leg.

Now in late April 2001, there was still no upgrade of the 'serious incident' to 'accident' and still no mention of an accident investigation. Once again, it can be alleged that BA appeared to be holding the broken leg under wraps and it now seemed they were going to keep it that way. At some time, however, this could come to a head and, if the drama of the previous situation with investigations was to be repeated, Mr Smart could very well be faced with another dilemma.

At Captain Hagan's first award ceremony in March with the Association of Retired and Persons over 50, his two co-pilots hadn't attended because they weren't old enough! Now the three pilots with their wives had been invited at BA's expense to receive an award at the end of the International Federation of Air Line Pilots Association (IFALPA) annual conference that had just started in Jamaica. All of them were to receive the prestigious Polaris Award, civil aviation's highest decoration for 'An act of outstanding Airmanship or Bravery'. This was only the second time the honour had been presented to a British flight crew member, the first being the award nine years earlier to First Officer Alastair Atchison, who had been the co-pilot on a BA BAC 1-11 when the captain's windscreen had suddenly failed and had blown out. The resulting rapid decompression had partially sucked out Captain Tim Lancaster and Alastair's highly skilled handling of the incident and his safe landing had won him the award.

It was now a great honour for the three BA2069 flight to attend the gala dinner that marked the end of the conference, which had been sponsored by Boeing. After dinner, the Polaris Awards were presented to all of them and the captain was delighted to make the acceptance speech to the several hundred representatives of pilots' unions worldwide. Bill concluded his speech by saying, 'This evening is sponsored by the Boeing Company and that gives me the opportunity to thank them. Not for this fine gala dinner, not for the great atmosphere here, but for building damned strong aeroplanes!' The applause had been deafening, not just for Bill, but for Boeing, for they knew he had meant it, and the international pilots attending had heartily endorsed his opinion.

Back in the UK, it was well into April and the aviation community at large was beginning to get restless over the lack of information from BA regarding their investigation of the BA2069 incident. It was normal practice as an investigation progressed for the professional pilot fraternity to receive preliminary reports from time to time, usually abbreviated and redacted, but from BA there was nothing. This issue was one of safety, for the more knowledge pilots had of the experiences of their colleagues the better prepared they were to manage, or avoid, a similar experience and they were getting impatient to know what had happened. It was felt that the CAA was acting as if there had been no BA2069 incident and suspicions were continuing to grow that BA was involved in a cover-up for there certainly was circumstantial evidence indicating that they had not been telling the whole truth.

As April ended, the CAA received a letter from a firm of solicitors, Russell, Jones & Walker, who were representing the Passenger Action Group (PAG). They stated that, in spite of innumerable letters, four passenger forums and discussions with the PAG attempting to sue BA, no satisfactory answers had been produced. The legal firm also pointed out the obvious that, by BA's own admission, their report was being prepared, edited and published by the same company, and that had placed BA in the unsatisfactory position of affording them the opportunity to obscure any failures in 'duty of care and attention'. The letter also pointed out that the CAA security inquiry, which had been ongoing since February, would also be relying on details from the BA report, and the solicitors argued that 'an objective and independent investigation by the CAA is therefore imperative'. They were not the only ones who did not trust BA to produce an unbiased report.

The CAA's Deputy Secretary & Legal Adviser responded by stating that 'the CAA was considering the implications of this incident and will take any necessary action'. It also declared that 'the purpose of the CAA's inquiry has been to identify as quickly as possible what actions might need to be taken in the interests of public safety. It has sought and obtained the full cooperation of British Airways in the course of this inquiry.'

Additionally, the author of the original risk assessment from the Threats Office, DM, had prepared his Annual Report for 2000 entitled 'A statistical Analysis and Summary of Major Incidents Affecting Aviation World-wide' and, on publication, had circulated the report to eight other internal offices and to fourteen police units and government departments, including the National Aviation Security Committee (NASC). When preparing this report, unlike the original assessment, DM was now aware that Mukonyi had actually been in contact with the controls for the period of the incident and he had recognised that the National Aviation Security Programme (NASP) protocols had in fact been breached. To compensate, therefore, he had included in his annual report a retrospective 'profile report' entitled, 'Attempted sabotage incident involving... Flight no. BA 2069.' The significant amendment to his original assessment was that, 'Although BA and the Kenyan authorities have ruled out hijack as a motive, this incident cannot simply be classified as air rage, in that the safety of both the aircraft and passengers were endangered by his actions. Had the attacker continued unabated the aircraft would probably have crashed with the loss of all those on board.' In response to the amendment in the annual report, and to possibly other reappraisals, the incident was re-categorised under 'Attacks on aircraft' by the Threats Office for the annual review meeting of the National Aviation Security Committee (NASC). The meeting held on 2 May in Great Minster House confirmed the opinion that 'the aircraft had come very close to being lost'.

In Kenya, the jurisdiction to criminally investigate Mukonyi's 'unlawful interference of an aircraft' under the Tokyo Convention had appeared to have been properly managed by the Kenyan state. There were many in the UK, however, who had been concerned that the diagnosis of the psychiatrists was anything but proper and that the exonerating of Mukonyi from all blame on the grounds that the young Kenyan had said he had no recollection of any violent behaviour was unacceptable. As a result, he had not stood trial, and for the first time, in early May, enquiries had been made in Whitehall questioning the Kenyans taking jurisdiction and the criminal investigation by the Kenya Police. It seemed that someone in the chief offices of government was now taking an interest.

Captain Hagan had now taken a few weeks of his annual leave in May and a short while after his return to the UK, nearer the end of May, he received a call from a Captain Mike Vivian, then deputy Head of the Flight Operations Department (FOD) of the Civil Aviation Authority (CAA). Captain Vivian was interested in a website about the BA2069 Nairobi Incident and he had wondered if Bill Hagan had known of its existence. On receiving the reply that Bill did not, he elaborated by saying that some of the website seemed to be based on fact, while other details seemed less so, but, if they were true, they would be of some concern. Captain Vivian also wanted Bill to know that since February the CAA had been reviewing cockpit security and now wanted to launch a full review of the BA incident report. Captain Hagan would be informed of its completion, but whether or not the CAA report would be made available to the public would not be a CAA decision but that of the Department of Environment, Transport and Regions (DETR), who had ordered the review. Either way, he added, Bill would be able to view it, but, unfortunately, the CAA would not be able to commence their review while BA was still conducting its own investigation and the CAA would have to wait for BA to complete its findings. It had seemed that the discovery of the nairobiflight2069.com website, having been built to share information primarily within the passenger's legal action group, but also with those who had already accepted the enhanced offer of £2,000, had been the catalyst that had cajoled the DETR into ordering the CAA to conduct their own security review. It had appeared that the DETR had also not been content to accept only BA's report.

Now at the end of May, the BA report had been completed at last and had been dispatched to the printers so, almost three months late, it would be finally ready for release in June 2001. Following Mike Vivian's phone call, Bill checked online for the Passenger Action Group's website and at his first visit was staggered to find that the passengers knew more about some aspects of the incident than he did. He had no idea from where what had seemed like genuine 'inside' information had come from, but it looked as if someone within BA had been providing accurate details, not only at the forums, but also by leaks from within. Since its inception, the website had grown to numerous chapters, but the first two chapters had described the actual incident with remarkable accuracy. The details of elapsed time, g-forces experienced and the aircraft flight path had been more comprehensive than any previous public report. The information had been clearly derived from the Digital Flight Data Recorder (DFDR) and had accurately quoted the duration of 2 minutes and 30-40 seconds, the climb into the first stall, entry into the steep dive, followed by the fast roll from 30 degrees right bank to 94 degrees left bank which had been incorrectly described as a 'barrel roll' through 124 degrees. The prolonged rattling, juddering and shaking of the aircraft had also been well reported but had used the BA nomenclature of 'switchback manoeuvre'. Other data had appeared to have originated from the DFDR with some small errors, like using units of miles per hour instead of knots, but all the other detail was perfectly correct. Other accurate information that had been reported included the danger of over-speed and the loss of thrust in the steep descent, the danger of the bank angle going over vertical, the gentle decent and smooth landing into Nairobi, with apparently no use of auto braking or reverse thrust after touchdown, and all had been fully recorded, precise 'inside' information. The website had already provided a considerable amount of accurate data and it continued to be updated regularly as the legal action group pressed for more information in the hope of litigating successfully. The problem for the passenger group was that, although the detail had been accurate, they had no concrete written evidence to back up any claim in court, they knew nothing about the broken leg, and it seemed that there were others intent on keeping it that way.

Chapter 22

The BA Report Completed

A few days later into June, a copy of the BA report finally arrived at Captain Hagan's home and he eagerly opened it, noting that it had been dated May 2001 with the title 'Safety Services report on the investigation into the unlawful interference with flight controls by a passenger on the BA2069......involving aircraft G-BNLM'. At this juncture the BA report was only being distributed to the selected few so the reader should view this report as if one of the inner circle.

Bill had kept a copy of the draft report he had received earlier ready to cross check so he rapidly thumbed through the pages to compare the draft with the final copy, and he was not greatly surprised to observe that his requested amendments had virtually been ignored.

A few other amendments, however, had also been noted. It was known that the captain on the Lyon to Gatwick flight had stated that 'had all the information of Mukonyi's behaviour been communicated to him he would have not allowed him to board'. This remark had been removed, possibly because it could have been inferred that, had Captain Hagan been provided with the same details, he also would not have accepted Mukonyi, and this appears to have been considered too incriminating to include. A previous comment by Phil that 'he had turned round to see a big man standing behind the pedestal looking straight at him' had been changed to 'had turned round to observe Mukonyi lunging towards him', but this seemed to have been lifted from the Nairobi psychologists' narrative. The draft report had also described in full the aircraft upset and had clearly referred to the aircraft stalling twice, as observed in the computer animation, but a further significant amendment in the final report, apart from the mention of 'stall buffet', was omission of the word 'stall' from the description of the erratic flight path. It could be alleged, however, that this alteration had not just been a diminishing of the stall progression, but had been an attempt to distort the facts. Of those invited to suggest amendments there had been only about ten – the two pilots on BA2357 to Gatwick and the three on BA2069 to Nairobi, plus department heads from Operations, Technical/ Training, Security/ Safety, Engineering and Continuity – and it seemed that none of them were likely to have had requested such a revision. BA had also never at any time admitted that the autopilot had been disconnected with Mukonyi's first strong snatch, that his hands had tightly grasped the yoke and that he had fiercely fought to control the aircraft for the entire period of the upset and these details had also been omitted from the final report.

Recommendations, however, had also been made in the report including, not surprisingly, a review of company policy regarding the management of disruptive passengers, guidance on the handling of mentally unstable persons and procedures that should be adopted by sub-contractors. BA was also going to assess for adoption the Defence Evaluation and Research Agency (DERA) passenger database that had already been established to enable information exchange on certain categories of passengers. Crew communications on board were also reviewed to ensure that crew members in the rest areas would have full access to the crew communications system at all times. Further training for cabin crew in the use of restraining straps was also recommended, as was a review to establish cabin crew complements for every aircraft fleet throughout the entire airline. It was also proposed that a review of cockpit security should include the locking of flight deck doors with cabin crew vigilance, and Captain Hagan was also delighted to note that the recommendation to consider locating flight crew rest seats adjacent to the flight deck had been retained.

Critics had claimed that BA's internal investigation was unlikely to be as full and open as it should have been and that their report would be less than adequate and, in some aspects, that's how it had appeared to have turned out. The prime purpose of their report, however, was to examine the circumstances surrounding Mukonyi, how he was able to board and to subsequently attack, and to implement changes to prevent a reoccurrence. The intention was not to provide a detailed analysis of the aircraft upset but it was significant and, in the absence of any investigation by Sudan or the UK, more could have been provided. Disappointingly, the details included had not only been minimal but had been amended, and some of them, it could be alleged, in a manner that was questionable. Apart from these allegedly deliberate manipulations of some facts, however, it mostly did appear that BA had not been untruthful, but it could be said that they were, perhaps not surprisingly, not telling the whole truth.

Near the end of the report, Captain Hagan would also have read a very short paragraph giving brief details of the injuries sustained during the incident where he would have noted that his own cuts and damaged little finger had been mentioned, then the wound to Mukonyi's eye, but, immediately afterwards, he would also have seen BA's revelation that: 'One cabin crew sustained a broken leg and was hospitalised.' Of the selected few in receipt of the full report, this detail of the broken leg would have been insignificant, but its mention in the report did indicate that BA's Safety Services, who had contributed extensively to the BA report from the outset, did know about the broken leg and had done so all along. BA's Safety Services, more than anyone, however, would have been well aware of its significance and would have known of the legal requirement to update the AAIB with details of the broken leg. Under the circumstances, this was an astonishing admission by BA and a very risky strategy, but perhaps BA had thought that the more brazen they were about it the more it would be considered of no consequence. The AAIB would also have received their copy of the BA report and, as it had appeared they had not previously been formally notified, only now would they have learned of the broken leg, but Mr Smart and the AAIB would most certainly also have known of its significance.

Fortunately for BA, the importance of the broken leg bone would only have been obvious to those with specialist knowledge and, as there had been no mention whatsoever of how this detail would have influenced an investigation, it would have meant nothing to almost everyone else reviewing it. Also, owing to the broken leg not having been reported to London from the aircraft shortly after the aircraft upset, no one outside the inner circle would have known about the broken leg, including the passengers, never mind of its significance. Pilots, too, were not familiar with the intricacies of accident investigation or of the differences between serious incidents and accidents and the rules and regulations governing each. Even if it had registered with others how serious the consequences of the broken leg had been, their hands were tied, as no one was at liberty to divulge any information from the report. Those who did know of the significance of the broken bone, BA's Safety Services included, had refrained from commenting.

Otherwise, BA's report had been much as expected for it appeared to have been 'economical' with the whole truth and seemed to have played down the severity of the aircraft upset in order to protect the company from litigation. Up to a point, that could be understandable, but failing to update the AAIB in a timely manner with information of the broken leg was different. BA's Safety Services had sat on this for many months and had consistently failed to submit a report. It is very difficult to imagine that Safety Services would have, of their own volition, acted in this way, and, almost certainly, it can be alleged that this instruction had come from a senior level within the airline.

The AAIB had allegedly colluded with BA to save the airline from serious financial harm by declining to investigate the serious incident when it was first reported, and that had avoided a damaging report being published and had given BA the opportunity to self-investigate their own serious incident, a rather bizarre scenario, but no regulations or laws had been broken. Now with the broken leg having been exposed to a few selected groups, including the AAIB, this was a whole new ball game, for the AAIB would most certainly have known its significance and that it should elevate the serious incident to an accident. BA Safety Services had clearly not formally reported the broken leg to the AAIB as required by law for, if they had, Sudan's AAICD or the UK's AAIB would, by now, have been obliged to commence an accident investigation, but they had not. It can, therefore, be alleged that BA Safety Services had deliberately refrained from reporting the broken leg to the AAIB by instruction from above with the intention of avoiding a full accident investigation and a damning report that could have resulted in substantial financial damages for BA. In that case, those responsible would have committed a criminal offence.

At this stage, however, if BA had formally reported the broken leg, they would have exposed themselves to censure. The UK regulations state that the report must be submitted as soon as possible after the incident, as well as by the fastest means available, and the airline would have had some explaining to do. Since the evidence had been clear that no formal note of the serious injury had been submitted to the AAIB, it can be alleged that BA had deliberately continued to withhold the broken leg from the AAIB in the hope that it would pass and that they would get away with what could be alleged to have been a criminal act.

The AAIB were in the same position, as they now had knowledge of the broken leg from the copy of BA's report that they had just received and, as anyone knowing of a serious incident or accident was legally obliged to report it, it did not matter who or by what means the AAIB had received the information. The AAIB, therefore, also had a legal responsibility to update the serious incident to an accident and to relay the details of their actions to the Department of the Environment, Transport and the Regions (DETR) and the Civil Aviation Authority (CAA) in the UK, to the International Civil Aviation Organisation (ICAO) in Montreal and to Sudan's Air Accident Investigation Central Directorate (AAICD) in Khartoum.

Once again, unfortunately, another perplexing drama had fallen on the shoulders of the Head of the AAIB, Mr Ken Smart, for he had to face another dilemma. How would he react? The facts are that, had he acted on the information of the broken leg by updating the 'serious incident' to 'accident' and had reported it to all concerned, it would have been considered he had done the right thing, but in doing so he would have jeopardised BA, who could have faced being charged with a criminal offence for not reporting it earlier. And, as he had only just been made aware of the broken leg, he would not yet have done anything wrong himself. With the aircraft upset being classed as an accident, however, this would be treated as a new case and, once again, Sudan would be in pole position for jurisdiction of the investigation to be conferred upon them. Article 26 of the Chicago Convention states quite categorically that 'the State in which the 'accident' occurs will institute an inquiry'. No choice in the matter! Annex 13 of the Chicago Convention, however, was also relevant, as it states that 'the State of Occurrence [Sudan] may delegate investigation to another State [in this case there only was the UK as the State of Registration] by mutual arrangement and consent.' If the AAIB had informed ICAO of the updated status of an accident, they would have alerted Sudan's AAICD, but, as Sudan had previously declined to investigate the serious incident, they would almost certainly have asked the AAIB to accept jurisdiction in their place to investigate the accident. It really was a UK show, and the AAIB was in a much better position to investigate than Sudan. As the AAIB had also already declined to investigate the serious incident, however, it would have been likely they would have, since they were second in line, refused to investigate the accident and would have insisted that Sudan investigate. The AAIB would still be in a situation where they could, as was their right, appoint a representative to observe and assist Sudan's investigation, but it was likely they would also have declined to do that.

Once again, however, it wasn't that simple, as ICAO regulations were not going to let a state that was in a position to help, not to do so. At Clause 5.22 of the Chicago Convention, it states that, 'When a State conducting an investigation of an accident requests participation of the State of Registry, that State shall appoint an accredited representative.' No chance then of the UK as the State of Registry being left to decide on appointing someone of their own volition as Sudan could insist that they did. At Clause 5.14 it also states that, 'On request, any State shall provide all the relevant information available to the investigating State', and, at Clause 5.1, the overriding statement is that: 'In any event the State of Occurrence shall use every means to facilitate the investigation.'

So, even if the intention of the AAIB was to refrain from getting involved, Sudan could have changed that, and the AAIB could have found themselves heavily entangled in the investigation. If Mr Smart was to respond to the broken leg, therefore, no matter what he did he would have been drawn into investigating the accident and the AAIB might even have ended up doing most of the work. Since Mr Smart's original intention in declining to investigate the serious incident was alleged to be to avoid BA facing substantial compensation payments, his only option, if he was to continue protecting BA from the same risk, was not to get involved in investigating the accident. All he had to do then was what he had done before, and that was to do nothing and ignore the broken leg. Since the evidence had been clear that nothing did happen, it can be alleged that the AAIB and BA once more deliberately colluded, this time by their silence, to protect BA from financial damage by preventing an accident investigation being conducted. It can also be alleged that BA and the AAIB hoped that this would pass and that they would get away with, not only what could have been alleged to have been a disreputable act and a criminal offence, but with what could have been alleged to have been, for the AAIB, a monumental breach of ICAO protocol and trust, and a scandal of international proportions. States just cannot go around the world having accidents in other nation states and not reporting them and not investigating them, especially a leading aviation state like the UK that should have been setting an example.

Chapter 23

Release of the BA Report Imminent

During the first week of June the BA report had been delivered to only selected groups and at the same time, by coincidence, Mukonyi had been making his way back to France on Emirates Airline, flying via Dubai to Paris Charles de Gaulle then on to Lyon where he had planned to resume his studies. It was now a month since preliminary questions had been asked in Whitehall about Mukonyi's circumstances and his journey to Lyon seemed to have been the catalyst for the UK Government to consider whether he should be arrested if he ever entered this country. BA had also been quoted as saying they were strongly in favour of prosecuting Mukonyi if he returned to the UK so the young man had now placed himself at risk by leaving Kenya.

As the UK was the State of Registration it had the right, like Kenya, the State of Landing, to claim jurisdiction under the Tokyo Convention. As the Kenyan state had already concluded their claim for jurisdiction without legal action and had released Mukonyi without charge, the UK was in the position to also claim jurisdiction under the Tokyo Convention in their own right, if required, to investigate the same offence. UK law also extended to on board British registered aircraft wherever they might be so, if Mukonyi did enter the country, the UK had the right to arrest him and to try and prosecute him through the British courts.

It was unlikely to have been a coincidence, therefore, that at the precise moment of Mukonyi's return to France, the Gatwick Airport police, having also shown a renewed interest in the affair, had contacted Captain Hagan for a statement about the incident. The phone call had been from a Detective Sergeant Mick Jones stationed at Gatwick and he suggested he could fly to Scotland to interview him, the next day if possible, so clearly something about the event was urgent. It had been almost six months since the BA2069 upset and the captain had been more than a little surprised at this sudden rise in interest. At the interview, DS Jones gave no reason for his visit and, as Bill was totally unaware of Mukonyi's whereabouts, he did not associate it with a possible apprehension. Other documentation also showed that, around that time, the Gatwick police had been in contact with the CAA and with BA, and that an approach had been made to the Crown Prosecution Service. A few days after giving his statement, Bill received a letter of acknowledgement which mentioned the possibility of Mukonyi being prosecuted by the Sussex Police if he did turn up in the UK, and it appeared that, at least briefly, the UK had been considering apprehending the young Kenyan. There was one group that would have been delighted to see the attacker brought to trial and that was all those on board the BA2069, for the evidence appeared to support their long held, strong feelings that Mukonyi had got away with trying to kill them all. The simple fact, however, was that Mukonyi was in France, not the UK, and BA might now have kicked themselves for refusing to carry him on his return, for Mukonyi could have been arrested and charged when transiting Gatwick. In the end the UK Government, not surprisingly, decided to abandon any thought of going down that route and it was never raised again. This may also have been the best outcome for BA as an attempted prosecution of Mukonyi would have made public a great deal of information, not all of which would have been of benefit to the airline, and some of which might have assisted those intent on litigation.

With BA's report now distributed to the selected few, Flight Operations also tried to have the full BA report released to all pilots, but BA had refused and they had lost that battle. The latest news was that Flight Ops had also lost the battle over the position of the flight crew rest seat, and it appeared that the Safety Group's policy on locking cockpit doors in flight had also been ignored. BA's behaviour withholding the report was also making pilots in general suspicious of the company for they suspected that the restriction was a deliberate cover-up. And, in some ways they were right, for BA's own report was unlikely to be too critical. The last thing the company wanted to do was to provide prospective litigants with the ammunition they would need to press their claims.

Previously, in May, however, the Department of Environment, Transport and the Regions (DETR) had appeared to have been uncomfortable about the circumstances of BA's efforts and had instructed the Civil Aviation Authority (CAA) to conduct their own review of the incident with the airline's report in mind. With BA's report now completed and delivered to the CAA, however, BA decided that, owing to growing threats of litigation, they would not release their own report for public viewing. This was a huge blow to BA's fed up passengers, who were now angry and upset at being let down again. BA was supposed to be investigating the accident along the lines of ICAO's Chicago Convention, but now they were using their status as a private company to withhold their report. The Freedom of Information Act only applied to public authorities, so there was nothing anyone could do to compel BA to release it. Also, with only very few being aware of the significance of the broken leg, the action of BA and the AAIB in allegedly deliberately covering it up now seemed to be paying off and their alleged behaviour was now likely to remain undetected.

The CAA, with the BA report completed, could now begin to conduct their own analysis and investigation by their Flight Operations Department (FOD) and, on the publication of the CAA review, the broken leg would all come out in the end anyway, or so one might have thought. The CAA's FOD and BA's Safety Services then began a serious of meetings, through June to August, with a final meeting for 13 September, to confer and discuss matters relating to BA2069's aircraft upset as well as BA's actions and recommendations. BA's Safety Services would, of course, have known about the broken leg, as would have the CAA FOD, but, although the former would have known of its significance it is almost certain that the latter did not, and, allegedly, Safety Services must have been very wary of raising the matter at meetings in case it attracted attention. These sessions with the CAA FOD must have been interesting!

All airlines in the UK are obliged to promulgate their flight deck security procedures in their Operations Manuals, which form part of their Air Operators Certificate (AOC) assigned by the CAA, and without which they cannot fly. The CAA Flight Operations Department (FOD), having initiated their review of flight deck security procedures in February, had also begun contacting airlines as part of their oversight responsibility. In order to formulate its strategy and recommendations, the CAA FOD involved all UK airlines, including BA, and, additionally, agreed to meet with representatives of the BA2069 Passenger Action Group (PAG) on 4 July. The UK had been stuck now for over six months in the situation where there had been no accident investigation. Kim Parker's broken leg had been mentioned in the BA report but it appeared that no one had been sufficiently interested in broaching the subject. BA Safety Services were responsible for reporting it to the Air Accident Investigation Branch (AAIB) and, with CAA/ BA meetings scheduled to continue throughout July and August, the last thing Safety Services would have wanted would have been a discussion about the broken leg.

In June 2001, the government decided to shuffle departments, and Environment was moved to another department and the

Department of the Environment, Transport and the Regions (DETR) became the Department for Transport, Local Government and the Regions (DTLR).

On 4 July, the CAA Flight Operations Department (FOD) met Passenger Action Group (PAG) representatives to discuss the present situation but as they had only received the BA report a few weeks previously and had just commenced their own review, there was little to bring them up to date on that matter. They were able to assure them, however, that they had already begun a full review of flight deck security procedures. The CAA FOD found the passenger representatives to be well informed but very critical of BA and this gave cause for concern.

In the meantime, on 11 July 2001, BA had posted a synopsis of the BA report to all passengers, this time including Captain Hagan's wife. The accompanying letter stated that it was only a brief outline of events and, perhaps as an explanation for its almost complete lack of information, ventured that the 100+ passengers who had attended the customer forums had already been made fully aware of the background to the incident. In support, however, it also included a summary of the questions most frequently asked at the forums. It then referred to the CAA review of BA's security recommendations but, owing to the details being confidential, they could not be included. The letter also stressed that there had been no investigation of the incident, either by the CAA or the Air Accident Investigation Branch (AAIB), but that the CAA had approached airlines as early as February concerning flight deck security and, with the release of the BA report, had then taken a more active interest.

BA's final report had consisted of twenty A4 pages of text and fifty pages of appendices, but the synopsis in the letter had been abbreviated to just two. The first page was entirely devoted to technical details of the two flights, i.e. from Lyon to Gatwick and Gatwick to Nairobi, and consisted only of irrelevant facts such as aircraft registrations, departure and arrival times, numbers of passengers on board, etc. The second page contained only the most basic details of the upset and struggled to fill the A4 paper. A further two and a half pages then followed with questions but with minimal answers. As an example, one good question asked was, 'What actually happened to the aircraft during the incident?' and was answered by, 'During the struggle with the controls the aircraft banked to the right and pitched up. The aircraft then entered into a steep turn to the left during which it descended and dropped altitude. The handling pilot recovered the aircraft fully and completed all the safety checks before continuing.' Finally, in a half page summary, it mentioned that procedures were being implemented in response to the incident but, for security reasons, these could not be revealed. Many angry and dismayed recipients of this skeletal report posted comments on the Passenger Action Group's (PAG) website stating that, having waited several months for information, they were extremely scathing and highly critical of being fobbed off by what they considered to be a totally unsatisfactory and inadequate response. Needless to say, Captain Hagan was also completely dissatisfied with BA's letter and synopsis.

After Stewardess Kimberley Parker's surgery earlier in the year she had been offered counselling at BA's expense, but that proved not to be successful as the counsellor was afraid of flying! BA then eventually provided limited sessions of treatment with a clinical psychologist and she was able to help Kim. In August 2001, however, Stewardess Parker was having trouble with her right leg and had to undergo further surgery. Her body had been rejecting the pins which were protruding from the injury and surgery site on her right ankle and the pins and a plate had to be removed and the damage reset. Neuromas in her right foot were also causing pain and had to be removed and that resulted in permanent nerve damage and the loss of feeling in three toes.

Discussions between the Civil Aviation Authority Flight Operations Department (CAA FOD) and BA's Safety Services regarding the CAA had continued throughout the summer months, with a planned final meeting on 13 September 2001, and it was hoped by then that the CAA analysis and investigation would be completed.

In the first week in September 2001, news was spreading that the CAA review was nearing completion. Since February, the CAA Flight Operations Department (FOD) had been liaising with the major airlines, but especially with BA, about the policy of flight deck security, including the pros and cons of locking cockpit doors. BA's report had recorded its own recommendations, which also included a review of in-flight security, but which mostly concerned preventing a reoccurrence by enhancing the handling and supervision of suspect passengers and by improving communications in these circumstances.

In spite of the fact that the release of the CAA review was still imminent, CAA recommendations had already been disseminated to individual airlines allowing each company to implement them in their own way. The BA2069 aircraft upset had galvanised minds worldwide towards the enhanced security of locking cockpit doors in flight and BA chose to change their standard procedures to permit captains to do so if they considered it appropriate. Captain Hagan thought this a bonus, for with the door secured in the cruise he now felt much more comfortable during the periods of low activity in the cabin that he had previously regarded as being vulnerable for flight crew.

On 9 September, Captain Hagan received a call from the BA Press Office informing him that he had been invited to an annual awards evening to be held in Glasgow on Saturday, 15 September. The event was for the 'Great Scots Awards' which was sponsored by the *Scottish Sunday Mail* and was acknowledged as being the county's biggest annual awards ceremony. Since Bill was from Northern Ireland, he had been nominated to receive an 'Honorary Great Scot' award which was occasionally awarded to resident non-Scots. A further invitation he received directly was to be nominated as one of the 'People of the Year' at a royal charity reception organised by The Royal Association for the Disabled and Rehabilitation (RADAR) to be held on 1 November at the Savoy Hotel in London and he had received BA's approval to attend. Up until now the awards he had received had been the Association of Retired and Persons over 50 (ARP050) Award, the British Airways' Award for Excellence (to all three pilots), the International Federation of Air Line Pilots Association (IFALPA) Polaris Award (also to all three pilots) and, more recently, the Queen's University of Belfast (QUB) Award. He was, of course, delighted to be further honoured, but he was also aware that BA's Press Office were more than a little concerned that if there was a press conference he may inadvertently let something slip that could be damaging to BA.

On 10 September, the next day, he had a late evening departure for a five-day trip to Bangkok and back, so he would fly down to Heathrow that day for the overnight flight and would be back in Glasgow on the morning of the fifth day, 14 September, in time for the event on the evening of Saturday 15th. Little did Captain Hagan realise that on his arrival in Bangkok on Tuesday, 11 September 2001 the world would change forever.

Chapter 24

The CAA Review Delayed Indefinitely

After an overnight flight of eleven and a half hours from Heathrow, Captain Hagan touched the 747-400 down smoothly on Runway 03 Left at Bangkok International Airport (Don Mueang) at 1500 local time, 0900 UK summer time, on Tuesday, 11 September 2001. The journey had been uneventful but, for other pilots and passengers on four US domestic flights, it would shortly be aviation's darkest day. In New York the local summer time was 0400, eleven hours behind Bangkok, and in a few hours the residents of that great city, and the entire planet, would be experiencing a day that would remain in peoples' memories for the rest of their lives. A terrible tragedy, totally unprecedented in world aviation history, was about to unfold.

Bill had managed to snatch a few hours' sleep on the flight from London so, after a shower, he went out for an early evening meal. An hour or so later, when about to return to the hotel, he first heard news of the attack on the Twin Towers of the New York World Trade Centre from someone talking about it loudly in English on a mobile phone. Unable to believe what he was hearing, he took a taxi to the hotel, on arrival went straight to his room to catch the news on TV and, when switching on at about 8pm local time, saw to his horror the second tower being hit. Shocked by what he was witnessing, he recalled Mukonyi trying to crash his aircraft with all on board and a cold chill ran up his spine as it dawned on him that those committing these heinous crimes in New York might very well have nurtured their plan on what they had learned from the

Nairobi Incident. About an hour after the second hit, the horror he was watching then unbelievably turned for the worse when to his astonishment the South Tower collapsed, followed about 30 minutes later by the North Tower also crashing to the ground.

Bill was aware that parallels would be drawn between the Nairobi Incident and the Twin Towers disaster, and it wasn't long until his phone began ringing with the press asking for his opinion on the atrocity. The reporters were asking him to comment on any comparison between the Twin Towers assault and the Nairobi Incident attack, but he, of course, declined to say anything beyond mentioning his shock and expressing his sympathies. In the afternoon of the next day in Bangkok, 12 September, a large envelope from BA containing a fax was pushed under his door which he assumed would be relative to the attacks the day before, and it was, but not what he expected. The fax read, 'A Corporate decision has been made that you should not attend the award ceremony on Saturday' (15 September)!

Captain Hagan arrived back at Heathrow on the morning of the 14th and, before signing off to catch his flight to Glasgow, he took a moment to check the latest flight crew notices. In light of the recent circumstances, he was not surprised to read that the pilot's rest seat for the longer flights had been relocated back to adjacent the flight deck door. Although he had been pushing hard for this, it had taken a terrible disaster to achieve the move and it gave him no pleasure.

In the meantime, on the day before, 13 September 2001, the supposed final meeting before completion of the CAA review between the Civil Aviation Authority Flight Operations Department (CAA FOD) and BA's Safety Services, would certainly not be the last as the only topic for discussion had been 9/11. This would now involve a massive rethink of flight deck security and the CAA review would not be published any time soon.

A week after the Twin Towers attacks, the Civil Aviation Authority (CAA) decided that the twelve recommendations that had been discussed in detail with the airlines and that had previously been disseminated should now be upgraded to requirements. The first six related to access to the flight deck with the instruction to lock the cockpit door in flight except for essential access, while the other six dealt primarily with certain groups of passengers, general surveillance, communications and the use of crew rest facilities. Flight deck doors had also to be of reinforced construction but it was acknowledged that these modifications would take time to implement. It was also mentioned that the notified requirements 'may be modified in the light of further information or circumstances, or in conjunction with other agencies'. At the time the media had also reported that other security issues had been discussed for possible implementation in future months, such as the placing of sky marshals on board flights.

On 19 September, just over a week after 9/11, a note from the CAA that had been forwarded to unknown departments stated, 'For the record, the CAA has not yet completed its report on the Nairobi Incident and you should avoid giving anyone the impression that they have. That is because there is a threatened court action against BA and pressure from various people for copies of said report. However, the report will, in first instance, be sent to DTLR [the renamed Department for Transport, Local Government and the Regions] and we will then consider implications, etc, before deciding to make it available to others.' The CAA review would now have to be updated in the light of the Twin Towers disaster and, as it would address serious security issues, it would not be released to the public, but here was a clear indication of concern about the financial implications for BA and a consideration that, to protect the national airline, the CAA review might also be withheld on that account.

The tragic events of September 11th (9/11 as it became known in the US and beyond) had a dramatic and traumatic effect on the financial viability of airlines as passengers evaporated and it was an uncertain time for aircrew worldwide. In an effort to minimise costs, almost overnight airlines began to shrink their fleets by grounding aircraft and by furloughing staff. In the UK, Virgin Atlantic laid off many pilots and BA stopped the intake of new pilots who had been previously planned to replace the large number of pilots approaching the then BA retiral age of 55. Some UK airlines, like British Midland, were close to collapse and facing uncertain futures but BA, fortunately for its staff, was better placed. The company had previously introduced cutbacks a year earlier in anticipation of a turndown in business travel, although, of course, not of this magnitude, but it did help, and there was also some comfort from opinions circulating in the City that BA had been considered 'too big to fail'. In this now perilous financial environment, the last thing BA needed was a damaging accident investigation report that could result in them having to pay out large compensation sums to passengers, and it can be alleged that this was likely to harden the resolve of BA and the AAIB to keep the broken leg under wraps.

In early October, Bill was pleased to receive the news that all three flight crew were to receive the Hugh Gordon-Burge Memorial Award and doubly pleased for Phil for he still felt that the co-pilot, who he considered was undoubtedly the real hero as he had saved the day, was not receiving the recognition he deserved. The honour was presented for the flight crew's contribution to air safety at the Guildhall in London by the Guild of Air Pilots and Air Navigators (GAPAN), and BA Flight Operations had provided a very complimentary citation that was read out prior to them being presented with their awards.

Earlier in September, Captain Hagan had accepted an invitation to be nominated as one of the 'People of the Year' at a royal charity reception which had been organised by The Royal Association for the Disabled and Rehabilitation (RADAR) at the Savoy Hotel in London on 1 November.

On the evening at the Savoy, the event began with a champagne reception and Lady Annabel Goldsmith, as was now her practice, had also attended the ceremony in support of Captain Hagan. Press photographers were on hand to take shots of them together and, with a press conference following, Bill was aware he could be asked some tricky questions. Regards 9/11, he successfully dodged mentioning any connections with the Nairobi Incident by saying that there were probably more differences between the events than similarities and concluded by saying that he was very supportive of improvements in flight deck security. That seemed to have had the desired effect with BA's Press Office.

In November 2001, the BA2069 flight crew were informed that they had all been awarded the British Airline Pilots Association (BALPA) gold medal for airmanship and the three felt it a special honour to receive the award in the presence of other pilots who were all closely associated with the aviation industry.

November was also the time of year with BA's Bidline system when pilots bidding for lines of work over the Christmas period on a seniority basis would take particular care of their choice in the hope of being home for the festivities, but the BA2069 flight crew were delighted to be excused the drama. The Chief Pilot of the Boeing 747-400 fleet, Captain John Leahy, aware that the first anniversary of the upset would have a significance personal impact on the three pilots, kindly arranged an extra week of leave for all of them at the end of December, a gesture which they all very much appreciated.

In the meantime, the Passenger Action Group (PAG) website had been very vocal in its comments ever since the September 11th terrorist actions and this continued well into the winter months. Once again there were many complaints about the treatment of the passengers and lack of corrective action from BA. Correspondence from BA Customer Services continued to show that complainants reacted positively to BA's attempt to engage retrospectively and passengers were assured that the airline had learnt many lessons on how to deal with such an occurrence if anything similar happened again.

Now at the beginning of December 2001, the CAA review, having been almost completed back in September, was still not ready as the limited numbers of staff available had been overwhelmed by the 9/11 disaster and the additional demands of updating security protocol.

The CAA had also been concerned about passenger attitudes so a further meeting was arranged with a representative of the Passenger Action Group (PAG) and questions had been answered as best they could. The meeting, however, had also raised concerns about what appeared to be small contradictions and minor errors in the BA report, and the CAA had decided that these needed to be addressed. Matters raised related to what had actually happened on the flight and so the CAA decided to do the sensible thing, which was to talk to the crew, something that should have been done right from the very beginning by the Threats Office before DM's ill-informed risk assessment at the end of December 2000 had been released. Interviewing crew members would delay the report further, of course, and would be frustrating for all concerned, but it was only right that due process should be observed.

Organising the crew interviews took some time and Captain Hagan's appointment was scheduled for mid-December with the last crew member to be interviewed in early January 2002. On the day, Captain Mike Vivian, Deputy Head of CAA Flight Operations Department (FOD), who had spoken with Bill on the phone at the end of May about the Passenger Action Group's website, was to conduct the interview and he was accompanied by Mr N. J. Butcher, Head of Cabin Service Operations (CSO), and, on this occasion, by a British Air Line Pilots Association (BALPA) solicitor, Tony Hows. Although the interview had been designated as a non-jeopardy encounter, BALPA had requested that their representative attend. It was explained that the CAA regarded the Air Operators Certificate (AOC), without which airlines cannot function, as falling under their normal oversight and they were looking at the aircraft upset and BA in general, not at individuals. They wanted to establish exactly what had happened prior to and during the incident, and what were the subsequent BA actions, mentioning that the CAA had been in contact with both the Gatwick police and the Passenger Action Group. It was also stated that the passengers were very angry at how BA had treated them, but the CAA FOD wanted to resolve some inconsistencies.

One of their important areas of interest concerned Mukonyi's movements during the 40 minutes prior to the flight deck intrusion and, as a matter of concern, BA's procedures for monitoring passenger cabins in flight. For Bill's own part, the CAA wanted to verify the level of communications between the cabin and the flight deck and requested confirmation that he had been unaware of the developing situation between departure time and the moment of the intrusion. Finally, Captain Vivian spoke to Bill for a little while about the extent of the aircraft upset, saying that in many ways he was fortunate as a pilot to have witnessed such loss of control and to still be able to tell the tale. Overall, Captain Hagan found the interview very relaxed, and he felt he had been given every opportunity to say exactly what he thought about the incident and how BA had handled it.

In the last week of December 2001, the three BA2069 flight crew enjoyed their extra days off over the festive season, and Bill's first trip in the new year was to Nairobi on 5 January 2002, this time from Heathrow with the new flight number of BA65. It would be the first time he had traced his steps on the same route since the incident. On 5 January on BA65's overnight journey to Nairobi, the captain had elected to take the middle rest period so he would be awake in the region prior to El Obeid. It turned out that the position and timing of BA65 were almost exactly the same as BA2069's had been and the sun also began to rise on cue. Fortunately, the trip proved to be completely uneventful and, having revisited the area of the aircraft upset, Bill was content to have coped without undue concern and he felt more settled with the experience.

On Captain Hagan's return to London, the news was that the Civil Aviation Authority's (CAA) review was soon to be completed. A rocky ride and many delays had resulted in it spilling into 2002 and, a week or so into January 2002, the CAA review was finally ready. The full report, however, not only included exerts from BA's Safety Services investigation of the incident but also, in response to 9/11, recommendations and requirements relating to safety and security issues. As these details were of a sensitive nature, the Department for Transport, Local Government and the Regions (DTLR), not surprisingly, considered it not in the public interest to publish the review in its entirety. The full report, therefore, was retained by the department and was not to be published, this time with good reason, but much to the disappointment and further annoyance of the long suffering passengers. Just before 9/11, however, the CAA, in response to mounting pressure from BA2069 passengers, had compiled, but not completed, an abridged review of BA's report, and they now decided to update and modify that report to produce an abridged CAA review for publication.

The Department for Transport, Local Government and the Regions (DTLR) had been responsible for ordering and withholding the full CAA review so, at the end of the third week in January 2002, when the abridged CAA review was completed, it was also duly delivered to the DTLR. The CAA had been able to quickly produce an abridged review as much of the preparation had been done earlier and it had been compiled for publication with the passengers in mind, but the DTLR would have the final say in whether or not the abridged CAA review would now be released for public viewing. In the meantime, however, the abridged CAA review was made available for viewing to the selected groups involved, including the AAIB.

On 23 January 2002, therefore, the three flight crew, Bill, Phil and Richard, were privileged to be invited to the CAA's library at their Head Office at Gatwick Airport for a private reading of the abridged CAA review. The pilots' first response on viewing the CAA's abbreviated version, unfortunately, was one of disappointment. Rather than it having been a report based on the CAA's own investigations, the document contained only the watered down account of BA's final report which had omitted all references to excessive stalling of the aircraft and to the danger to which the flight had been exposed. The feeling was that, with respect to BA's reasons for constraint, the review had not done the passengers justice and they had deserved more.

Chapter 25

The Abridged CAA Review

The distribution of the abridged CAA review, for the time being, had, like BA's report, been restricted to only those privileged few in the inner circle, and the reader should, once again, view this detail as if being part of a selected group. Others would have to wait for the department's decision. The abridged review also contained numerous extracts from the BA report which had previously been briefly mentioned, so only the salient points relevant to the abridged CAA review have been included.

The abridged CAA review was a compilation of information and reports from different sources including BA and their Safety Services, the CAA's Safety Regulation Group (SRG) and their own Flight Operations Department (FOD), the Air Accident Investigation Branch (AAIB), divisions within the Department for Transport, Local Government and the Regions (DTLR) and, also, from the CAA's own enquiries. Approximately the first half of the review consisted of details of the BA2069 event which had mostly been lifted from BA's report and the second half detailed BA's conclusions, safety recommendations and actions and the CAA's conclusions, recommendations and requirements.

The report began with the DTLR appearing not to have been content with the reasons that Mr Smart, the Head of the AAIB, had provided for not getting involved in investigating the 'serious incident'. He had stated that the AAIB had been 'unable to appoint a representative', but the DETR had considered that it was 'due to the lack of jurisdiction'. Neither mentioned the Tokyo Convention and both reasons appeared to have been invalid.

In regard to the injuries, after the Air Accident Investigation Branch (AAIB) had been informed of the incident on 29 December 2000, they had notified the Civil Aviation Authority (CAA) that 'there had been two minor injuries to the aircraft crew', but 'it had subsequently transpired that this was incorrect in that one cabin crew member sustained a serious injury to a lower limb, as stated in the British Airways Report'. This was somewhat euphemistic, however, for although medically the injury had been considered serious the critical detail of the broken bone had been omitted.

It also mentioned that, on the day of the incident, 'BA orally advised the CAA's Safety Data Unit and raised a Mandatory Occurrence Report (MOR) that was sent to the CAA.' It then added, significantly, that, 'Additionally, BA immediately instigated an investigation into the event.' As BA's MOR would have been faxed only a short while after the airline informed the CAA's Safety Data Unit, BA's announcement that it would investigate the event must also been made just after that, also at a very early stage. The AAIB's decision to decline had not been taken until after Mr Smart had, in error, called the Kenyan Directorate of Civil Aviation (DCA), so the chronology provided by the abridged CAA review seemed to indicate that all these important communications had occurred in the very early morning, shortly after the incident, but before BA had announced it would conduct its own investigation. Unfortunately, with all the AAIB records of communication traffic having been destroyed, it was only possible to deduce what exchanges of contact had been made, and with whom, from the information available. From these contact details, however, beginning with Captain Hagan's radio call to Khartoum and ending with BA's declaration to investigate the incident, it can be deduced that the time span could only have been about 25 minutes, and in that short period the stage had been set for the performance to begin.

The abridged CAA review provided a very brief summary of the incident and continued with the progress of events from Mukonyi's behaviour in the terminal at Lyon Airport all the way to his admission to the hospital in Nairobi under police escort. This detail, plus extensive additional information, has been provided in Part 1 of this book.

Later in the abridged review, under the heading, 'Events immediately after the incident', was repeated the astonishing revelation of the injuries sustained during the incident that had been extracted from BA's withheld report, the most striking being 'One cabin crew sustained a broken leg and was hospitalised.' This statement had been considered by the CAA to be suitable for a review that was intended to be released to the public, and it did appear to indicate that the CAA was unaware of its influence. It can be alleged that BA's Safety Services would most certainly have been aware of the risk of mentioning the broken leg, but also aware that insisting the CAA remove it could have increased the risk of giving the show away. It appeared, therefore, that the airline allegedly thought it safer to do as they had done before and that was just to do nothing. Significantly, although the broken leg had been openly acknowledged amongst the few in these reports, there had been no mention anywhere of BA complying with their legal duty to update the AAIB with this information.

It had also been acknowledged in the abridged CAA review that, throughout the BA2069 event, communications had not been at their best. Apart from the BA2357 flight from Lyon to Gatwick, exchanges of information could have been better at Lyon Airport, at Gatwick Airport – with BA, Aviation Defence International (BA's agent), and the Gatwick police – and, during the flight, with the poor monitoring of Mukonyi's behaviour and movements, as well as Kim's serious injury being incorrectly reported as minor.

The review also quoted the company's conclusions from BA's report that, 'If all the information available at the time of boarding the Nairobi flight had been collated by British Airways at a central location, it is more likely that Mr. Mukonyi would have been denied boarding and a more informed assessment would have been made of his mental state.' There were others involved at Gatwick, of course, the security company, Aviation Defence International, their agent and the Gatwick Police, so this was not just down to BA, but the airline could be the one left to pay the price.

A further BA conclusion noted that, 'The best way to prevent disruptive and dangerous passengers causing problems on a flight is to prevent them boarding the aircraft. In this specific event, the assumption that Mr. Mukonyi was a deportee or a nervous flyer breached the existing defences and procedures. The current culture seems to be that the 'default' is for the ticket holder to travel unless reasons are found to deny them carriage. The culture should be that if there is any doubt about a passenger's suitability to travel, reasons should be established for why they should be allowed to board the aircraft, and not the converse.'

The report continued by noting that, 'The procedure should be that ground staff can identify potentially disruptive passengers for additional checks during any point of the boarding process. The captain must be briefed if a passenger has been subject to such checks and subsequently deemed suitable to board. This does not affect the captain's authority in denying carriage.' Assurances were given by the CAA's Flight Operations Department (FOD) that these matters had been dealt with by British Airways.

The full CAA review had been close to completion by September 2001 when events were overtaken by the 9/11 terrorist attacks. As a direct result of the Nairobi Incident, a wide range of safety recommendations to airline operators in the UK in regard to in-flight security that the CAA's Flight Operations Department (FOD) was about to issue were, following extensive consideration, upgraded to requirements and were issued to UK Air Operations Certificate (AOC) holders on 18 September. These requirements were based on months of reviewing the circumstances surrounding the Nairobi Incident as well as the ongoing work conducted by the CAA's FOD in conjunction with the Department for Transport, Local Government and the Regions (DTLR) in respect of disruptive passengers.

The abridged review then supplemented and commented on the information in the BA report where required, or where there was ambiguity. An attempt had been made to ascertain why information about Mukonyi's behaviour during the flight had not been reported to the Cabin Services Director (CSD), or to the captain, and these were partially resolved by interviewing staff members and air crew. More information was also gleaned from interviews with the cabin crew covering Mukonyi's whereabouts immediately before the attack. It then ascertained that eight was the number of cabin crew that BA had stated were taking rest just before the upset. A brief discussion then followed about the number of cabin crew permitted to be on rest at any particular time combined with the need for regular monitoring of the cabin. There was also a considerable number of comments about information exchange prior to boarding. The CAA's Flight Operation Department (FOD) agreed with BA that the captain, who is not best placed to make a decision, should not be responsible for denial of carriage but should still retain the right to refuse carriage. That was followed by an analysis of additional factors that had been itemised by BA and then by conclusions and recommendations from both BA and the CAA.

The abridged CAA review then finished with twelve flight security requirements, with the first six of these being directed to flight deck security, while others referred to monitoring of passengers and information exchange between ground staff and aircraft operating crew. It was also stipulated that all airline operators should review their crew rest procedures including specific cabin crew surveillance duties and their locations in the cabin at all phases of flight.

As the abridged CAA review had been compiled with the public in mind, there was some hope that it would soon be released for everyone to view, but suspicions of a cover up were still circulating. A few selected groups did have access to BA's report but, in 2002, that was still restricted and they were not at liberty to divulge details. Any open discussion, therefore, would have to wait until the abridged CAA review was released to the public.

In the meantime, during the early months of 2002, the Department for Transport, Local Government and the Regions (DTLR) had to consider if the newly prepared abridged CAA report was suitable for public release. The CAA and the DTLR were aware, of course, that in addition to the physical injury claim by Stewardess Kimberley Parker, passenger groups were also currently pursuing legal action against BA on both sides of the Atlantic, so the DTLR were wary of going public with the review. On the other hand, the CAA had produced the abridged review to be published for general release to the passengers and the public and, having written it with that in mind, it could be made available to all.

The injury Kim Parker had sustained on the BA2069 aircraft upset had been very serious and, on return to the UK, she had initially been medically certified as unfit for work for ten months, but that had to be extended for more hospital treatments. Finally, in 2002, Stewardess Parker had been declared fit to return to work but, in regard to her claim for injuries, she had been obliged by BA's solicitors to undergo several medical and psychiatric examinations in order to assess her condition. At an early stage she had been medically diagnosed as suffering from Post Traumatic Stress Disorder (PTSD) and, in January 2002, she had been examined by a psychiatrist, Dr Paul Mallet, who had been provided with all her medical records. As a result of her litigation and consultations, Kim Parker's claim against BA for her broken leg had attracted the attention of the press and information of her serious injury had begun to spread further afield into the public domain. It was also obvious that some in BA had known of her broken leg, cabin crew managers for one, and details of the broken leg may also have seeped from within to beyond the airline. Of those who had knowledge of the broken leg, whether those of the selected few who had received a copy of BA's report, or those others within BA, or the passengers and the public without who had learned from the press of Kim's claim, only a handful of specialists would have been aware of its significance. As Kim began her struggle with BA for compensation, therefore, for almost all there was never any consideration that there might be more to her broken leg than a serious injury. There were still many on the outside, however, who were eager for more information and they waited in anticipation of the abridged CAA review being published.

In the UK, BA had offered compensation of £2,000 per passenger plus one free return trip to anywhere in the world and many had settled on that account. A group of about seventy UK passengers, however, were still holding out for more and they were determined to press their case on the grounds of psychological trauma and Post Traumatic Stress Disorder (PTSD). For a successful outcome the litigants in the UK needed evidence to press their claim, and it was hoped that some information supporting their cause might be available in the abridged CAA review when it was released for the public scrutiny.

In the United States, in a legal system somewhat different to the UK, a group of sixteen passengers in an ongoing class action lawsuit, Osborne v British Airways Plc Corporation, in Houston, Texas, had claimed for bodily and psychological injury, in spite of the fact that only four of them had been admitted to hospital in Nairobi for minor injuries. Their lawyers had attempted to engage Bynum and Shaw knowing that their evidence would underline the seriousness of the incident and would strengthen their case, but they refused to join any litigation, firmly believing that God had been instrumental in saving the aircraft. The two Osborne plaintiffs representing the group in Houston were also missionaries but they apparently were less convinced of divine intervention.

In London, the Department for Transport, Local Government and the Regions (DTLR), having carefully considered whether or not the abridged CAA review was suitable for publication, eventually concluded that, as it contained some sensitive details in regard to litigation, it was still a risk and it would not be made available for public viewing. If published and released to the public, they considered, BA could face a substantial legal challenge. If that was the only drawback, however, it seemed that if they had redacted some of the salient text it could have been released. BA, after all, was a private company, having been privatised way back in 1987, and it operated independently from the government. If a government department withholds a sensitive document on the grounds that 'it is not in the public interest' to release it, that, of course, is understandable. In this particular case, however, the DTLR appeared to have withheld the abridged CAA review on the grounds that 'it was not in BA's interest' when it was most certainly 'in the public interest' to release it, for the public wanted to know what had been going on. The DTLR's action not to release it was, therefore, at least debatable. It was also somewhat ironic, however, that in supporting BA, both the DTLR and the CAA had been unwittingly aiding and abetting alleged criminal offences. In the end, strangely, the DTLR did decide to publish the abridged CAA review, but with publication limited to only two copies. These publications, however, would not be released to the general public to view but would be placed in the Houses of Parliament, one copy in the library of the House of Lords and the other in the library of the House of Commons. This was a very British way of declaring the abridged CAA review published while at the same time protecting it from the public.

Abruptly, on 24 April 2002, the case of Osborne v British Airways Plc Corporation in the United States ended when a BA motion to dismiss the complaint on the grounds of lack of jurisdiction of the court was unopposed, and the action progressed to a discussion of an out of court settlement. The maximum award for negligence in the US then was $150,000 and settling the case with sixteen litigants could have amounted to a multi-million-dollar sum. A settlement was later agreed and substantial amounts, rumoured to be around $100,000 for each of the sixteen passengers, was awarded for bodily injury and psychological trauma in spite of the fact that only four had suffered minor injuries. The total sum was never disclosed, however, as all litigants had signed confidentiality agreements, and that effectively eliminated the possibility of a further legal challenge in the USA. In that case, therefore, the total cost to BA would have been of $1.6 million/£1.02 million but, had these same sums been paid out to the seventy remaining passengers holding out for a better settlement, it would have been closer to $7 million /£4.7 million in 2002. The passenger group of seventy or so in the UK were still striving for a greatly enhanced settlement and they were hopeful the outcome in the United States would also improve their chances of a successful claim.

After the announcement of BA's USA compensation awards, it had been reported in the UK press that the seventy passengers holding out for an improved offer 'had been furious with BA for the multi-million dollar settlement in the States'. A Passenger Action Group (PAG) spokesperson, Nick Reid, had charged BA as having treated them with 'callous contempt and disregard'. Reid and his group had also 'accused BA of bias, covering up data and not doing enough to prevent the incident, claiming the Kenyan, Paul Mukonyi, had been behaving strangely both before boarding and during the flight'. While praising the crew, he was 'angry with the airline, and had claimed it had offered little assistance to the traumatised passengers when they arrived in Nairobi and had been grudging with information and comfort since. The settlement with the US passengers was the last straw,' Reid added.

Chapter 26

The Reckoning

In London, in the House of Commons on 7 May 2002, the MP for Manchester Central, a Mr Tony Lloyd, requested information on the progress of the abridged CAA review of the BA2069 Nairobi Incident and the then Minister for Transport, Mr John Spellar, who had succeeded Lord Macdonald in 2001, announced his response.

> The CAA has reported to me on the outcome of its review.... and I have today placed in the libraries of both Houses a report of the Authority's findings. I am satisfied that the security and safety lessons from the incident for the travelling public have already been fully taken into account with the actions implemented since the terrorist attacks of 11th September 2001.

The two copies of the abridged CAA review were duly shelved in the Houses of Parliament libraries and the opportunity for the UK passengers to litigate for increased compensation was lost. All three investigation appraisals of the aircraft upset, the BA report, the full CAA review and now the abridged CAA review, had been completed and withheld, and the lack of any written evidence effectively put paid to the passengers claiming further compensation in court.

Many were very angry and bitterly disappointed that, having suffered what they had considered to have been a near death experience and a close disaster, they had not received the fair treatment they had deserved. Not surprisingly, almost all the BA2069 passengers perceived this to be a deliberate cover-up, and, of course, it could be alleged they were right, but without evidence they couldn't prove it and others were still making sure they weren't going to get it.

An attempt to protect BA from financial damage could be understood, but the participants had allegedly gone too far and they were taking a staggering risk. It is alleged, however, that those involved knew what they were doing, that they were aware they had to maintain their silence and that the cover-up of the broken leg and its significance had to be concealed at all costs. That in some way explained the isolating of the flight crew in First Class on their return, the registering of Kim in hospital in a false name, Ken Smart allegedly not telling the truth about declining to investigate the serious incident, a 'minder' for Bill on his first supernumerary flight, BA's report and the abridged CAA Review being withheld and all AAIB communication files relating to the BA2069 incident being destroyed.

With all three of these important documents now having been banned from release, those in BA and the AAIB who had been in positions to assert authority, and who allegedly took part in the 'broken leg cover-up', must have been relieved that their allegedly criminal actions had avoided exposure and that their alleged attempt to protect the company from serious financial damage had saved the day. In the aftermath of 9/11, when air traffic had plunged and airline finances were in dire straits, some may have thought that BA had been fortunate. Almost everyone, however, had thought that the payouts in the USA had been excessive but that the BA compensation offer of £2,000, plus a free return flight anywhere, the latter being useless to the many suffering from PTSD, was totally unfair. That settlement, it was felt, had been more in keeping with 'air rage' than the traumatic, terrifying, near death experience the passengers had actually endured. In the end, however, they were left with no choice but to take or leave the compensation offered and it can be assumed that most would have accepted and would have signed settlement agreements. Some may have held out to make their own claim later but they would have to submit it within three years of the aircraft upset, with a deadline at the end of 2003, so they didn't have a lot of time.

It now seemed that BA had won the day, but at the cost of alienating their passengers, for all felt very bitter about the way BA had treated them and no one had a good word to say about the company. BA's stance from the beginning had appeared to have been defensive and intransigent, but had they attempted with diplomacy to engage the passengers, that may have been avoided. For the alleged participators who thought they had got away with it, however, this was their moment of the crossing of the Rubicon, for whatever happened now they had passed a point of no return. One day, it might just come back on them!

To quote from Robert Burns, 'The best-laid schemes of mice and men go oft awry,' and it's often the smallest of items that give the show away. One line of only ten words – 'One cabin crew sustained a broken leg and was hospitalised' – could be the participants' Achilles' heel, for, in June 2001, Safety Services had revealed the injury in the BA Report to which they had contributed to substantially. That admission had proved that Safety Services had known all along, but had not reported the broken leg to the AAIB, and that, allegedly, exposed the criminal offence. It was not enough just to state that, however, for what was needed for anyone intent on revealing the 'broken leg cover-up' was hard copy written evidence that Safety Services had known, but that was buried in the abridged CAA Review.

The abridged review had been published, albeit just two copies, but they represented something tangible, and there was still the possibility that, one day, copies could be made available by the Houses of Parliament for public viewing. If a copy was released, it would still be clasping its secret of the broken leg, and the concrete written evidence within would expose the truth of the 'broken leg cover-up' and may even bring the paticipators to justice.

In the absence of any further possible claims for compensation, therefore, there was still the matter of the suspected cover-up, and, amongst those with a vested interest there was someone with the knowledge and inclination to research the case, and that was Captain Hagan. He had been amongst the select few who had viewed reports in spite of the fact that it did not appear that BA had considered him as part of the inner circle. He had received a copy of the BA Report but that had been withheld, and it was now not available for evidence. He had not received a hard copy of the abridged CAA Review but, instead, had been invited to read it at the CAA headquarters in Gatwick. Since two copies had been lodged in the libraries of the Houses of Parliament, however, he thought it quite possible that one day they could be released for public scrutiny.

Soon after the aircraft upset, Captain Hagan had started keeping notes about the incident and, over time, he had been compiling a journal of information about the event. His intention was not to write a book, but to keep as a memory of events, and maybe something he could pass on to posterity. In 2000 the Blair Government had introduced the Freedom of Information (FOI) Act and it had received royal assent in the same year, but it was not expected to come in to effect for another two years or more, perhaps in late 2004. The FOI Act when implemented would allow members of the public to request copies of documents from all public authorities, of which the Civil Aviation Authority (CAA) was one, and, if approved, the documents could be made available online. This was a significant change for Bill Hagan and his interest in pursuing answers to the suspected cover-up of the Nairobi

Incident, for it meant that the CAA could be requested to provide documents. They would, however, only be made available if the time was right and if the documents requested were considered suitable for public viewing. Since the abridged CAA review had been withheld only recently, however, it would be many years before it could be considered suitable for release.

On 9 May 2002, two days after depositing of the abridged CAA reviews in the Houses of Parliament, Bill, Phil and Richard, were presented to the BA board to receive the British Airways Air Safety medal. It had been a long time since the incident, but BA had wanted the abridged CAA review to be finalised before the reward and they now wasted no further time. It was very much a private event at BA's Waterside headquarters as it was just the pilots accompanied by their wives. They were met in the boardroom by Captain Lloyd Griffiths, the newly appointed Director of BA Flight Operations who, as Chief Pilot, also sat on the board, and he introduced them to the other board members present. Captain Griffiths then addressed the members by emphasising that all three had saved the company from experiencing a 'hull loss'. They were then asked to assemble in the hall where a plaque, now with the addition of their names, was displayed and, as they posed beside the marble plaque for the BA News photographer, they all regarded the accolade as a prestigious recognition of what they had achieved.

In October 2002, Captain Hagan completed his last trip in BA and then, at the beginning of November at the age of fifty-five, the then compulsory retirement age for BA pilots, he left the company. Nine days later he joined easyJet as a direct entry captain and his intention was to fly with them for the rest of his career if he could. On joining BA, he had been obliged to sign a contract stating that he could not publish anything of an aviation nature without first obtaining permission from the airline. This prevented him from writing about the Nairobi Incident, but now he had joined easyJet he had been obliged to sign a similar contract and his hands were once again tied for many years to come. In the meantime, he could continue with his journal hoping in the future that he could complete it by obtaining a copy of the abridged CAA review with a Freedom of Information request.

Dr Paul Mallet, the psychiatrist who had examined Kim Parker in January 2002, had submitted his psychiatric report to BA in May 2002. Now, later in the year, in November 2002, Kim was examined in Harley Street by a Mr William Toar, this time a consultant orthopaedic surgeon, to assess the condition of her injured leg. His medical report stated that the damage caused by her injury was irreversible. In December 2002, Kim was also examined by a consultant neuropsychiatrist, Dr R. R. Jacobson, and he also provided a report. In 2003, Kimberley was examined again in Harley Street by the same consultant orthopaedic surgeon, Mr William Toar, and once more his medical report confirmed irreversible damage.

In January 2004, it was taking so long to resolve Kim's claim that even the *Mail on Sunday* reported that the settlement with Kimberley Parker, the stewardess whose leg had been badly injured on BA2069, had not yet been agreed. Later in 2004, Kim was once again sent by BA to Harley Street, this time to a different consultant orthopaedic surgeon, a Mr J.T. Coull, for yet another assessment.

On 1 January 2005 the Freedom of Information Act finally came into effect, but the abridged CAA review had been withheld from viewing in May 2002, only about two and a half years ago, and it wasn't going to be released to the public any time soon. Bill was also constrained by his easyJet contract so he had to be content to bide his time for some years yet.

Also in 2005, about four and a half years after the incident, Ken Smart, the then Head and Chief Investigator of the AAIB, retired in April, and two months later he was appointed Chairman of BA's Safety Review Committee. At the following AGM he was then duly elected to serve on the board as a non-executive director. Mr. Smart was an able and competent air accident investigator and he was certainly a suitable candidate for chair of the Safety Committee. Ken Smart, however, was also the same person who had made his own decision not to participate in investigating the 'serious incident' and that was questionable, as demonstrated by the CAA Safety Regulation Group's (SRG) question. That had avoided BA from facing an AAIB serious incident investigation and, with no one left, had allowed them to make their own offer which was accepted. BA was then at liberty to conduct their own investigation and most considered that unsatisfactory, with the airline's refusal to release their own report to the public being the final ignominy. Ken Smart had allegedly been involved from the beginning and it could be also be alleged that he, unwittingly, was the architect of the broken leg cover-up, for he had started the chain of events. Mr. Smart's participation had then allegedly continued and, in an alleged turn for the worse, on reading about Kim's broken leg in his copy of the BA report in June 2001, he had allegedly turned a blind eye and had done nothing. This failure to act was, allegedly, a criminal offence. Mr. Smart had also allegedly presided over the deliberate act of destroying all AAIB's records of communication exchanges between them and all the others involved in the Nairobi Incident. That was highly suspicious and the evidence does appear to suggest that the AAIB did have something to hide. How history might perceive Mr. Smart is open to debate but, as applies to all with a long service in public life, perceptions are important.

At about the same time in 2005, Stewardess Kim Parker's claim for damages, finally, after all these years and numerous medical and psychiatric examinations later, was at last settled. It had taken more than four years of waiting, a ridiculous period of time to settle a claim when the damage caused by her injury had been assessed as irreversible by a consultant in November 2002. Needless to say, the compensation paid to Kim was at a level somewhat less than her American counterparts. Her right foot was also affected by permanent nerve damage owing to ligaments being torn at the time of the incident and by the necessity to surgically remove painful neuromas which resulted in permanent loss of sensation to three of her toes. She still also suffers to this day from PTSD.

In 2007, to put the UK passengers' claims for compensation into perspective, BA was fined a total of £270 million for fixing fuel charges with other airlines in 2006, and had set aside £350 million to cover these fines and the costs of possible legal challenges by customers on both sides of the Atlantic. By contrast, the costs of settling claims for all of the Nairobi Incident UK passengers would have been a fraction of these amounts, and, whatever the payments, the total would have been miniscule compared to the sum had the aircraft gone down.

In March 2012, Martin Sinclair of the *Business Traveller Magazine* stated that, in regard to a discussion about the Nairobi Incident, 'it is remarkable that it has been kept under wraps for so long' and stressed that even outside the aviation industry the apparent non availability of information had not gone unnoticed.

In November 2012, Captain Hagan reached the age of sixty-five after which he could no longer continue as an airline captain and he ended his flying career by retiring from easyJet. He then wasted no time in seeking documents related to the BA2069 incident and, on 21 January 2013, with help from the volunteer organisation 'What do they know', he submitted a Freedom of Information (FOI) request to the renamed Department for Transport for a considerable number of documents. In the middle of February 2013, the Department for Transport responded by saying they 'did hold some of the information you are seeking' but 'your request raises complex public interest considerations'. The 'public interest test' took time to resolve, but, eventually, all but three of the documents requested were released. The abridged CAA review, however, could not be provided as the copies were being held in the Houses of Parliament.

In November 2013, the captain then submitted a further FOI request to the House of Lords for a copy of the abridged CAA review that they held and, almost 13 years after the event, Bill was delighted to be informed that his request to the House of Lords had been approved and he finally received a copy. Now he could complete his journal but, more importantly, he could also publicly use the content without constraint. It had been feared that the abridged CAA review would never be released, until now, but had it not been for the two published copies in the Houses of Parliament's libraries and the Freedom of Information Act, it might never have seen the light of day. The two abridged CAA reviews published are still shelved in the libraries of the Houses of Parliament to this day.

There is now concrete written evidence available that BA and the AAIB did allegedly collude in criminal acts to protect BA from paying substantial funds in compensation to passengers.

To date, however, no one has been held to account, but, if the alleged criminal offences are considered sufficiently serious, they may be indictable with no statute of limitation, and the alleged offenders could still be prosecuted. The UK is a signatory to the Convention on International Civil Aviation, like 200+ other nations, and it is alleged that the behaviour of both BA and the AAIB was also in breach of the International Civil Aviation Organisation's (ICAO) protocol. As the UK is a leading aviation nation, this alleged breach is a scandal of international proportions.

Almost all who were associated with the Nairobi Incident had felt that BA was covering up, but no one could put their finger on it or find the evidence to prove it. Now, in the year of its twenty-fifth anniversary, the alleged scandal of the 'broken leg cover-up' has been uncovered and, allegedly, the truth has now been be told.

END OF PART 2

Bibliography

Convention on International Civil Aviation. 8th Edition, 2000.

International Civil Aviation Organisation (ICAO) Chicago Convention Annex 13. Aircraft accident and incident investigation. 9th Edition, 1999.

International Civil Aviation Organisation (ICAO) Tokyo Convention. Offenses and other acts committed on board aircraft. 1963.

UK Guide to the Tokyo Convention.

International Civil Aviation Organisation (ICAO) Annex 17 Security – Safeguarding international civil aviation against acts of unlawful interference.

Air Accident Investigation Branch (AAIB) Aircraft accidents and serious incidents – Guidance for airline operators.

Civil Aviation Act UK 1982.

Statutory Instruments UK – The Civil Aviation (Investigation of air accident and Incidents) – Regulations 1996.

Department of Transport, Local Government and the Regions (DTLR) - Disruptive passenger working group – March 2001 and November 2001.

Civil Aviation Authority (CAA) – 'Cockpit coup at 37,000 feet over Sudan' – Synopsis of event with details from different sources.

Civil Aviation Authority (CAA) – Debrief of meeting with Mr Reid of the Passenger Action Group (PAG) – November 2001.

Department of Transport, Local Government and the Regions (DTLR) – abridged CAA Review – May 2002. Released from House of Lords by Freedom of Information (FOI) request November 2013.

Air Line Pilot: A Long-Standing, Successful Aviation Safety Reporting System (BA), Captain Thomas Duke, January 2001.

The Regulations of Civil Aviation (UK) Operational Selection Policy OSP26, 1972-2002.

International Civil Aviation Organisation (ICAO) Manual of Aircraft Accident and Investigation, 1st Edition, 2000.

Laws of Kenya: Protection of Aircraft Act 1982, Revised Edition 2012.

United Nations Treaty Series: Convention on Offences and Certain Other Acts Committed on Board Aircraft 1969.

Freedom of Information (FOI) requests – numerous documents.

Internet – numerous documents.

Addendum

Sources

The narrative of this book has been formed by substantial information and primary evidence of the aircraft upset and the cover-up provided by Captain Bill Hagan, as a professional witness, as well as extensive detail from the abridged CAA review and from Freedom of Information (FOI) requests. Crucially, hugely valuable primary evidence from Stewardess Kimberly Parker, also as a professional witness, provided vital detail of her broken leg and of her experiences. The two copilots on BA2069, Phil Wilson and Richard Webb, were in their mid to late thirties at the time of the incident and, with the BA retirement age having been raised to sixty-five, they are now in their early sixties and still flying as captains in BA. Regrettably, it goes without saying that BA would not have approved of them contributing to this book.

In addition, further research, investigation and detective work added significant details that were vital to the quest of establishing the truth. In the end, by wading through ICAO and other regulations, it transpired that the conclusion was more obvious than suspected and it was surprising that no one had worked it out before. It was like the invention of the vacuum cleaner, so simple when working but astonishing that no one had thought about it till then.

British Airways and the Air Accident Investigation Branch

It is important to mention that, in spite of this book, British Airways (BA) has been for decades, and still is, a world class airline with a deservedly high reputation and the Air Accident Investigation Branch (AAIB) for decades has been a renowned aviation accident investigation authority that is admired throughout the world, so it is unfortunate that references throughout are made to BA and the AAIB in general, for they are only really referring to certain individuals within these organisations who had the authority at the time of the aircraft upset to influence policy.

Mr Kenneth Smart, Head and Chief Investigator of the AAIB

An interview with Ken Smart by email was attempted in order to give him the chance to tell his side of the story, but he declined and refused to correspond. Sadly, he died in the spring of 2024 before this book could be published and, regrettably, he is no longer in a position to defend himself.

Mukonyi

After Paul Mukonyi had returned to France to repeat his year at Lyon Université Lumière, he was unsuccessful in his exams and he returned to Kenya where he struggled to find a post as a teacher. Eventually he gained two part-time positions, one as a lecturer at Daystar University and the other as a teacher at a nearby private high school. In 2011, Mukonyi eventually gained employment as a language lecturer in a local university in western Kenya where he settled, got married and had two children, Bernard and Ble. The university? Moi University, of course!

Final review

In the aftermath of the Nairobi Incident, BA2069's accident early on the morning of 29 December 2000, and ever since, wherever two or more aviation people gather in its name, there will be, always, these points of discussion; that it was the biggest aircraft upset in aviation history and that it was the biggest cover-up in aviation history. It will take a public enquiry to unearth the whole truth and that is unlikely to happen, but there is much that is disturbing about this event.

THE END

Index